ECONOMIC LIFE IN GREECE'S GOLDEN AGE

ECONOMIC LIFE IN GREECE'S GOLDEN AGE

BY

H. BOLKESTEIN †

Professor of Ancient History in the University of Utrecht

NEW EDITION

REVISED AND ANNOTATED

BY

E. J. JONKERS

LEIDEN
E. J. BRILL
1958

PRINTED IN THE NETHERLANDS

CONTENTS

PREFACE

Bolkestein's "Economic Life in Greece's Golden Age" was published in Dutch in 1923 in a popular edition, with no notes and it has found a great number of readers in this country.

Will—after thirty four years— a republication be justified of this book for an international circle of readers?

The question rose when the editor consulted me about an English edition of the book. And I have with full conviction given an affirmative answer.

Hendrik Bolkestein was born in Amsterdam in 1877 from Dutch parents; he was a student of classical philology and history at the University of Amsterdam and took his doctor's degree there in 1906 on a thesis called "De colonatu Romano eiusque origine". For some months he attended Eduard Meyer's lectures and in 1915 became professor of ancient history in the University of Utrecht; this office he helt till his death in 1942.

The young scholar was deeply impressed by Eduard Meyer's lectures, in which Meyer carried on a fierce controversy against Karl Bücher expressing the view that 5th and 4th century Athens should have had an economic system that resembled modern capitalism. At the same time these lectures urged Bolkestein on to criticism and he took Bücher's side where he demonstrated that as to its economic life Greece had a very low degree of development.

On the other hand, however, in opposition to Bücher, Bolkestein clearly showed the very particular structure of the ancient society and that Bücher's scheme did not in the least cover the Greek situation. Regarding this he built on the thoughts of the great Max Weber and on those of P. Guiraud and H. Francotte. Especially however he feeled himself related with the English scholar A. E. Zimmern and he was proud to have introduced Zimmern's "The Greek Commonwealth" to his Dutch students. But neither he did follow Zimmern hand and foot, nor did he take over all his views. On the contrary he often showed his independent spirit by combating some of Zimmern' views also and putting his own against them. We need only think of the causes Zimmern believed to have found in Greece for marriage in a man's advanced age, and those of Bolkestein, which shows the latter's sound realism.

In 1923 Bolkesteins ideas were those of a pioneer and often revolutionary. The chapters on trade and commerce and on the state and industry were written when no separate study or book on these subjects yet existed. Presently the works of the German scholar J. Hasebroek on this material were published, who admits being acquainted with Bolkestein's theories and experienced their influence. Further Bolkestein's views of slavery were—after the publications of H. Wallon and Ed. Meyer—often very original.

Therefore it is regrettable that Bolkestein's pioneering book was edited in Dutch. His successor in the University of Utrecht Professor J. H. Thiel mentioned this in his commemorative oration in the Royal Academy of Science as "a serious omission" and "little less than a catastrophe". Thiel also regrets the lack of a scientific adstruction [1] which before him already C. L. W. van Hille had stated in a review of the book [2].

Since 1923 several publications on conditions in economic and social life in the 5th and 4th centuries B. C. have appeared; nevertheless Bolkestein's book has not yet become antiquated, owing to the original vision of its author.

My task has been in re-editing this book to find together as much as possible the documentary evidence and to expunge some views overtaken by science. I have often referred to later works by other scholars, if their views corresponded with Bolkestein's.

In searching for the evidence I have found much aid in the numerous theses which had appeared under Bolkestein's direction and which further developed Bolkestein's theories.

I have made it my task merely to serve: the book had to remain the work of my master Professor H. Bolkestein.

Winschoten (Holland), September 1957.

E. J. JONKERS, Litt. D., LL.D.

---

[1] Herdenking van Hendrik Bolkestein. Jaarboek der Nederlandse Akademie van Wetenschappen 1942-1943, p. 16.

[2] Weekblad voor het Gymnasiaal- en Middelbaar Onderwijs 1924, p. 397. Compare also E. J. Jonkers, In memoriam H. Bolkestein. Tijdschrift voor Geschiedenis LVII, p. 163.

LIST OF THESES IN THE DOMAIN OF ANCIENT ECONOMICS WRITTEN UNDER THE DIRECTION OF PROF. H. BOLKESTEIN

J. J. B. MULDER, Quaestiones nonnullae ad Atheniensium matrimonia vitamque coniugalem pertinentes. 1920.

O. VAN DER HAGEN, De Clementis Alexandrini sententiis oeconomicis, socialibus, politicis. 1921.

P. HERFST, Le travail de la femme dans la Grèce ancienne. 1922.

J. HEMELRIJK, Penia en Ploutos. 1925.

H. KNORRINGA, Emporos. Data on Trade and Trader in Greek Literature from Homer to Aristotle. 1926.

J. J. VAN MANEN, Penia en Ploutos in de periode na Alexander (Penia and Ploutos in the Period after Alexander). 1931.

H. HÖPPENER, Halieutica. Bijdrage tot de kennis van de oud-Griekse visscherij (Halieutica. A Contribution to the Knowledge of Fishing in Ancient Greece). 1931.

J. C. A. M. BONGENAAR, Isocrates' Trapeziticus vertaald en toegelicht (Isocrates' Trapeziticus translated and annotated). 1933.

E. J. JONKERS, Economische en sociale toestanden in het Romeinsche Rijk blijkende uit het Corpus Juris (Economic and Social Conditions in the Roman Empire apparent from the Corpus Juris). 1933.

J. KORVER, De terminologie van het crediet-wezen in het Grieksch (The Terminology of Banking in Greek). 1934.

P. J. T. ENDENBURG, Koinoonia en gemeenschap van zaken bij de Grieken in den klassieken tijd (Koinoonia and Communal Trade in the Classic Period of Greece). 1937.

CHAPTER ONE

LAND, SEA AND CLIMATE

Though the civilization and the history of a nation can by no means be wholly explained by the nature of the country in which it lives, yet the development of its economic life depends to a very large extent on its geographical conditions [1]. Progress in civilization is often considered as an increasing dominion of man over nature [2]. This, however, does not imply that man succeeds in becoming more independent of nature in general, but of that special part of the world in which he lives, owing to the growth of commercial intercourse. The more we go back in the history of a nation, the more we see the direct influence which it undergoes from its immediate surroundings. Consequently the knowledge of these surroundings is highly important for the appreciation of its entire civilization, and not only of its material side. The object of the following pages is to indicate those particularities of land, sea and climate which have been significant for the economical condition of its people.

In Greece the settlements were established in the valleys as everywhere else, but here the valleys were no long narrow plains watered by a river, but for the greater part small valleys surrounded on all sides by mountains or especially by sea and mountains. In this way no extensive state could come into being, at least not without the interference of a power from without [3]. A great many tribes or small states continued living side by side, politically apart. But as soon as the

---

[1] R. J. Holland, The Mediterranean in the Ancient World. Cambridge 1934; E. Churchill Semple, The Geography of the Mediterranean Region, its Relation to Ancient History. London 1932; E. H. Warmington, Greek Geography. London-Toronto 1934; H. J. Lulofs, Geographie in de spiegel der Oudheid (Geography in the Mirror of Antiquity). Tijdschrift van het Kon. Ned. Aardrijkskundig Genootschap 1917, 6 and 1918, 1; A. Wünsche, Die geschichtliche Bewegung und ihre geographische Bedingtheit bei Carl Ritter. Thesis Leipzig 1899; Carl Ritter, Erdkunde im Verhältnis zur Natur und zur Geschichte der Menschen. Berlin 1817/1818; M. Cary, The Geographic Background of Greek and Roman History. Oxford 1949; H. E. Burton, The Discovery of the Ancient World. Cambridge 1932; J. H. Rose, The Mediterranean in the Ancient World. Cambridge 1931; J. Myres, Geographical History in Greek Lands. Oxford 1953.

[2] Cf. K. Bücher, Die Entstehung der Volkswirtschaft p. 12; Ed. Meyer, Geschichte des Altertums I, 1^5: Elemente der Anthropologie p. 66.

[3] Cf. F. Ratzel, Politische Geographie^2. München 1903, p. 402.

wants surpassed the first necessities of life, they were thrown on each
other's resources and traffic ensued. This traffic was considerably
facilitated because most territories bordered on the sea. The contrast
between political independence and mutual dependence in matters of
supply determined the development of economic as well as political life.

The contents of the ground have had a more direct influence than
the nature of its surface. In Greece, in contrast with Palestine e.g.,
the ground contained treasures of various kinds. There was no district
which did not produce *loam* for the manufacture of earthen ware, an
important product in a country with little wood and for a people to
whom cast iron was unknown. *Marble* is found in the most beautiful
shades and in great quantities: the island of Paros is one block of
marble! It procured an easily workable and durable material for archi-
tectural and statuary arts. It constituted moreover an important article
of commerce, as certain species were highly valued and in great
demand. *Gold* is found too, in fairly large quantities at the northern
coast of the Aegean sea, in Thrace and Macedonia [4]; the mines in the
island of Thasos [5] seem to have been little known before the 5th
century; the gold which in the Mycean time was used in such large
quantities by way of adornment must have been imported from the
east [6]. As regards *silver* it is principally found in the Laurium district
in the south of Attica [7]: the lead-ore dug there contained 0.1-0.3 %
of silver, so a profitable working was only possible by the cheapness
of slave-labour. *Copper* was only found near Chalcis in Euboea [8] and
had to be imported from Cyprus [9] or Spain. Most *iron*-mines were
not worked; this was only possible if sufficient fuel were available or

[4] Her., VI, 46; VII, 112; IX, 75; Thuc., I, 100; IV, 105; Xen., Hell. V, 2, 7;
Strabo, VII, fr. 33 and 34; Athen., II, 42 b; Diod., XVI, 8; Plin., N. H. XXIII, 21.

[5] Her., III, 57; VI, 46 sqq.; Paus., X, 11, 2. Cf. Klio X, p. 1.

[6] To this may point the legend of Pelops, who is said to have come with great
treasures from Asia to Greece.

After the Mycenaean Era gold cannot have been but rare in Greece. For a votive
offering the Spartans wanted to buy gold from Croesus (Her., I, 69). Only with a
lot of trouble could agents of Hiero of Syracuse get gold in Corinth for a tripod
(Athen., VI, 232 b).

[7] E. Ardaillon, Les mines du Laurion dans l'Antiquité. Paris 1897; A. Boeckh,
Über die laurischen Silberbergwerke in Attica. Abh. der Berliner Academie der Wis-
sensch. 1815, pp. 85 sqq. = Gesammelte kleine Schriften VI, pp. 1 sqq.; S. Lauffer,
Die Bergwerksklaven von Laureion. Akademie der Wissensch. und Lit. in Mainz,
Abh. der geistes- und soz. wiss. Klasse. Wiesbaden 1955. N. 12 (Erster Teil). Cf.
also Her., VII, 144; Xen., Vect. IV, 2; Strabo, IX, 399.

[8] Strabo, X, 447; Plin., N. H. IV, 64; Steph. Byz. s. v. Aidepsos.

[9] Strabo, III, 163; XIV, 654; 684; Plin., N. H. XXXIV, 2.

could be imported without difficulty. Iron is, moreover, not easily workable, consequently it played an unimportant part in antiquity. In Greece, Laconia was richest in this mineral [10]; the inhabitants of the towns in this region, the so-called perioeci, made it into arms for the Spartans and into the few agricultural implements for which iron was indispensable. Steel was no more known than cast iron.

As much as Greece abounds in minerals, so poor it is in agricultural produce. According to our standards it is an unfertile country — the Greeks themselves, however, as for instance the inhabitants of Palestine, viewed the national soil with different eyes [11]. Very large part consists of *rocky ground* and does not produce anything. The thin layer of humus which hardly covers the rock is caused by weathering and disappears only too quickly, when no precautions are taken, because no regular rainfall fixes it. Moreover, whenever rain falls, it oozes rapidly away through the porous limestone. In Antiquity *woods* covered a much larger surface than they do now [12]. Enormous quantities of wood were needed for the construction of houses and still more so as fuel; besides the goats wrought great havoc among the young shrubs, no wonder that many of the old forests have now disappeared. It is certain that the aspect of the country was very different from what it is at present. But formerly too the high trees with spreading leaves, the pride of the forests in Central Europe, were mainly lacking [13]. Therefore Greece was dependent for the import of wood for its shipbuilding upon the countries on the north coast of the Aegean Sea [14]; its small but numerous vessels had often to be renewed or replaced.

Pasture-land, as we know it, with its fresh green and tender grass did not exist in Greece, the grazing herds had to be contented with the soil which was not good enough for cultivable land [15]. So there was not sufficient food for the larger cattle [16]. Consequently there was

---

[10] Steph. Byz. s. v. Lakedaimōn.

[11] Exodus III, 8; Xen., Vect. (ed. Thiel) 1; Thuc., I, 2.

[12] Soph., Ai. 1217; Theophr., Hist. Pl. V, 2, 1; Dicaearch., II, 2; Aristot., Pol., V, 211; Plato, Critias 111 c.

[13] Hylè means bush as well as tree.

[14] Plato, Critias 111 c; Leg. IV, 706 b; Plut., Sulla 12. Cf. Guiraud, La propriété pp. 503 sqq.

[15] The fixed phrase, that bad weather was desired for the hay-harvest, because at the same time rain was needed for the arable land, shows, that the hay-harvest was considered to be of little importance. Plut., Qu. Nat. 14.

[16] Strabo, VIII, 366; Isaeus, X, 42; Plato, Critias 111c with scholia; Aristoph., Nub. 71 with schol.

not enough manure to improve the ground [17], already poor in itself, and thus the consumption of meat could not be but small; it was reserved for festival times: sacrifice and slaughter were identical to the Greek [18]. The herds of sheep and goats, animals with small demands with regard to food and drink but which gave man milk and meat for his maintenance, leather for his shoes and wool for his clothing, grazed on the slopes below the forests or failing these under the bare rocks.

The *arable land*—at the end of the last century it did not yet occupy a fifth of the Greek area—is almost entirely confined to the valleys. Plains of some extent are found in Thessaly round Larissa and east of Pharsalus—this is by far the most extensive valley of the country—; the Spercheus-valley east of the Malian bay; in Phocis south of Elatea; in Boeotia north of Thebes; in Attica near Eleusis, west of Athens, between the Hymettus and the eastern coastal mountains, and round Marathon; in Argolis round Argos; west of Argos the valley round Mantinea and Tegea; in Laconia south of Sparta; and almost the whole western coast of Elis. The islands are absolutely devoid of plains, Euboea excepted [18a]. The most important products were corn, wine and oil.

Cereals formed the staple food of the population; they were sown in October, the barley was reaped in May, the wheat in June. Bread was baked of wheat-flour; barley-flour was eaten as a kind of porridge with water [19]; rye and oats were unknown. Many towns had recourse to grain produced in more fertile neighbouring regions round Greece.

The -vine grows everywhere in the country, every district grew enough for its own consumption; people only dealt in the choicest marks as wine from Chios [20], Lesbos [21] and Thasos [22]. In Antiquity the currant, nowadays the most significant article of export, was

[17] On manuring: Hom., Od. XVII, 297 sqq.; Theophr., Caus. Pl. III, 6, 1; III, 9, 3 and 17, 5; Hist. Pl. II, 7, 4; VIII, 9, 1; Geopon., II, 21, 6 sqq.; II, 22, 2; III, 8, 10; Xen., Oec. 20, 11; 18, 2; 17, 10.

[18] Hom., Od. III, 454; Pind., Pyth. 11, 23; Aesch., Choeph. 891; Eumen. 295; Soph., Ai. 231 and 292; Eur., Andr. 315 and 626; Or. 1199.

[18a] The best map of Greece on which the nature of the ground is clearly indicated is the volume *Graecia* of Murray's Handy classical maps.

[19] Archil., 2; Her., I, 133; IV, 42; Plato, Rep. 372 b. Of course this does not preclude the possibility of there having been choicer kinds of bread. Athen., III, 112 c.

[20] Strabo, XIV, 645 and 657; Athen., I, 28 sqq.; Pollux, VI, 15; Plin., N. H. XIV, 73.

[21] Strabo, XIV, 657; Athen., I, 28 e sqq. and 30 b; Plin., N. H. XIV, 73.

[22] Aristoph., Plut. 1022; Lysistr. 196.

unknown; this way of using the grape was not known till in the 14th century.

The olive was most important on account of the varied uses made of it; the fruit was used as a food; the oil was indispensible for the preparation of all the dishes for which butter or its substitutes are used in central Europe; scented on unscented it served as a cosmetic indispensable in a dry climate [23]; finally the lamps were filled with it: so it constituted the principal means of lighting [24]. The frontier of the olive-tree runs not far from the north and east coast of the Aegean Sea, along the south coast of Asia minor. No olive-tree was found on the whole coast of the Black Sea [24a], and the numerous Greek colonies founded there were absolutely dependent on the import from the mother country on both sides of the Aegean. Especially the olive-oil from Attica was renowned, it became the principal export product there [25]. Though one of the sources of Athens' welfare, the possession of olive-groves formed at the same time a weak spot. When raiding the country the enemy could easily destroy the fruit-trees [26]. In contrast with grain olive-trees take many years before they come to maturity.

Cotton was unknown in Greece [27], flax was but cultivated in small quantities [28] and linen garments were only worn by well-to-do people. As regards fruit: figs, apples, pears and pomegranates were found in Greece, but—at least before Alexander—cherries, oranges, tomatoes, as well as peaches and apricots, were not grown. Instead of sugar honey was used, but coffee, tea and tobacco, nowadays to be found in the simplest households, were unknown articles.

This country rich in minerals, but rocky and unfertile, is situated very favourably with regard to the surrounding *sea*. Of all parts of

[23] W. H. C. van Esveld, De balneis lavationibusque Graecorum. Thesis Utrecht 1908, pp. 111 sqq. and pp. 18 sqq.; Theophr., Char. XXIV, 11; Aristoph., Eccl. 625; Xen., Conv. I, 7; Hom., Od. III, 466; VI, 96; VII, 454.

[24] Th. Fischer, Der Oelbaum. Seine geographische Verbreitung, seine wirtschaftliche und kulturhistorische Bedeutung. Petermanns Mitteilungen. Ergänzungsheft 147. Gotha 1904.

[24a] Xen., An. VI, 4, 6; [Aesch.], ep. 5.

[25] Plut., Solon 2, 24. Solon forbade the exportation of all agricultural products except olive-oil. Thuc., III, 263. Cf. Plin., N. H. V, 3.

[26] Thuc., I, 108, 2 and IV, 69, 2. Such-like methods are more met with in Antiquity: Moses for instance forbade the Jews to cut down "trees for meat" in warfare. Deut. XX, 19-20.

[27] Herodotus did know it in Egypt (III, 47. Cf. 106).

[28] Thuc., IV, 26.

the world Europe has the most broken coastline and in Europe Greece has this advantage to the greatest extent. The bays which penetrate deeply into the land and the numberless islands in the surrounding sea (on the west coast 116, in the Aegean Sea 483!) together with the tranquillity of the water over which regular winds blow, at least during a great part of the year, could not but stimulate fishing and shipping and also brought about traffic between tribes whose differences in civilization were neither so great nor so slight as to make interchange of intellectual and material values impossible. No place in the Peloponnesus is farther removed from the sea than about 32 miles, in Middle Greece not farther than about 38 miles; most bays are well protected from the prevailing winds. Finally, the eastern part of Greece, richest in marble, also possessed the most favourable coast-line, because this part was turned towards the country with the oldest civilization. The Aegean sea, far from raising a barrage, offered in its countless islands the finest harbours for navigation: a sailor was always within sight of land.

In the meantime traffic by sea was subject to many restrictions; the principal reason was that it ceased during the whole winter [29]; the boats were laid up in October when the moist notos (south-western wind) with its rain and clouds and the boreas (northern wind) with hail and snow made the sea dangerous, and they were not launched before April [30]. During the whole of Antiquity the compass remained unknown, so the Greeks had no means of localization, when the sky was overcast. This circumstance alone sufficed to compel the navigator seldom to venture out of sight of land. Besides, they dared not navigate in the dark; they only rowed or sailed by daylight, as much as possible along the coast [31]. It goes without saying that they cut deep bays and that they had to cross the sea from one island to another! Every evening the ship was hauled ashore, where the sailors took their meal. In this manner it was not necessary to take many provisions, the cargo capacity of the boats was too small to allow this: vessels of more than 300 tons will have been an exception in the period which we are discussing [32]. One of the largest ports in later

[29] Cf. Philippson, Das Mittelmeergebiet. Leipzig 1922, p. 159; A. Köster, Das antike Seewesen. Berlin 1923; A. Lesky, Thalatta, der Weg der Griechen zum Meer. Wien 1947; J. H. Thiel, De Grieken en de zee (The Greeks and the Sea). Tijdschrift voor Geschiedenis, 1949, pp. 1 sqq.

[30] Dem., XXXIII, 23.

[31] Xen., Hell. II, 1, 17.

[32] Cf. Her., I, 194; II, 96; Thuc., IV, 118.

days, the port of Delos, had a quay-length of about 834 feet; even when taking into account that the sailing-boats were moored with the prows to the quay (a thing not very conducive to rapid discharging and loading!), it indicates little traffic with small vessels in comparison with modern times. The fact that they were not only provided with sails, but could also be arranged as rowing-boats proves as well that their cargo-capacity was very moderate.

The *climate* in Greece is the same as the Mediterranean climate with which it has in common the distribution of rain over the year: the summer is dry, the winter is the rainy season. In Greece the annual rainfall is not less than in Central Europe, but of all the rain the winter gets 78 %, the three summer-months June, July and August together only 7 %. The persistent drought is accompanied by intense heat during which all plants wither.

The unequal rain-fall also affects the nature of the rivers. Greece hardly knows rivers as such: in winter they are swollen torrents [33], in summer dry beds. In one of Demosthenes' pleas [34] it is a controversial question, whether a piece of ground is a brook, a road or an orchard! The rivers are therefore unnavigable, the Achelous [35] on the border of Acarnania and Aetolia, the Alpheus and the Pamisus [36] in Messenia excepted. As regards commercial intercourse the rivers only form a serious impediment in winter, when they are swollen and difficult to cross. Transport in so far as it takes place by land, is carried on on the roads along the riverbeds [37].

In a country without rain in summer and where the water of the rivers is undrinkable on account of the mud which the rapid current carries along [38], people had to settle in the vicinity of wells. Many a village was as proud of its excellent well-water as a connoisseur of

[33] In winter some rivers can flow like roaring bulls, as which they are sometimes represented on coins. For instance Head, H. N. pp. 86-87. (Probably a symbol for the Xanthes), and p. 140 (Gela at the mouth of the Gelas. Cf. Virg., Aen. III, 702); Hom., Il. XXI, 237; Soph., Trach. 9 sqq.; Strabo, X, 458.

[34] Dem., LV, 13 and 16.

[35] Strabo, X, 450.

[36] Pausan., IV, 34, 1.

[37] Consequently the ports in the Mediterranean are not situated at the mouths of the rivers that get rilted up time after time, but they are often situated near them, if the river-valley is a road: Venice (Po), Marseilles (Rhone), Salonica (Axius), Alexandria (Nile), Smyrna (Hermus).

[38] E. Curtius, Griechische Quell- und Brunneninschriften. Abhandlungen der Kgl. Ges. der Wissenschaften zu Göttingen VIII (1860), pp. 153-184.

a good mark of wine [39]; as a rule special magistrates were charged
with their supervision [40]. Before the Hellenistic time the Greeks hardly
knew waterworks; Herodotus describes those of Samos [41] and Pisistra-
tus [42] built those of Athens. The Romans alone were skilled in laying
out cities on a soil destitute of water [43]. Even in olden times, however, the Greeks went in for artificial inundation; their whole agriculture and gardening system depended on it [44]. The water supplied
by the Cephisus near Athens was used in summer for irrigation of
adjacent olive-groves.

In Greece the temperature is naturally higher than in our regions,
the average temperature in July being 80° F. in Athens (in Central
Europe 64° F.), in January 46° F. (in Central Europe 30° F.).
Summer and winter are very divergent: the latter, which is short, is
only an interruption of the summer; the entire Greek life is based on
this season. In winter, war and navigation come to a standstill [45]
and the shepherds as well as the merchants live in the city. Whereas
in towns of more northernly situated countries, people as a rule spend
their days indoors, only leaving their homes for their occupations,
in Greece and the whole Mediterranean territory people spend their
public and private lives in the open. They only betake themselves to
their homes when this is inevitable. The higher temperature and the
life in the open engendered by it considerably influenced the nature
and the extent of the necessities of life.

When a man spends a large part of his life outdoors, he does
not care much for the comfort of his *home*. In the fifth century at
any rate the greater part of the town-population in Attica was contented with airy houses, made of wood and clay dried in the sun-
shine [46]. As to their adornment it goes without saying that nothing

---

[39] Curtius, l.c. Cf. also C. I. G. 6256.

[40] Themistocles was epistatès hydatōn. Plut., Vit. Them. 31. Cf. Pollux, VIII, 113;
Photius s.v. Krènophylakion.

[41] Her., III, 60; Strabo, V, 235. Cf. Esveld, De balneis p. 173 and Esveld, De
watervoorziening in de Oudheid (Watersupply in Antiquity). Water en Gas 1930,
pp. 8-10.

[42] Cf. Esveld, De balneis p. 173; Daremberg et Saglio s.v. Aquaeductus.

[43] Strabo, V, 235.

[44] Oldest instance of irrigation: Hom., Il. XXI, 257.

[45] Cp. p. 6, 29.

[46] Xen., Mem. III, 1, 7; Plut., Conv. sept. sap. 12; Plut., Dem. 11; Plin., N. H.
XXXV, 172; Thuc., II, 3. Yet there must have been many fine and more substan-
tial houses. Cf. Xen., Oec. III, 1; IX, 2; Mem. III, 8, 10; Plato, Rep. II, 373 a;
Andoc., c. Alcib. 17; Dem. XXI, 147 and 158; Olynth. III, 29; XXXIII, 208; Plut.,
Alcib. 16.

of all the rubbish to be found nowadays in "fancy-shops" was used by the Greeks! [47]

As humble as the houses of most Greeks were, so little precious and ornate was their *clothing*. The climate allowed people to wear very little: they wrapped a woollen piece of cloth round their bodies; in this way it was hardly necessary to make it to measure; the fleece of the sheep could become an article of dress without its leaving the house: people spun and wove the wool themselves [48]. They were also very slack in changing their linen. The typical capitalistic phenomenon of fashion which in our days forces men and especially women to discard clothes before they are worn out, was unknown. Theophrastus mentions as one of the dandy's characteristics: "he will have his hair cut repeatedly, he will keep his teeth white and will discard his clothes while still good" [49].

In the subtropical climate of Southern Europe the population needs but little *food* as long as no factors from without influence it, because the body sustains itself with less. It is a well-known phenomenon of this present time too: Baedeker warns his compatriots, who intend travelling in Italy for a long time, as follows: "der nordische Appetit verringert sich im Süden allmählich" (the nordic appetite grows gradually less in the South). In Greece farinaceous dishes formed the staple-food; everything else, meat included, was considered as dessert [50]. The Greeks were and are still extremely frugal about their food and drink: most of them have only two meals a day, lunch towards midday and supper in the evening.

We may well imagine what this frugality and these moderate wants of the population which could be supplied for the greater part by

[47] For the contents of a well-to-do fifth-century Athenian bedroomfurniture cf. Zimmern p. 216.

[48] Hom., Od. XXII, 422; Xen., Oec. X, 10; Plato, Alcib. 216 e; Eurip., Hec. 363; Aristoph., Lys. 567 sqq.; Lucian, Fug. 12.

[49] Theophr., Char. V.

[50] All side-dishes taken with bread are called *opson*: Schol. ad Hom., Il. XI, 629; Photios s. v. Opson; Aristoph., Pax 123; Plato, Rep. II, 372 c and VIII, 559 b; Gorg. 518 b; Xen., Comm. III, 14, 2; Plut., Mor. 99 d; Lucian, Timon 56; Mnesimachus II, 437, 27 sqq. (K). These side-dishes can be vegetables, olives, cheese, meat, fish etc. It is striking how Plato ignores the most appreciated *opson*, and forbids his phylakes the consumption of fish. That was a Spartan custom (cf. Agatharchides, F. H. G. III, 193). The *opsa* of the sea push the others into the background to such a degree that the word *opson* simply becomes a synonym of *ichthys* (fish). This narrowing of a concept is put on record by Plutarch (Qu. conv. IV, 4, 2. Cf. Alexis, II, 314 and 378 (K.). The fish-market is called *to opson* in contrast to the meat-market, *to mageiron*.

every district itself, meant for the degree of development of production and traffic. Especially when we think of our days where even the humblest household consumes products imported from all parts of the world: wool from Australia, cotton from America, rice from the Indies, coffee from Java or Brazil. Further on [51] we shall discuss more in detail the great significance of slavery which reduced its victims still further to the lowest standard of living.

But this low standard of living of the mass of the people was not the only reason why wholesale production was not remunerative. Part of the traffic was seriously handicapped by the geographical conditions of Greece and its surrounding countries. We have explained above [52] the limitations of navigation, interrupted as it was during the whole winter and by night. Inland navigation did not exist on account of the unnavigability of the rivers. And the transport by land was extremely difficult in default of proper roads. Their lay-out in this stony country was excessively onerous. The Greeks speak of cutting roads! [53]. They chiefly confined themselves to the construction of roads for processions to the well-attended sanctuaries, where, for that matter, markets were also held at the time of the great yearly festivals[54]. The political dissension of Greece impeded its economical development in this respect too, since it was in the interest of every little state to hamper the enemy wanting to invade it. Only the Romans, when they ruled the world, laid out for the quick transport of their armies that admirable net of high roads which, at least in the Balkan, remained the only valuable ones till far up in the 19th century. All the same, even these roads were not very suitable for the conveyance by carts as every visitor to Greece may know from experience. Transport by land of all perishable articles and of bulky goods was impossible. This means that all the districts not situated on the sea were deprived of all but local traffic. We shall discuss below [55] the other impediment which had less to do with the geographical situation: the piracy by land and sea, facilitated here by the multitude of bays on the coast.

We have already explained that the political dissension of Greece

---

[51] Pp. 61 sqq.

[52] P. 6.

[53] Thuc. II, 100, 2 (*temnein hodon*). On Cyprus *keirein hodon* (Hoffmann 99).

[54] Paus., X, 32, 5; Pollux, III, 126 (cf. 78); VII, 11.

[55] P. 106. Cf. E. Ziebarth, Beiträge zur Gesch. des Seeraubs und Seehandels im alten Griechenland. Hamburg 1929; H. Ormerod, Piracy in the Ancient World. Liverpool 1924.

on account of the nature of its soil checked the progress of its economical life in various aspects, a.o. because not one state was powerful enough to secure the safety of the traffic by sea. This is the more serious for an unfertile country as Greece is, whose prosperity depends to a large extent on trade. The historical development has been fatal to this country in so far that in the days when Philip and Alexander created a central power able to protect its traffic they also conquered the fertile and rich regions in Asia and Egypt. In this way the economical centre was transposed from the countries around the Aegean sea to the East which drew a large part of Greece's most enterprising and energetic men. And Greece profited little by the traffic, which ensued later on between these prosperous districts and the then powerful states in the Western part of the Mediterranean on account of the progress in nautical technique by which it was no longer necessary to avoid the open sea. The history of Greece after Alexander the Great offers, as far as its economical life was concerned too, a disconsolate picture of a hardly interrupted decline and pauperization.

CHAPTER TWO

AGRICULTURE AND CATTLE-BREEDING

It is a well-known theory that everywhere at the beginning of the economical life of communities the ground, from which private possession gradually emanated, was first common property [1]. Does this theory hold good for Greece and is it sustained by our knowledge about its earliest known conditions?

Before trying to answer this question, we must first explain the difference between the earliest known economical relationships and the oldest known conditions in Greece. For Greece—that is to say the country and islands round and in the Aegean Sea—before being inhabited by the tribes to which it owes its name later on, had other inhabitants with a very different degree of civilization. First of all the tribes of the neolithical period who only knew the use of wetted and pierced stones. Numerous finds have proved their existence in Northern and Middle Greece. But from excavations in Southern Greece and in Crete we also know of a non-Greek civilization between 2000 and 1200 B.C., whose architecture, statuary and painting greatly surpass the first stages of later Greek art; the centres of it were nobly built palaces adorned with refinement. They point to the existence of absolute monarchs in the Oriental style, a civilization and a form of government wholly incompatible with the primitive economical development which probably attended original communism.

But are traces of it to be found with the "Greeks" who later penetrated the country? The question can only be answered when we describe first what the exact meaning of original communism is.

We speak of *communistic* or *common landed property* when a bigger or smaller territory inhabited either by a would-be or a really kindred group of men, tribe or race, or by a purely local community, a village e.g., belongs to that community without distinction of families or individuals. It happens that the soil is either cultivated jointly or that it is distributed at set times; in the last case a single household

---

[1] For Greece compare about this: Büchsenschütz, Besitz und Erwerb pp. 28 sqq.; Guiraud, La propriété pp. 1 sqq.; Ed. Meyer, Gesch. d. Allertums III. Stuttgart 1937, pp. 272 sqq.

may use it for a time. It can, however, in no way alienate this property, neither through sale nor through donation nor through legacy. It changes sometimes into *household-property,* the first state of private possession where the ground is the property of the males of the family who cultivate it together, that is to say the father as long as he is capable and the sons as soon as they are capable of work [2]. Finally we can speak of *individual property* when the soil and the rest of the property are exclusively in the hands of the father and pass on to the sons only after his death. Here we need not speak further about the particulars and later development of this stage; about the possibilities of common possession by brothers, who leave the inheritance undivided, and about the origin of the will.

When talking of common landed property we mentioned the tillage of the soil; this characterizes the stage in which a tribe ceases from living exclusively on cattle-breeding, but passes on to regular agriculture. As long as the herds of cattle form the principal assets and means of subsistence, private property must have been nearly impossible: the extent of the land needed for it, the inevitable alternation of summer- and winter-pasture ground and the want of common guards and defenders of precious property, which might easily be stolen, must have led to a form of communistic property. But the Greeks, whose oldest traditions we owe to Homeric poetry, had already got beyond this stage, though it was not unknown to the historian Thucydides [3]. Undoubtedly cattle formed still a large part of the assets of the rich in epic poetry [4]: in many passages it is the principal means of exchange, the only standard of value because it formed the most important part of the movables [5]; but, just as often, cultivable land and orchards are mentioned [6]. Ploughing [7] and sowing [8], mowing [9] and threshing [10] are the ordinary occupations of normal life. We cannot adduce a single evidence of communistic possession of this

[2] Cf. Xen., Cyrop. VIII, 3, 37.
[3] Thuc. I, 2.
[4] Hom., Il. 244 and 671; XX, 221; Od. XIV, 100.
[5] Hom., Od. I, 431; VIII, 278; Il. VI, 532 sqq.; VII, 474; XVIII, 593; XXIII, 703 and 885. Once cattle are mentioned as a medium of exchange, but side by side with iron, copper, hides, and slaves.
[6] Hom., Il. I, 156; V, 612; XIV, 121; XXII, 489.
[7] Hom., Od. IX, 122; X, 353; XIII, 32; XVIII, 365 sqq.; Il. XVIII, 542; XXIII, 538; Eust. ad Hom. Il. XVIII 550 p. 1162, 20.
[8] Hom., Il. VI, 195; XII, 314.
[9] Hom., Il. XI, 67; XVIII, 550.
[10] Hom., Il. V, 500; XX, 495.

arable land, which does not likewise allow of different explanation [11], whereas many passages ascertain that private property was normal [12]. Further intelligence gathered from statements or remarks of later authors about situations and habits, which have been considered as traces of communism, can be explained in a different way and have nothing to do with it. We think here of conditions in the Liparian islands, in South-Italy, the later temple- and state-properties in Attica, the convivial dinners in numerous Greek states and other so-called remnants of juridical nature [13]. Already in Homeric poetry and moreover always in classical times, an inheritable piece of land in private possession is described by a word "kleros" [14] which means "lot". This undoubtedly points to a period during which the ground was the property of a community and plots of it were allotted by the drawing of lots at set times [15], but a direct example proving these old conditions has not been handed down to us. We can only trace something about household property from an article of the law of Gortyn [16], and perhaps also from an earlier inscription from Naupactus [17], but here private property has already set in and we may therefore conclude as follows: as far as our knowledge of Greece and its inhabitants goes, private property of the soil exists.

In Homeric poetry agriculture naturally predominates [18]; the work of the farmer as well as the arable land itself are indicated here with the general word for work: erga [19]. Some other trades also were prosecuted independently [20] and traffic by sea, never failing at any period, was also practised by the Greeks, but it is the profession of the few and did not require a special name.

The society known from the poetry of the Boeotic poet of country-life, Hesiod, dates probably from some centuries after the Homeric world, yet it is more primitive, as it belongs to the Greek interior, than the poetry of the coastal district where the epic originated. Agri-

---

[11] Hom., Il. XII, 421. Cf. XXI, 403 sqq. (Virg., Aen. XII, 896 sqq.); Il. XVIII, 541 sqq.

[12] Hom., Il. I, 156; V, 612; XIV, 121.

[13] Diog. Laert., VIII, 1, 23; Jambl., Vit. Pyth. 20; Gellius, N. A. I, 9, 12; Diod., V, 9. Fustel de Coulanges, La cité antique, Chapters I and II.

[14] Hom., Od. XIV, 64; Il. XV, 498.

[15] Cf. p. 12.

[16] Law of Gortyn IV, 23 sqq. Cf. Guiraud, La propriété p. 99.

[17] Ditt. Syll.3 47.

[18] Hom., Od. XVI, 140; XXIV, 226 sqq.; XIV, 222; Il. XVIII, 566 sqq.

[19] Hom., Il. II, 751; Od. II, 22; IV, 318; VI, 259; X, 98, 222 and 344; XI, 140.

[20] Hom., Il. XII, 295; IV, 187; XVIII, 601; Od. III, 432; XIV, 391.

culture is the principal source of welfare there [21]; by *ergazesthai* "to work" agricultural work is meant here too [22]. But the poet is also cognizant of navigation and trade by sea—here he uses a separate word for it, *"emporia"*, for the first time [23]—but apparently only as an auxiliary profession of the farmer: he warns emphatically against making this dangerous and insecure occupation one's only means of subsistence. In his simple society the self-sufficient household prevails: the farmer manufactures everything needful to his trade, his cart, his plough, his wooden mortar and pestle [24]; he does not yet know the use of the mill-stone with which Homer is quite familiar [25]; the independent crafts, which broke up the self-supporting household, are identical with those in the epic of Asia-Minor, the trades of blacksmith [26], potter [27], and carpenter [28].

Homeric poetry was written for the people of note, the world of the lower classes is only mentioned incidentally, often in comparisons [29]. The fact, however, that only wealthy landowners are mentioned and not the little husbandmen, the freeholders or tenants, does not prove in the least that they did not exist in the days when this poetry was made. They will undoubtedly have existed, as in the days of Hesiod who, a small farmer himself, described their life and toil, in pithy verses, without idealizing them [30]. The exhortation which he had learned from bitter experience, occurring again and again, is to work incessantly; "if not, you will have to beg along the houses" [31]. It is really inconceivable how this poem, the *"Erga"*, has been considered as a eulogium of labour [32].

Little is known of the situation of the farmer; it is not certain whether next to the land-owner and the small farmer tenants also existed. A thing which we do know is that slaves, *dmoës*, also took part in the work in the fields especially as shepherds [33]. The farmer

---

[21] Hes., Erg. 405 sqq.
[22] Hes., Erg. 630 sqq. and 689.
[23] Hes., Erg. 644.
[24] Hes., Erg. 423 sqq.
[25] Hom., Od. II, 355; VII, 104; XX, 106 and 111; Il. VII, 270.
[26] Hes., Erg. 10; Hom., IL. IV, 187; XII, 295.
[27] Hom., Il. XVIII, 601; Hes., Erg. 25 sqq.
[28] Hom., Il. XXIII, 712; Od. IX, 126; XVII, 384; XXI, 43; cf. Il. V, 59; XV, 411; VI, 315.
[29] Hom., Il. XXIII, 712; XVIII, 601.
[30] Hes., Erg. 300 sqq.; 404; 717.
[31] Hes., Erg. 299 sqq.
[32] This rests on Hes., Erg. 311. Cf. Ciccotti, Le déclin de l'esclavage antique p. 63.
[33] Hes., Erg. 428; 502; 573; 596; 767.

apparently no more used female slaves as he did in Homer's days [34], but free day-labourers, *thetes* [35], and female helps, *erithoi* [36], a word, however, by which Homer also indicates male labourers [37]. Though Hesiod repeatedly mentions debt resulting from laziness which may lead to a forced sale of land, yet the only consequences depicted by him are poverty, hunger and the necessity of begging [38]. The poet does not seem to know the sale of the debtor as a slave to the money-lender, debt-slavery.

We meet this form of slavery, already early extant in the East, in Attica, the only province properly known to us, towards the end of the VIIth cent. B.C. We know it from the preserved fragments of Solon's poetry: "of the poor many are sold to a foreign land" [39]. As the first and most important act of this legislator Aristotle mentions the prohibition to lend with the debtor as a security [40]. This system came into being under the influence of the first metal medium of exchange which can be heaped up in unlimited quantities and which develops the proprietor's thirst for money. The poetry of this time is full of it [41]. Solon, the father of Athens' democracy, led this phenomenon into lawful tracts; it lasted only a short time thanks to the farmer's resistance [42]. There was no question anymore of debt-slavery or any form of servitude in Attica in historical times. Outside Attica we find some traces of it [43].

In order to be able to learn the economic structure of a country, it is absolutely necessary to determine what part of the adult population is employed in the different branches of trade. Such direct data are wholly missing for any people and any period of ancient history; the numbers handed down to us concern as a rule the men capable of bearing arms; and in accordance with the place which war occupied

[34] In Homerus only men occupied themselves with agriculture. Even sheeps were not taken care of by women. Cf. P. Herfst, Le travail de la femme dans la Grèce ancienne. Thesis Utrecht 1922, pp. 13 sqq.

[35] Hes., Erg. 604. Cf. Schol. ad Hom., Od. IV, 644; X, 84; XI, 489; XIV, 102; XVIII, 357; Il. 444 sqq. About female thètes cf. Erg. 602.

[36] Hes., Erg. 600.

[37] Hom., Il. XVIII, 550 and 560.

[38] Hes., Erg. 404; 299 sqq.; 302.

[39] Solon, III, 23 sqq.

[40] Aristot., Ath. Pol. IX, 1.

[41] Hom., Il. IX, 231; I, 230; XVIII, 225; Hes., Erg. 39 and 221; Theognis, V, 1181 and 1157.

[42] Solon, XXXII, 7.

[43] Diod., I, 79; Lys., XII, 98; Isocr., XIV, 48.

in life, also in economic life, war-statistics are the only ones available. Consequently here also we are dependent upon the casual and un-intentional statements in preserved literature. Direct communications must be cautiously examined, the more so, when they refer to daily life, for it is a well-known phenomenon easily explained psycholog-ically that the normal things rarely attract the attention of non-scientific people, who are accustomed to consider the unusual and striking things with particular interest and describe them as a rule with an absolute neglect of the right proportions. In the regions in-habited by Greeks traffic by sea always was very brisk, partly under the influence of the geographical circumstances indicated above [44], partly on account of the economical position to be treated further on [44a]. Therefore considerable parts of the population in the coasttowns were involved in it. So it is usual to consider Athens as an "industrial" but also as a commercial town where the population made a livelihood chiefly through industry and trade. "Most of you draw your sub-sistence from the sea", Xenophon lets a foreign ambassador say in the Athenian Assembly [45].

This point of view which may be explained a.o. by the reasons men-tioned above is nevertheless inexact. For in the whole of Greece, also in the districts economically most developed like Attica, the soil and its tilling were the only or principal means of subsistence for the greater part of the population throughout Antiquity.

In Attica too. When in 403 the government of the oligarchs was abolished, one of the moderate conservatives, Phormisius, tried to prevent the return to the former democracy by an intermediate measure which had in view to grant civic rights exclusively to land-owners. By this measure 5.000 Athenians were to be excluded from their political rights [43]. Now the total adult male population is not known with certainty; the estimates of modern investigators for the year 431, the beginning of the Peloponnesian war, diverge between 35.000 and 55.000 [47], but at any rate we may assume that only a small part of the citizens had no share in the Attic soil. Aliens and outlanders

[44] Pp. 5 sqq.

[44a] Chapter III.

[45] Xen., Hell. VII, 1, 4. Cp. also J. Hatzfeld, Histoire de la Grèce ancienne. Paris 1926, p. 176.

[46] Dion. Hal., Lys. 32. Cf. A. H. J. Greenidge, A handbook of Greek Constitu-tional History. London 1920, p. 212.

[47] Cf. Ed. Meyer, Gesch. des Altertums IV, 1. 1939, pp. 704 sqq. Cp. also A. W. Gomme, The Population of Athens in the 5th and 4th centuries B.C. Oxford 1933.

were not allowed to own ground. It is true that we must take into consideration that not everybody in possession of ground was a farmer, but on the other hand part of the paupers worked as day-labourers and as such they took care of the cattle, the soil or the fruit-trees [48].

More facts may be adduced to prove the preponderance of agriculture and landed property as factors of economic life. Throughout history in Attica and outside it, the claims of the suppressed and lower class people are confined to these two: distribution of land and cancellation of (mortgage-) debts [49]. In some states the oath which a man had to take in order to be registered as a citizen, included a vow that he would not render himself guilty of these transgressions [50]. We cannot but doubt the exactitude of the communication that Pericles should have undertaken the construction of the splendid buildings to the eternal glory of Athens with an eye to procure employment [51]. On the other hand, it is certain that plots of land, *klèroi*, were allotted to poor citizens in the districts of Athens' so-called allies. Troops from the army as well as from the navy deprived of the supply from home, were at once ready and capable to till the soil and to earn their livelihood in this way [52]. The word *autourgoi*, selfworkers, does not generally mean *men* who work themselves, but in particular *farmers* who cultivate the land themselves; such were according to Pericles all Peloponnesians [53]. Aristotle's statement that most people support themselves by agriculture which satisfies all needs according to Socrates [54], tallies with reality in the Greek world.

So Greece was a country mainly subsisting on its agriculture, but at the same time it was covered by a very large number of towns, not only bigger ones on the coast, but especially smaller ones in the

---

[48] Hom., Od. IV, 644; XVIII, 357 sqq.; Il. XVIII, 550 sqq.; XXI, 444; Hes., Erg. 600 sqq.; Her., VIII, 137; Xen., Mem. II, 8, 1; Hell. II, 1, 1; VI, 2, 37; Plato, Euth. 4; Aristoph., Vesp. 712; Isaeus, VI, 39; Isocr., XIV, 48; Theocr. III, 35; Eur. Alc. 2; Apoll., II, 5, 5 and 9; Paus., V, 1, 9; Dem., LVII, 45; LIII, 21.

[49] Tyrtaeus in Aristot., Pol. 1307 a; Isocr., Pan. 259; Plato, Rep. VIII, 566 a; Leg. III, 684 d; Dem., XXIV, 149; Andoc., Myst. 88; Dio Chrys., XXXI, 70. Cf. Thuc., V, 4; Diod., XIX, 9; Plut., Agis 8. Bolkestein, Sociale politiek en sociale opstandigheid in de Oudheid (Social Policy and Social Rebelliousness in Antiquity). Amsterdam 1934; Bolkestein, Wohltätigkeit und Armenpflege im vorchristlichen Allertum. Utrecht 1939, pp. 248 sqq.

[50] Büchsenschutz, p. 36.

[51] Plut., Per. 12.

[52] Thuc., III, 50; V, 116; VI, 24; Diod., XII, 2; Plut., Per. 34; Strabo, VIII, 375; C. I. A. I, 31 b; IV, 22; Xen., Hell. II, 1, 1; VI, 2, 37.

[53] Xen., Oec. V, 4.

[54] Aristot., Pol. II, 3, 6.

interior. This circumstance was of great significance for its development and civilization. The frequent occurrence of towns in the midst
of an agrarian world already shows that the town-population was
different from that known in our European cities.

Of old the towns in Greece were the dwelling places of *land-
owners*. In the epic poems, viz. in the Odyssey where the normal life
of the upper classes is described, they live in towns, from which they
visit their grounds and herds at more or less frequent intervals [55].
The fact that some municipalities in Attics were called after families
out of the nobility [56] does not prove in the least that these families
were established there, for it may as well be explained from the circumstance that they owned land in those parts. The excavations in
Athens have shown that in olden days in the Ceramicus the residences
of the noble land-owners were situated next to the potters' workshops [57]. Ischomachus also, the gentleman-farmer in whom Xenophon
embodies his ideal, lived in the town [58] and most people of his time
did so though some of them possessed country-houses outside it.

It is worth while to pause a moment to consider the importance
of this fact of the proprietors living in the city. A first social and
political consequence is that the modern contrast between large scale
properties and trading and industrial capital and with it the opposition between conservatives and liberals, was lacking; party-demarca-
tions were based on different principles, for trading or industrial
capital, as such, hardly existed, at least not with the citizens. We shall
treat these two notions more at length in the following chapters. The
outlanders, however, were treated differently, because they were not
allowed to own land unless by way of favour [59]. The fortunes mentioned
in some pleas [60] were composed of various elements: landed estates,
houses, money lent on mortgage or bearing interest in an other way,
slaves either put to work by the proprietor or let out to a third party,
cash or valuables. The proprietors, the "powerful", *dynatoi*, form a

---

[55] Hom., Od. II, 77 and 154; VI, 383; XIII, 192; XVII, 206; II. IV, 474 sqq.
Also the mass of the common freeman, the demos, lived in town. Only the unfree
herdsmen and other unfree workers lived in country. Od. II, 384; VI, 274; XI, 293;
XVI, 27; XVII, 182; XIV, 372; XXIV, 210.

[56] E.g. the Boutadai (Boute(i)a).

[57] Lysias, I, 11, 20 and 22. However, many also lived in the country: Thuc., II,
14; Aristoph., Nub. 43 sqq.; Dem., XVIII, 38; LIII, 4; LV, 23; XLVII, 53.

[58] Xen., Oec. XI, XII, XIII, XIV.

[59] Xen., Vect. II, 6; Plato, Rep. 328 b; [Aristot.], Oec. II, 2, 3; IV, 9, 5; Lys.,
XII, 18; Dem., XXXVI, 6; C. I. A. II, 380; Plut., Per. 37; Athen., XIII, 577.

[60] Dem., I, 10 and 13.

unity and are, as a whole, politically conservatives; opposite to them are, on the one hand, the small farmers and tenants, on the other the "*banausoi*", the craftsmen, the shop-keepers, and all those who had to earn their living by manual labour; they form the common people, *dèmos*.

The social status comparable in its way of living and ideas to the mediaeval knights is missing therefore in Greek society; it did not know the gentry living in castles apart from the towns, granting themselves titles of their own and developing a feeling for standing and culture; we do not find a trace of ladies' worship or an exaggerated sense of honour in Greek civilization, which never submitted to the influence of the nobility or the clergy, whose nature was merely middle-class and town-like and whose men of note merely aspired to the exercise of power in the State, that is to say in the city.

But not only the bigger land-owners lived away from their estate; the main part of the farmers was not scattered in solitary farms either. Conditions still prevailing in South Italy and in Sicily may elucidate the ancient situation of the country: there we find at intermittent distances varying between three and twenty miles towns with 20 to 70.000 inhabitants, while in between there are no settlements except some cottages and barns; our hamlets or scattered farms are unknown. An observant traveller [61] tells us: "Early in the morning our farmer leaves for his land, while his donkey or, in absence of such, his wife carries the pitcher and the basket with food. For he lives far from his land, in the city. Only 11 % of the population of Sicily lives in the country, the rest of them in little towns of more than 500, more than half even in towns of more than 15.000 inhabitants. A quaint phenomenon for a state subsisting in the main on agriculture". In the Odyssey we read of men who travel regularly to and fro between the town and the land [62]. Even in Athens they live in this way: the principal figure in one of Lysias' speeches [63] owes his misfortune, his wife's infidelity, partly to the circumstance that he must till the soil far from the town in day-time. It goes without saying that not all the farmers in Attica lived in the capital; most of them had their houses close to each other in the centre of their municipality; many of them shunned the bustle of Athens and the comedies prove that the contrast between farmer and townsman was certainly visible in

[61] A. Bauer, Vom Griechentum zum Christentum. München 1899, p. 13. Cp., however, Ed. Meyer, Gesch. d. Alt. III, p. 304, 1.

[62] Cf. p. 18, 54.

[63] Lys., I, 11, 13, 20.

this most developed state [64]. But the solitary life at isolated farms was exceptional; the farmers had daily intercourse with each other in the *lesche* which was not lacking in any village. It was the meeting-place which, in day-time, protected the citizens talking politics from the sun, and which during the night offered a shelter to strangers without a guest-friend.

Scholars have suggested that this remarkable phenomenon of settlements in the city was due to the prevailing unsafety [65], but first of all it is not clear why this same factor did not apply to e.g. Central Europe during the Middle-Ages, and further they neglect the fact that the principal possessions which ran the risk of being stolen were the cereals on the land and the fruit on the trees [65]. The explanation will also have to be sought elsewhere. As we remarked above (pp. 7 sqq.) Greece is country poor in water; it hardly has any rivers which are not dried up in the hot season; there is no rainfall in summer, so wells are not sufficient for the whole year. A result is that every settlement is absolutely dependent on the presence of a spring. Many and small villages can only subsist in regions where numerous springs are found. Whereever they are scarce—and this is the case in all the countries round the Mediterranean Sea—isolated farms and villages are impossible and the population must dwell together in larger cities, often far away from the land which they must cultivate daily.

Thus the town is inhabited to a large extend by farmers, which means that in the Greek world the sharp contrast of the Middle-Ages between the country living on agriculture and cattle-breeding and the town, the centre of industry and trade, is lacking. The towns of Greece did not originate from markets: the word *agora* indicating market later on, meant first of all assembly or meeting-place of the people [66]. The Greek town came into existence as the centre of consumers, not as the centre of producers, and it has never lost its rusticity nor the character of centre of consumption, not even Athens. It has been justly said that the comedy of the fifth century bears the unmistakable smell of country-life and could never have pleased the modern townsman; the advantages of peace enumerated in these comedies are not restoration of business or ports full of vessels or

---

[64] Aristoph., Nub. 43 sqq.

[65] Cp., however, also Ed. Meyer, Gesch. des Alt. III, p. 302.

[66] Hom., Il. I, 305; II, 53-80 and 808; XII, 211-213; XIX, 50; Od. II, 69 and 257; VIII, 156 and 503; IX, 171; X, 188; XII, 319; Her., VI, 58; Xen., An. V, 7, 2.

workshops being reopened—no, they only refer to the benefits bestowed on the farmers: Dicaeopolis complains about vineyards cut down [67], Strepsiades liver happily without care or trouble in the country with his bees, his sheep and his olives [68], Philocleon's youthful recollections regard the stealing of grapes, and his being tied to an olive-tree [63]. For this reason alone Bücher's construction of "Stadt-wirtschaft" (self-sufficient town economy) cannot be applied to Greek life [70].

We must see Greece, Greece of the 6th to the 4th century too, as a principally agrarian society, but with a great number of, as a rule, small towns. This fact explains how it was possible that an intellectual civilization came into being inconceivable in a merely agricultural world, also how beyond the conception and worship of the gods characteristic of country-life, other ideas about world and life could exist in a townish community which were to disappear again with the decline of the cities and their culture.

Above [71] we have explained the nature of the soil in Greece; we have seen that a very large part of the ground, did not produce anything, and that an other part is used as pasture-land. In these circumstances one expects extensive *cattle-breeding,* but we must not forget that in Southern Europe only the ground too poor to be cul-tivated is used as pasture-ground. It follows that the number of cattle wanting high and tender grass is small. They were to be found especially on the Western slopes of the mountains where the Zephyros brings rain, in Epirus [72] (even now most cattle-breeders and butchers are Epirotes), in Acarnania with its alluvial land rare in Greece [73], at the mouth of the Achelous, in the plain of Elis, where Augias' herds grazed, in Eastern Greece especially in Phthiotis, in Thessaly, in the district formed by the valley of the Spercheus and the plain of Cran-non, further in the Peloponnesus in Messenia [74]. For the rest only

---

[67] Aristoph., Ach. 29 sqq.; 231; 994 sqq. Cf. Pax 1130; Nub. 43 sqq. Mosaic law forbade the Jews to cut down "trees for meat" in warfare. Deut. XX, 19-20.

[68] Aristoph., Nub. 43 sqq.

[69] Aristoph., Vesp. 449.

[70] K. Bücher, Die Entstehung pp. 91 and 116 sqq.

[71] P. 3.

[72] Eustath. ad Hom., Il. II, 633 sqq; Paroemiographi Graeci ed. Schneidewin I, App. I, 57. Cf. Plut., Pyrrhus 5; Varro, R. R. II, 5, 10.

[73] Schol. ad Theocr. XIV, 48; XXII, 157; Hom., Il. II, 605; Hymn. XIX, 30; Pind., Ol. VI, 100.

[74] Strabo, VIII, 366.

small cattle, goats and sheep were raised [75]. To day also in Greece cows do not live near the farm, but during the night in stables on the land; in the daytime they were driven to the river-valley in winter, in summer to the woods to eat the foliage. No wonder that the cows had hardly any milk for their calves, they only served as breedes for the oxen which were used beside the donkeys as draught-animals and which lived like our horses in stables. Moreover, they were used as slaughter-cattle or sacrificial animals which came practically to the same in Greek society where meat was only eaten at sacrifices and where probably the killing of each animal was treated as such. Horses were not used in farming and scarcely employed otherwise; as a rule only in battle and in games; but even the number of riding-horses was small and only the very rich could afford to participate in the Olympic chariot-races. Studs were only known in Thessaly [76] and Boeotia [77]. Pigs were kept in some districts in Arcadia and Aetolia [78]. Apiculture, on the other hand, must have been practised on a large scale, because sugar was unknown and honey the only sweetening material [79].

All this has little in common with our cattle-raising: dairy-industry is nearly wholly lacking; milk, butter and cheese do not belong to daily nourishment. It is also evident that it is not necessary to invest much money in breeding this kind of cattle; the food of goats and sheep does not cost anything, looking after them requires but a few hired labourers or slaves. Economically it did, therefore, not play an important rôle, except perhaps in some regions in the neighbourhood of Miletus, e.g., where they applied themselves to the breeding of more valuable sheep [80]; the sheep were either exported themselves or merely their choice wool destined for the making of clothes for the rich or for public worship [80a]. Socially too, cattle-business must have been of little importance. Perhaps we may estimate the number of

---

[75] Schol. ad Plat., Criti. 111c, Cf. Harpocrat. s. v. Phellea; Aristoph., Nub. 71; Is., VIII, 42.

[76] Strabo, X, 449. According to Isocrates (VIII, 118) the Thessalian could put more than three thousand men into the field, according to Xenophon (Hell. VI, 1, 8) six thousand. Her., V, 63 sqq.; Thuc., II, 9; Aristot., Ath. Pol. 19. In Attica there were few horsemen (Her., IX, 13). Cf. A. Hörnschemeyer, Die Pferdezucht im klassischen Altertum. Thesis Giessen 1929.

[77] Ps. Dicaearch., I, 13; Xen., Hell. VI, 4, 10; Diod., XII, 702; C. I. G. 1569 a.

[78] Athen., IV, 148 sqq.; Xen., Comm. II, 7, 6. Cf. K. Winkelstern, Die Schweinezucht im klassischen Altertum. Thesis Giessen 1933.

[79] Plin., N. H. XII, 32; XXI, 57; Diosc. II, 101 and 104; Strabo, IX, 399; Pausanias, I, 32, 1; Athen., XIII, 582 sqq.; Geopon., XV, 7, 11.

[80] Aristoph., Lys. 724; Ran. 542; Athen., XV, 691 a. Cf. also p. 44.

[80a] Cf. O. Brendel, Die Schafzucht im alten Griechenland. Würzburg 1934.

men necessary for the tending of the cattle in Attica at 5 to 6,000, a
number of little significance compared to an estimated total population upwards of 300.000.

From the above it is evident that cattle-breeding was a trade of
hardly any importance. The same may be said of the development of
agriculture. A good graduator for the standard of its development is
the measure in which the Greeks have been able to profit from the
ground. In leases [81] it is sometimes emphatically that half of the
leased land must remain uncultivated and must be delivered up uncultivated. Considering that a very small portion of the Greek soil could
be tilled we need not wonder that agriculture yielded but little profit.

We should wrong the Greeks by ascribing this either to their bad
insight or to neglect. They could not act differently in those times.
The soil was poor and could not possibly furnish a sufficient quantity
of food to nourish big cattle; consequently they had not enough
manure at their disposal to improve the quality of the land [82]. Agriculture merely depended on the natural fertility of the soil which was
very slight in Attica and elsewhere, though some enthusiastic admirers
of their country thought differently. "Greece has always had poverty
as a companion" duly remarks her most ancient historian [83].

So the grain-harvest was scanty, notwithstanding cereals (*sitos*)
formed the staple-food of the population. Barley (*krithè*) was cultivated most; the flour of it (*alphita*) cooked with water into porridge
(*maza*) furnished the daily meal; sown in the beginning of November [85], it could already be reaped in May. In this way much time was
left for other occupations: navigation and the waging of war. Wheat
(*pyros*) was sown more scantily, the flour of it (*aleura*) was baked
into bread (*artos*) [86]. Most of it grew in Asia-Minor and Boeotia; it
could be gathered a month later than the barley. The material for the
bread used by the Athenians, at least if they could afford it, was
imported from abroad. Below [87] we shall speak more fully about the
shortage of home-grown corn as well in Attica as in numerous other

---

[81] Bull. de correspond. hell. XVI, pp. 292 sqq. Cf. Guiraud, La propriété p. 436
and Büchsenschütz p. 94.

[82] Cf. pp. 3 and 4.

[83] Her., VII, 102. Cf. VIII, 111.

[84] Aristoph., Lys. 729; Athen., XII, 540 d; XV, 691 a; Plin., N. H. XXIX, 33.

[85] Her., IV, 42; Theophr., Hist. Pl. VIII? 1, 2-4; cp. Geop. II, 40, 2.

[86] Enjoyable is the place in Plato (Rep. 372, as far as d) about the meals of the
phylakes.

[87] P. 108.

more densely populated coast-towns, and the need of import of these commodities from surrounding districts.

Though the soil is little suitable for corn-growing, it is extremely good for some kind of fruit-trees, especially the olive-tree; its fruit and particularly the oil pressed from it were considered indispensable by the Greeks. We have already spoken of the frequent use made of it [88]. In Attica, which apparently produced a particularly fine quality of oil, oil and marble were the few articles of export yielded by the soil [89].

Next to the olive-tree the vineyard furnished the most important product lacking in no part of the Greek world. Almost every district supplied its own local wants; naturally the wine from some districts was considered better than the rest (the brands from Chios, Lesbos and Thasos were most in demand [90]; wine only used by the rich as a rule or on solemn occasions, also belonged to the articles of commerce.

The Attic farmer as we know him from Aristophanes' comedies [91], is different from the Dutch one in this respect that he resembled the Frenchman who is chiefly a vintager and an olive-planter too. With the increase of grain-import from the Black Sea the cultivation of corn at home will probably have diminished still more. However, we must not overrate the influence of the rivalry of grain-import from oversea too much in Greece (no more was this the case in Italy before the Gracchi); the considerable cost for the transport by land confined the import mainly to the coast-towns. In the country among the slaves and the poorer population in general, for whom barley-porridge formed the principal food, the inland product will always have found a ready market.

In the 7th century B.C. the ground in Attica was in the hands of a few, as Aristotle tells us, probably without much exaggeration [92]. In some parts of the Greek world this remained so: the few districts suitable for landed property were Sicily where it predominated, and where it has remained so throughout history, Thessaly, for the greater part flat arable land in the possession of some hundreds of noble families whose wealth, it is said, attracted the Persians, further

---

[88] P. 5.

[89] Plut., Sol. 24.

[90] Cf. p. 4.

[91] Aristoph., Nub. 45 sqq.; Ach. 987 and 1022-1023; Pax 557-559 and 1140-1148; Plut. 253.

[92] Aristot., Ath. Pol. 2; 4; 12.

Laconia, Messenia and Crete. For the rest, Greece was destined to be the country of small properties by the nature of its soil.

Attica too during the period of its greatest florescence. The cutting up of the land is apparent from the results which Phormisius' proposition mentioned above [93], would have had: with so many posessors the allotment of the greater part cannot have been large. And the data confirming this are not lacking either. Only small sums of money are mentioned in the mortgage-deeds preserved on stone. We learn from the same sources that it was usual to dispose of the soil in numerous and small plots [94]. This was especially the case when State-property was sold, obtained as a rule by confiscation, in contrast with what happened later on to the Roman State-demesne. The data in the Athenian pleas from the fourth century tally with the facts given above [95]: in all inventories about inheritances mentioned in law-suits only a small part of the property was invested in land; an estate of about 44 acres was considered big and the very largest property known to us had a size of 74 acres. Aristotle describes peasantry in general as the class of small proprietors [96]; naturally all this does not mean that bigger estates did not exist.

We must not forget either that the landed property of the wealthy Athenians, even when it was not situated outside the boundaries, was often scattered over sundry districts. Consequently the economic advantages attached to landed property in the pre-industrial period as for instance smaller cost for manual labour and guards, were lacking.

Finally, we must mention Aristotle's statement of general purpose in his Politics [97]; he scores it against Plato for a mistake that the latter, it is true, divided the landed property in his state in equal parts, but neglected to take measures to regulate the birth-rate so as to keep the population stationary. Exactly in his State such legislation would have been necessary because property could in no way be alienated and therefore nothing was available for an increase of the population. He continues: "in reality, nobody is lacking ground because the size of the plots depends on the number of the population".

So a large number of the population in Attica were farmers (far-

---

[93] P. 17.

[94] Cf. P. Guiraud, La propriété pp. 291 sqq.

[95] Isaeus, V, 34; VIII, 35; IX, 41, 42 and 44; II, 34; Dem., XLV, 28; Aesch., I, 97; Dem., XX, 115; XLII, 5, 7 and 20; XLV, 28; Lys., XIX, 29.

[96] Zimmern p. 227.

[97] Cf. Guiraud, La propriété pp. 588 sqq.

mers especially in the sense of vintagers and olive-planters[98]), either as freeholders or as tenants; it follows that small properties prevailed, here and in the other democratic states of Greece. It is important to indicate now some social phenomena probably connected with this fact.

Not only theorists like Plato [99] and Aristotle [100], but also men of action like Hesiod [101] and Solon [102] were of opinion that a man should not marry before his thirtieth year; from the legislation [103] it appears, indeed, that the marriage of an older man with a young girl was considered normal. These late marriages have been taken as a consequence of social life and of the mutual friendship between young men by which the need of intellectual intercourse was completely satisfied [104]; but it is an evident mistake of intellectuals to think that it is this need which, either now or formerly, prompts men to marry. As a rule late marriages have a social reason which may perhaps be indicated in Greece too. As we have seen above a large part of the population consisted of petty farmers [105]; the quantity of land to be cultivated or to be prepared for cultivation was small; the young farmer will probably have been able to found a family of his own merely as a successor to his father, that is to say when the father had grown too old to perform the necessary labour himself. For that part of the population a marriage before their 30th year will hardly have been possible [106].

The late marriages of the men combined with the institution of slavery sanctioning the purchase of human bodies, and the frequent cohabitation of country people in the city too must have been a spur to sexual intercourse before marriage afterwards continued: the circumstance that this illegal intercourse was accepted by public opinion[107] may perhaps also be explained by this fact. The considerable difference in age between married couples (the wife was often still a child) will undoubtedly have aggravated her subservient position. The high tone

[98] P. 25.
[99] Plato, Leg. 721 b and 785 b.
[100] Aristot., Pol. IV, 16, 1334 b-1335 a-b. Cf. L. v. Bortkiewicz, War Aristoteles Malthusianer? Zeitschr. f. d. gesammte Staatswissenschaft LXII (1906), p. 436.
[101] Hes., Erg. 695.
[102] Solon, fr. 27. Cf. J. J. B. Mulder, Quaestiones nonnullae ad Atheniensium matrimonia pertinentes. Thesis Utrecht 1920, pp. 7-19.
[103] Mulder p. 5-7.
[104] Zimmern p. 29.
[105] P. 17. Cf. pp. 25 and 26.
[106] Mulder pp. 28-34.
[107] Mulder pp. 34-35.

which Xenophon's ideal husband Ischomachus takes with his young
wife (she was only fourteen years old when they were going to found
a family) is very instructive on this point [108].

There is another phenomenon to be mentioned possibly connected
with the late marriages. Scholars have been astonished that Greek
writers of ideal forms of government did not take into account the
increase of the population which seems normal to us [109]. They
forget, however, that the Greeks solved this problem by despatching
and forming settlements. We get the impression that a stagnate population was a natural phenomenon to the Greek: Aristotle [110] for that
matter ascertains this once and for all. To explain this exceedingly
remarkable fact it does not suffice to point to the undoubtedly high
infant-mortality in the Greek world. According to a hardly credible
statement in a pamphlet on natural science from the 4th or 3rd century most babies were wont to die before the seventh day [111]. But
there is no reason to admit that in this respect conditions here were
more favourable than with the Romans, e.g., where very large families
were no exceptions as appears from their children's names [112]. Not
only the war [113] nor the party-strife [114] which moved down many
young men had this effect on Greece only. We may sooner suppose
that the late marriage of the men and the small amount of children are
connected with each other without our being able to explain this
fact [115]; statistics have proved of late, however, that these things are
connected [116]. Furthermore we must not forget when treating the
problem of the slight population-increase in Greece that it was also
partly due to slavery [117].

The question now arises in what manner agriculture was carried on
and the different statuses of the men concerned with it. We must
distinguish two classes of land-owners: the one who did not work

[108] Xen., Oec. VIII, 4 sqq.

[109] Mulder p. 126 sqq.; Zimmern pp. 324-326. Plato, Leg. V, 737 c and 740. Cf.
Malthus, An Essay on the Principle of Nations pp. 115 sqq.

[110] Zimmern pp. 324-326.

[111] Aristot., Hist. An. VII, 12 588 a. Cf. Chr. Hack, Die Geschichte der Säug-
lingskrankheiten im Altertum. Diss. Jena 1914.

[112] Mulder p. 125: An probabile non est nomina quae sunt Septimus, Octavus,
Decimus, olim liberis indita esse quibus ordo eorum designaretur? Cf. Weise, Charak-
teristik der lateinischen Sprache p. 23.

[113] Schol. ad Hom., Il. I, 5; Eurip., Hel. 38 sqq.

[114] Thuc., II, 44; III, 73; Lys., XXI, 24; Dem., XVIII, 205.

[115] Isaeus, II, 4-5 and 7-9.

[116] Mulder p. 131.

[117] Cf. below p. 78.

himself and the small farmers-proprietors. The tenants, the working-managers or stewards (freemen or slaves) and the labourers (likewise free men or slaves) belong to this last class.

Though big landed properties at least in Attica were of little importance, yet it does not mean that every land-owner worked himself as a farmer on his land: there were plenty of them who left the cultivation of their ground either to tenants or to men whom we call working-managers (*epitropoi*) who might be slaves or free men [118]. Xenophon says of this last group of men that they "farmed with their supervision" (*tèi epimeleiai geōrgountes*) in opposition to the small farmers who tilled the soil with their own hands (*autourgoi*) [119]. In Ischomachus he describes his ideal gentleman-farmer living in the city: "every day he goes on horseback to his estate in order to regulate the work" [120]. Others, however, did not interfere at all with the work and confined themselves to a rare visit now and again. In one of Sophocles' [121] tragedies Deianira compares her consort Heracles, who neglects his children, to the farmer who only looks at his distant fields during sowing and reaping-time, and in one of Demosthenes' pleas [122] a piece of land is mentioned neglected by its proprietor "who prefers the town to his land". The phenomenon is perfectly comprehensible when we think not only of the fact that the landed-property of many of them lay wide apart, but also of the circumstance that many proprietors were all but exclusively land-owners. On an earlier page [123] we saw that there was hardly any fortune in which no land was included. Most of these owners will have had their real occupations—and these certainly not only of political nature!—in the city, and they will especially have appreciated the revenues of their land.

By far the greater part of the land-owners in Attica and other regions was composed of small farmers, who tilled the little fertile soil with their own hands [124] with or without the help of hired labourers or slaves. We need not be astonished that so little has been handed down to us of just these men who formed the pith of Greece's population; everywhere and at all times, before social researches became

[118] Xen., Mem. II, 8, 2-3.
[119] Xen., Oec. V, 4. Cf. Aristot., Pol. VI, 5, 6; Aristoph., Eccl. 432-434; C. I. A. I, 31; IV, 1a. Bullet. de Corresp. Hell. XII, p. 3. Dem. II Argumentum Libanii; Diod., XIII, 78; XV, 46.
[120] Xen., Oec. XI.
[121] Soph., Trach. 32-33.
[122] Dem., LV, 11.
[123] Pp. 17-18.
[124] Aristoph., Nub. 43 sqq. Cf. Lucian., Het. dial. VII, 3. Thuc., II, 14 sqq.

a special science, the normal life of the masses hardly excited the
attention of the authors, least of all when they rose almost exclusively
from the propertied and non-working classes. We learn the character
of the farmer best from the description of those very rare poets who
knew themselves the necessity of earning their bread by manual labour.
Hesiod as he describes his ideal farmer will have been for ages the
normal type in large parts of Greece; he knows that only through
steady toil and with the sweat of the brow poverty is to be avoided[125],
that in the most auspicious circumstances some welfare may be attained and that honesty is the best policy. He holds hospitality in
esteem but for the rest he acts like the ground his master; he only
gives to those who give back; as every farmer he brings the ox and
the labourer on the same level [126].—In the 5th century too we must
go to the poets in order to know country-life; in Euripides [127] we
meet the honest poor *autourgos* to whom Aegisthus gave the noble
Electra in marriage; like Hesiod he knows that only constant labour
and not speaking about the gods procure a reasonable livinghood [128];
he is as hospitable, as open-handed towards strangers [129] as only a
man can be in a world cognizant of little bartering and little money;
a rich man's stomach cannot contain more than a poor man's [130].
Aristophanes [131] draws a picture of the sturdy Dicaeopolis who originates from the same sphere of the self-sufficient household and longs
for his *demos* (village) where he need not buy anything but obtains
everything from his own land.

Among the small farmers there was a part which did not cultivate
its own land but that of others. Literature is almost completely silent
about the position of these tenants; fortunately, some leases engraved
upon stone are preserved for us [132]. From the circumstance that all
these leases, with one exception all originating from a town in
Lycia [133], relate to land owned by the State or by a temple, scholars
have inferred that lease of land by private persons did not occur in
Attica. It is easy to ascertain that in this case even less than usual in
ancient history with its extremely lacunary traditions the "argumentum

125 Hes., Erg. 297 sqq.; 395; 404; cf. 647.
126 Hes., Erg. 403.
127 Eur., El. 1 sqq.
128 Eur., El. 80.
129 Eur., El. 357 sqq.
130 Eur., El. 431.
131 Aristoph., Ach. 34 sqq.
132 Cf. Guiraud, La propriété pp. 423 sqq.
133 Cf. Guiraud, o.c. pp. 423 sqq.

e silentio" must not be applied. Lease of land owned by the State was a matter of public concern; so it had to be fixed on a document accessible to the public: on a stone; the more so because the leases were given at long date and the magistrates alternated every year. Agreements between private persons, on the contrary, were fixed in a cheaper way and on more perishable material, on potsherds—a mutilated lease has come down to us in this way— [134]. No wonder that they were easily destroyed. Though an agreement concerning bottomry must have been made numerous times [135], not a single original copy has been handed down to us. For the rest we need not restrict ourselves to eliminate this "argumentum e silentio", no more need we refer exclusively to the above-mentioned conditions which made the leasing of land by private persons also unavoidable; from the authors of the time, Xenophon [136], Lysias [137] and Isocrates [138], passages may be quoted proving the existence of this renting.

The preserved leases teach us something of importance about the position of the tenants. Aristotle in his Constitution of Athens [139] communicates that in Attica the lease of government-ground was concluded for a period of ten years and that the rent was payed yearly in the tenth prytany i.e. about June. A lease found in the Piraeus confirms this [140]; the temple-land of Delos was regularly leased for the same period [141]; an Attic lease mentions a term of twenty [142], one even of forty years [143]. In Delos the tenant had the right—which was not obligatory—to renew his lease if he were willing to pay one tenth extra of the original rent; in that case a new public leasing was omitted [144]. The long term of the lease shows the tenants' firm position, for the shorter it is, the more he approaches the labourer, as is evident in Oriental states, because he can be expelled from it every year. It goes without saying that the tenants are subject to all sorts of obligations, as a rule purporting to assure the

[134] Cf. Guiraud, o.c. pp. 423 sqq.
[135] Below p. 112.
[136] Xen., Vect. IV, 19. Cf. Harpocration s. v. apo misthomatōn. Soph., Trach. 238; Plato, Leg. VI, 759 b; Andoc. I, 92; Ditt., Syll. I³, 93, 153, 28, 29, 64, 65, 100.
[137] Lys., VII, 9-11.
[138] Isocr., VII, 31-32.
[139] Aristot., Ath. Pol. 47.
[140] C. I. A. II, 600.
[141] C. I. A. I, 283.
[142] C. I. A. IV, 53a.
[143] Inscriptions Juridiques XIII², 2-3.
[144] Bullet. de Corr. Hell. XVI, p. 431.

quality and the value of the soil, and a certain security is demanded for the observance of these obligations in the shape of superintendence [145]. But the independence of the tenant and in general the liberty of working the farm in his own manner is not impeded. In Greece no example has been handed down to us in this period of the so-called half-culture (except for serfs) where the landlord stipulates a certain part of the proceeds to have a more direct interest in the way in which the farm is managed and the tenant has to submit to his supervision and directions [146]. The case is different when the landlord and the tenant agree to go halves when the harvest is partially destroyed by superior power, that is to say not by force of nature, as hail or inundation, but by destruction or by the menace of an invasion [147].

The particulars of the lease need not to be mentioned in this sketch; we must, however, still pay attention to the stipulation that the tenant is always obliged to give a security when concluding the agreement, as is usual in all the domains of business. The question may be raised how it was always possible to find people willing to go bail, especially in a country where one of the most famous proverbs was: "go bail and disaster is at your elbows [148]. The explanation may be that the farmers and tenants went bail for each other; if so, we must consider this mutual help as one of the forms in which the principle of insurance expressed itself in primitive economical life.

Also in the districts in which small farming was preponderant, the farmer, freeholder or tenant, had assistants for his work, servants. We may, however, assume that many a farmer was both; besides his own piece of land he will often have leased another plot. The general word for workman in Greek, *ergatès,* indicates as a rule the land-labourer [149], thanks to the predominant place which agriculture occupied in Greek life; for this matter, the small farmer also is often called by this name [150]. This much is certain that freemen as well as slaves served as such, but it is impossible to say who predominated, because the terms used leave us the benefit of a doubt. Without

---

[145] C. I. A. II, 600; 564; IV, 53 a; II, 1060; Bull. d. Corr. Hell. XVI, pp. 278 sqq. and 292 sqq; III, p. 242 A.

[146] Tyrtaeus, fr. 5. Cf. Pausan., IV, 14.

[147] Insc. Jur. XIII, 2, 12-14. Cf. XII, 1, 152.

[148] Insc. Jur. XIII, 1, 100 and 108; XII, 320-22; Bull. de Corr. Hell. IX, p. 412; XIV, pp. 430 sqq.

[149] Aristoph., Ach. 611; Xen., Inst. Cyr. V, 4, 24; Dem., XXXV, 32; LIX, 50; Plato, Polit. 259.

[150] Aristoph., Ach. 611; Xen., Inst. Cyr. V, 4, 24.

exception the free labourer and the slave employed in farming are both called *ergatès* as well as the hireling or *misthōtos,* for slaves were also let out by their masters for certain services and were then called *misthōtos*[151]. Meanwhile, after reading the scattered and hidden indications, one retains the impression that slaves as a rule did the work in farming, though free labourers were never absolutely lacking [152].

In agriculture—taking the word in its widest sense—female labour seems to have been of little importance. From what we have said above we know that cattle-raising did not involve dairy-farming; it follows that most of the work, done by women on the farms in Northern Europe, was lacking [153]. They can neither have been used on a large scale for the guarding of herds, because here drastic measures were often required; the occupations of the shepherdess will have been more glorified extolled in the poetry of the townsman than on the land among the goats; a word for female swine-herds, however, existed [154]. It is significant for the little important rôle of woman in farming that Hesiod compares her in general to the drones which pile the labour of the bees in the hive in their bellies [155]. In busy times, in the harvest period e.g., especially during the gathering of olives and grapes, women were also engaged as assistants; but hardly a trace is to be found of regular labour of female slaves on the land.

Besides the citizen-farmers, either independent farmers or tenants, free labourers or slaves, another category of men, the *serfs* [156], also tilled the soil in some parts of Greece. This institution seems to have developed chiefly from the circumstance that the conquerors of some districts appropriated the fertile land and compelled the natives to cultivate it for their benefit. These situations are best known in Thessaly where the agrarian population consists of the *"penestai",* in Lacedaemonia where the reigning class of the Spartiatai imposed the working of their farms on the *Helots* [158], and in Crete where the serfs were called *"mnōitai"* in the State demesne and *"klarōtai"* in

---

151 Plato, Polit. 290 a.
152 Cf. Guiraud, La propriété p. 454.
153 Cf. P. Herfst, Le travail pp. 15 sqq.
154 Pollux, IV, 56.
155 Hes., Theog. 589 sqq.
156 Cf. Guiraud, La propriété pp. 407 sqq.
157 Hes. s. v. Penestai; Athen., VI, 264 a. Greenidge, A Handbook pp. 83-84.
158 Paus., III, 2, 5-7; IV, 23, 1 and 24, 5; Athen., VI, 272 a. Cf. VI, 278; XIV, 657 d; Plut., Luc. 8 and 24; Inst. Lac. 41.

the private estates [159]; of other regions we only know that this institution existed.

While their position shows many a difference juridically with
respect to their relation to the landlord, the way of adjudication and
the like, they all have this in common that they are attached to a
certain plot of land from which they cannot be severed. For the rest
they resembled each other in so far as they worked their farms as
tenants on their own account and owed a fixed amount to their
landlords, either money or a share in the crops; they were allowed to
keep the rest of the proceeds [160]. Their position slightly resembles
that of the slaves to whom an opportunity was given to make their
labour pay (see chapter IV). In so far they differed greatly from the
slaves as the serfs were not at the absolute disposal of the proprietors,
they could not be sold nor be liberated; only the ruling citizens as a
whole possessed this right [161]. For the rest we know, if it is only from
one inscription regarding agrarian situations in the region of the
Eastern Locrians, that slaves were also tied down to the ground and
were either sold with it or changed hands with the sale of the land.
The circumstance that for the serfs a general and separate term never
arose also points to the fact that there was not always a clearly defined
difference between slaves and serfs.

Though not juridically, there was, however, a real difference with
great social consequences. As we shall discuss below [162] more at large,
the great majority of the slaves consisted of aliens kidnapped or
bought from everywhere; a feeling of solidarity could hardly be
expected among them and so the first condition for a united resistance
failed [163]. The serfs, on the contrary, came forth from the original
native population whose unity need not be consolidated by the common fate of subjugation. Among the *"penestai"* [164] as well as the
Helots [165] dangerous rebellions broke out repeatedly. Aristotle says of
the Helots that they were continually on the look-out in order to take
advantage of every mishap of their masters [166]. A large part of the
Spartan policy may be explained from the fact that they always had to

[159] Pollux, III, 83; Athen., VI, 263 and 267.
[160] Athen., VI, 264 a.
[161] Athen., VI, 263 sqq.
[162] Pp. 79-80.
[163] Plat., Leg. VI, 777 c; Aristot., Pol. VII, 9237; [Aristot.], Oec. I, 5.
[164] Aristot., Pol. II, 6, 63; Xen., Hell. II, 3, 36. Cf. Aristoph., Vesp. 1271 sqq.
[165] Aristot., Pol. II, 7, 63. Cf. Thuc., I, 32. Strabo, VI, 280; Paus., IV, 24, 5;
Thuc., IV, 41; Xen., Hell. I, 2, 18.
[166] Aristot., Pol. II, 6, 53; Xen., Hell. III, 6, 3; Thuc., I, 101; IV, 80; V, 14.

pay regard to the inland foe. Undoubtedly many communications about
their treatment are inventions as so many other stories about the Spartans' mysterious world,—e.g. if a serf was sturdier than beseemed a
man of his kind, he is said to have been put to death while his master
also was punished because he had not been able to prevent such an
unwished-for growth—[166a]. But highly instructive for our knowledge
of their relations is the scene enacted during the siege of Pylos: according
to Thucydides' credible narration [167] the presence of armed Athenians
roused the non-imaginary fear of a revolt of the Helots. The Spartans
called up volunteers for military service, they held out the prospect of
freedom as a reward; the two thousand who sent up their names
disappeared, nobody knows how, because the Spartans were convinced
that those who were most keen on their freedom would also be
inclined first to rebel.

As we have mentioned above [168], the slight development of cattle-
raising implied that the consumption of meat could not be large and
regular. *Hunting,* however, tried to supply this want to a certain
degree. From literature [169] and vase-paintings [170] we get the impression that hunting was mainly a distraction and an amusement [171]. It
possessed, indeed, the character of sport already at the princely courts
of the Mycenean time—a well-known fresco of Tiryns [172] proves it—;
hunting was especially pursued where the aristocracy dominated as in
Lacedaemonia and in Thessaly; the Hellenistic monarchs were to
continue the Macedonian and Persian traditions later on. We are not
astonished to see that men like Xenophon [173] and Plato [174] considered
and appreciated hunting only from this point of view, as an excellent
bodily exercise by which moral qualities as courage and perseverance
were also stimulated. But some of Aristotle's [175] statements where he
mentions hunting beside piracy and fishing as one of the means of

[166a] On the arbitrary treatment of the helots: Isocr., XII, 181.
[167] Thuc., IV, 80.
[168] P. 22.
[169] Hom., Od. XIX, 428 sqq.; XIX, 464 sqq.; Il. V, 49 sqq.; XVII, 725 sqq.;
X, 360 sqq.; XI, 324 sqq.; XII, 41.
[170] Cf. also M. Rostovtzeff, The Social and Economic History of the Hellenistic
World. Oxford 1941. p. 1387.
[171] Büchsenschütz p. 314.
[172] H. Th. Bossert, Altkreta p. 162.
[173] Xen., Cyn. passim; Inst. Cyr. I, 2, 10. Cf. VII, 1, 35. E. Scharr, Xenophon's
Staats- und Gesellschaftsideal pp. 260 sqq.
[174] Plato, Leg. 823 c and 763 b. Cf. also Rep. 412 b.
[175] Aristot., Polit. I, 2 and 3.

subsistence make us realize that it was as much of economical significance, a conclusion also to be drawn from general considerations. In so
far it is different from agriculture and fishing which we are going to
discuss presently, that only very few will have regarded it as their
exclusive trade. The Greeks no more than any other nation in Antiquity knew "shooting-licenses"; every one was allowed to kill and
appropriate a wild animal; neither was a fence-season fixed by law.
In these circumstances every farmer must have been a hunter at certain
times in the numerous regions where mountain and wood produced
a profusion of game. Attica, according to the antique standard inten-
sely cultivated, where hardly anymore a hare was to be caught, will
have been an exception. The farmer was compelled to protect the
growing crops from the voracity of the game: he will not always have
confined himself to guard his crops, but he will often have pursued
it on his own ground, especially the hares, the deer, wild goats or
fowl; on the other hand he will probably have left the more dangerous
boar-hunting to skilled hunters. And the shepherds too must have
considered the setting of traps and snares, and the digging of pits
as a welcome diversion in their monotonous lives; the fact that the
shepherd's crook was called *"lagobolon"* [176], hitter of hares, may
also prove it.

But however important hunting was to the public house-keeping,
it was by far surpassed by *fishing*. In a country like Greece, where
water and land are so closely connected through hundreds of bays and
spits of land, and hundreds of islands in the midst of a tranquil sea,
fishing must at all times have procured food to a considerable part
of the population [177]. The significance of the sea and its live con-

---

[176] Theocr., IV, 49.

[177] *West coast of Greece*: Plin., N. H. IX, 115; XXXI, 94; XXXII, 18 and
150; Aristot., Hist. An. II, 504 b 32; Strabo, VIII, 3, 19; Ael., N. A. XIV, 1;
XIII, 9; Xenocr., De alim. aquat. 44 and 62; Arch., Fr. 53; 23, 43, 46, 24 (R);
Paus., X, 9, 3; Athen., III, 91 b and 30 d; VII, 288 c; Democr. of Ephese, F. H. G.
IV 383.

East coast of Greece: Aristot., H. A. V, 548 b 25; VI, 569 b 11 sqq.; VIII, 602 a
8; Plin., N. H. IX, 149; Ael., XV, 10; Philemon, II, 500, 21 K.; Aesch., Ag. 959;
Alciphr., Ep. III, 10, 4; Strabo, VIII, 6, 11; Athen., VII, 317 b; Paus., II, 34, 1, 2;
I. G. IV, 752; Arch., Fr. 25; 28; 15 (R); Isocr., VIII, 117; Pluf., Sol. 9; Xen., Hell.
V, 1, 20; Aristoph., Av. 76; Athen., VI, 244 c; IV, 135 a; Poll., VI, 63; Aristoph.,
Ach. 901; Eq., 815; Criton, III, 354 (K); Cratinus, I, 80 (K); Nausicrates, II, 295
(K); Antiphan., II, 92; 105; 115 (K); Eubulus, II, 186; 177 (K); Ptol. Euerg.,
F. H. G. III, 186; Agatharchides, F. H. G. III, 192; Ps. Dicaearch., F. H. G. II,
260; Hegesander, F. H. G. IV, 415; Aristot., H. A. IV, 531 b, 12.

tents finds expression in the adornment-motives of the Cretan-Mycenean art [178]; the fishers of Phylakopi became celebrated in a very short time. It has often been said that this must have been different in the Homeric world, the Greeks of this period are supposed to have had an aversion to fish: this supposition could only hold good as long as people were not aware of the extremely limited sphere socially speaking of the epic poem. Its heroes undoubtedly preferred fragrant roasted meat, but the comparisons which often borrow their material from daily life, also of the lower classes mention fishing time after time [179], and in the description of the situations characterizing welfare under a just monarch is also mentioned: the sea produces fish [180]. Fish was the principal animal food to such a degree that the general word for it, *opson*, as a rule only means fish [181].

In the Homeric epic poem the epitheton "abounding in fish" is given thirteen times to the sea and once to a river [182]; for certain a poetic proof that fresh-water fishing was in no way to be compared to salt-water fishing, which may be easily understood in a country where rivers with ever running water are well-nigh lacking. Except in some sacred lakes or temple-ponds, inland fishing was practised exclusively in the Copais-lake in Boeotia, well-known on account of the eel which it provided [183].

North coast of the Aegean Sea: Arch., Fr. 24, 43, 44; 46; 15; 28; 50; 56 (R.); Diod., V, 47; Aristot., H. A. V, 548 b, 15; V, 549 b, 16-17; VIII, 598 a, 22; Her., VII, 109; Paus., VI, 11, 2, 8; Cratinus I, 13 (K); Aristoph., Ach. 671; Athen., VII, 329 b; Poll., VI, 63; Plin., N. H. IX, 149; Hegesander, F. H. G. IV, 420; Anthol. Pal. VII, 739; Antiphanes, II, 52 (K).

The Cyclades: Ditt. Syll.[3] 1024, 103; Philostephanus, F. H. G. III, 29; Herophytus, F. H. G. IV, 428; Aristot., H. A. V, 548 b, 19; Plin., N. H. IX, 149 and 180; XXXI, 131; Xenocr., De al. aquat. 53; Suidas s. v. Phaselis; Plut., Soll. An. 32; Ael., N. A. 28.

[178] Evans, Knossos I, pp. 519 sqq., fig. 377-380; fig. 390; 397-399; Brit. Mus. Cat. of Gems 80; Xanthoutides, Vaulted Tombs of Mesara p. 114, pl. XIV, n. 1079; Phylakopi p. 123, pl. XXII and p. 72, fig. 61-62; Rodenwaldt, Tiryns II, pp. 222 sqq., Taf. XXI and Abb. 80 sqq.; Bossert Abb. 236 c and 238 ab.

[179] Hom., Il. XVI, 406 (Cf. Finsler, Homer I, p. 81); XXIV, 80; Od., XII, 251; XXII, 383. Cf. Her., II, 92 and 77. Il. V, 487, cf. Hes., Scutum 213 sqq.; Od. X, 124; V, 432; Il. XVI, 745.

[180] Hom., Od., XIX, 111. Cf. Hes., Theog. 411-452.

[181] Above p. 9, 50.

[182] Hom., Il. XIX, 378, cf. Od. IX, 82. Od. IV, 516; V, 420; XXIII, 317, cf. Il. IX, 4. Od. IV, 381 and 390; 424; 470; X, 540, cf. III, 177; Il. IX, 360 (Hellespont); Il. XX, 392 (Hyllus).

[183] Aristoph., Ach. 880; Lys. 36 and 702; Strattis, I, 724 (K); Antiphanes, II, 92; 105; 115 (K); Eubulus, II, 186 and 177 (K); Athen., VII, 297 c; Poll., VII, 63; Ptol. Euerg., F. H. G. III, 186; Agatharchides, F. H. G. III, 192.

The character of sea-fishing was determined by the kind of fish which was caught and by the climate, keeping fish for a long time or transporting it a long way off was out of the question through the heat, therefore all fishing was mainly exercised at the coast and every region made use of the fish caught in its immediate surroundings [184]. In this way the conditions for a whole-sale trade were lacking, merely the poorer people found here a scanty subsistence. In literature [185] as well as in art, especially in later art, the fisherman was the type of the poor and fagged-out toiler [186]. It was unimaginable for a Spartan to profess such a trade [187] and Plato's contempt [188] may be explained in the same way; if ever he visited the market he will un-doubtedly have avoided the fishmongers' corner; it is remarkable that here woman did not act as a sales-woman [189]; in Athens bread-sales-women had the reputation of being the noisiest market-people [190].

One branch of fishery to be compared in some sort to herring-fishing in the North Sea is the fishing and salting of tunny. The tunny is a big fish: it can obtain a length of about 4 yards; they migrate in enormous shoals along the coast of the Mediterranean and are caught there from the middle of May till the end of October; they are also found in the Black Sea, especially in the Sea of Mar-mora and the Straits of the Dardanelles. On the coast conning-structures are built from where the people watch the arrival of a shoal; the fishermen are warned, they put out to sea in their boats, catch the fish in large nets and kill them with tridents [191]. Poseidon's

---

[184] On a red-figured pelike from the middle of the fifth century a bearded fisher-man sits angling from a rock. A boy withdraws at full trot, on his shoulder the carrying-pole (asilla) with two baskets (phernia, spyrides, Herodianus, I, 36, 24; cf. Ammon., p. 144; Poll., VI, 94; Hes. s. v. phernia), in which he takes away his father's catch. Another boy is still waiting for a load (Arch.-epigr. Mitteilungen aus Oesterreich III (1879), Taf. III, pp. 25 sqq.). Simonides, III, 503 b 4: The rough carrying-pole on the nape of his neck, this Olympic victor had in former days carried fish from the Gulf of Argolis to Tegea, a distance of over twenty miles in a bee-line. Cf. Arch. Eph. 1918 p. 168; Menander, III, 132, 8 (K); Alciphr., I, 1, 4.

[185] Anthol. Pal. VII, 505; Ael., N. A. XIV, 20; XV, 23; Athen., VII, 283 b; Alciphr., I, 3; Theocr., XXI, 31; Eur., Fr. 670 (N²); Soph., Ai. 879 sqq. Cf. Anthol. Pal. VII, 11. Fishery is the only trade in Antiquity that knows night-work. Buns-mann, De piscatorum in Gr. et Rom. litt. usu. Thesis Münster 1910. Cf., however, also p. 55.

[186] Cf. picture in R. Ménard and C. Sauvageot, Le travail dans l'Antiquité (Agri-culture-Industrie), p. 25; H. Bulle, De schöne Mensch, p. 188 (right with literature).

[187] Plut., Mor. 236 b.

[188] Plato, Leg. XI, 917 c.

[189] Pherecrates, I, 162 (K). Cf. Aristoph., Lys. 457 sqq.

[190] Aristoph., Ran. 857; Plut., 427 sqq.

[191] Ael., N. A. XV, 5.

the work of one individual, but how the organisation of the coopera-
also represented as the *retiarii*, netthrowers, in the gladiator's games
trident is probably the weapon of the tunny-fishermen [192], who are
in the time of the emperors. It is evident that this capture cannot be
the work of one individual, but how the organisation of the coopera-
tors worked has not been recorded. As a rule—we may suppose so
on account of what is known to us about Greek navigation—a certain
number of fishermen will have joined hands, and will have divided
the proceeds of their labour [193]. *Meritai*, partners, is mentioned in
one of the few passages from which something about the trade may
be gathered [194]. But it also happened that fisherman were employed
by a lord who collected the fish and the change so he was certainly
no whole-sale *entrepreneur*; next to slaves there were also free men
who offered their service in this trade [195].

The tunny-catch became very important to the public household
when the salting of fish, first cut into fillets, was invented [196]. The
Mediterranean Sea situated in the warm zone and characterized by
strong evaporation, possesses a high percentage of salt. By the laying-
out of salt-pans salt may be easily collected [197], a product the more
important for the preparation of food, because the farinaceous dishes
used by the Greeks are mostly in need of salt. Especially in the Black
Sea the presence of salt at the mouth of the large Russian rivers [198]
goes hand in hand with the abundance of fish; the salting of fish
could be applied on a large scale and besides corn [199] and slaves [200],
salted fish [201], *tarichos*, was the most important export-product of the

[192] Aesch., Sept. 131; Tillyard, Hope Vases p. 37, pl. 6.

[193] Ditt. O. G. I. S. 480 and 496. Mordtmann, Ath. Mitt. X (1885), pp. 206
sqq.; Ael., N. A. XV, 5; Theocr., XXI, 31; Plin., N. H. IX, 182; Anthol. Pal. VI,
33; VII, 295.

[194] Alciphr., I, 20.

[195] Alciphr., I, 5.

[196] Athen., III, 119 e and 121 b; Anaxandrides, II, 157 (K). Slaves' fare:
Lucian., Fug. 14; Gallus 29; De hist. conscrib. 20; Philippides III, 303 (K);
Aristoph., Ran. 558. Country-fare: Aristoph., Pax 563; Dem., XXXV, 32 sqq.;
Theophr., Char. IV, 12 sqq. Soldiers-fare: Aristoph., Ach. 967 and 1097 sqq.; Her.,
IX, 120.

[197] Her., IV, 53; Dio Chrys., XXXVI, 3; Schol. ad Aristoph., Ach. 760;
[Aristot.], Oec. II, 2, 3 p. 1346 b 13. Cf. Van Groningen, Mnemosyne 1925, pp.
211 sqq.

[198] [Aristot.], Oec. II, 2, 3 p. 1346 b 13; Her., IV, 53; Dio Chrys., XXXVI, 3.

[199] Isocr., XVII, 57; Thuc., III, 2; Dem., XXXIV, 36; Strabo, VII, 311.

[200] Polyb., IV, 38, 4; Strabo, VII, 304.

[201] Strabo III, 144; XI, 493; Dem., XXXV, 31 and 34; Athen., III, 116; VII,
278 c; Plin., N. H. IX, 50 sqq.

Pontus area [202]. Economically this is also significant, because it concerns an article of general use, the popular food *par excellence*; for *tarichos*, indicating all sorts of salted foodstuffs [203], practically has no other meaning than salted fish [204]. Moreover this product must have called into existence or must have supported all sorts of by-trades in the exporting districts: next to the catching and salting of fish the very large nets had to be made or mended, earthenware in which the salted fish had to be transported must be manufactured, the small but very numerous boats had to be constructed. Nothing, however, is known to us of all these trades, nothing of their economical arrangement, nothing of the labour-conditions. Another proof of the extent of the trade is Aristotle's statement that the number of fishermen is very large in Byzantium and in Tarent [205].

Nowadays the export of fish is out of the question though the Greek fishermen do not only sail in the Aegean Sea, but along the coast of Africa as far as Tunis and in the Sea of Marmora: North Sea herrings are eaten to-day by the inhabitants of the Piraeus. At present Greece exports one more Mediterranean product in great quantities: the sponge. Nearly the whole need of Europe is supplied by the capture in the Aegean and the surrounding seas. In Antiquity also the sponge was used for many purposes, but we learn little of the prosecution of this dangerous, but profitable trade, except some names used for that kind of fishermen of which *spongothèrai*, spunge-hunters, is the one occurring most frequently [206].

[202] Her., IV, 53; Mela, II, 6; Plin., N. H. IX, 45; Strabo, VII, 46 p. 311; Cratinus, I, 24 (K). Cf. Von Stern, Klio IX (1909), p. 142 and Hermes L (1915), p. 166.

[203] Zenob., I, 84.

[204] Her., IX, 120; Aristoph., Ach. 931; Vesp. 491.

[205] Aristot., Polit. IV, 4, p. 1291 b, 23.

[206] Ps. Dicaearch., F. H. G. II, 259; Aristot., H. A. V, 548 b, 15; Plin., N. H. IX, 149; XIII, 136; XXXI, 130 sqq.; Theophr., Hist. Pl. IV, 6, 5; Mart., IV, 10, 5. In Antiquity the trade of the sponge-fisher was considered to be the most miserable subsistence in the world (Opp. Hal. V, 612 sqq. Cf. Panaït Istrati, Le pêcheur d'éponges); for fright of this a slave ran away (Alciphr., I, 2, 3 sqq.). By living on a diet and extra sleep the divers train themselves for their arduous task (Opp. Hal. V, 614 sqq.; cf. Aesch., Suppl. 409). To smooth the surface of the sea, and to be able to see at great depth in the clear water, — for the softest and best sponges grow in deep places (Aristot., H. A. V, 548 b, 27) — they poured oil on it. (Plut., Mor. 950 b; Philostr., Apoll. III, 57; Theophyl., Coll. 7. Cf. Brehm, Tierl. I, p. 96). When it is said, that the diver took a mouthful of oil down with him, and by spitting it out made the submarine darkness light (Plut., Mor. 950 b; Opp. Hal. V, 638; 646 sqq.), this is probably due to a misunderstanding. With a rope tied round his middle the diver jumped into the sea. In order to sink quickly, he took a piece of lead with him. In his hand he had a curved knife (arpè) to cut the

sponges (Opp. Hal. V, 634 sqq.; Plin., N. H. IX, 152). By contracting themselves, the slime sponges slip from his hand. For Aristotle it is a problem, wether the sponge has feeling, while later authors contribute the contraction to the stimulus of a little resident animal resembling a spider (Aristot., H. A. I, 487 b, 9; Plin., N. H. IX, 148; XXXI, 124; Opp. Hal. V, 656 sqq.). When the diver cuts the sponge suffocating dirt is stirred up, the so-called blood of the sponge (Aristot., H. A. V, 548 b, 6; Plin., N. H. XXXI, 124; Opp. Hal. V, 656 sqq.). Numerous are the big sea-monsters, especially sharks and polyps waylaying him (sharks: Plin., N. H. IX, 151-153; Opp. Hal. V, 626 and 667 sqq.; Anth. Pal. VII, 506; Paus., II, 34, 1. Polyp: Plin., N. H. IX, 91), and the little ones hindering him on his work (Opp. Hal. II, 434 sqq.; Ael., N. A. II, 44; IX, 41; XV, 11). Therefore he welcomes the appearance of the anthias; for where this fish appears, there are no fishes of prey, and therefore the sponge-fishers call it the holy fish (Aristot., H. A. IX, 620 b, 31; Plin., N. H. IX, 153; Plut. Soll. An. 32; Ael., N. A. VIII, 28). In order to be less conspicuous, the diver blackens his feet and hands (Ael., N. A. XV, 11. Cf. Plin., N. H. IX, 152). But worst of all is the tightness of the cherk seizing him, and suggesting to him that there is a huge flat-fish over him, which cuts him off from the world above like a lid (Opp. Hal. II, 141 sqq.; Ael., N. A. I, 19; Plin., N. H. IX, 151). The enormous pressure of the water causes him ear-drum to tear (Aristot., Probl. 960 b, 8), wherefore he drops oil in the ears (Aristot., Probl. 961 a, 24), or binds sponges soaked in oil against them (Aristot., Probl., 960 b, 15) or makes an incision in ears and the sides of the nose (Aristot., Probl. 960 b, 21). The ancient divers, too, had already devised various apparatuses to supply themselves with air, and thus to be able to stay under water for a longer time. Either an upturned dish filled with air, and weighted, so that it could not overturn, was lowered (Aristot., Probl. 960 b, 31); or the diver remained in connection with the world above by means of a tube. Aristotle incidentally mentions this latter invention (De part. an. II, 659 a, 9), while in the sixth century A.D. it was employed by Slavonian divers in the Danubian area (Mauricius, Strategicum XI, 5, p. 274 Scheffer). On modern sponge-fishing cf., however, W. Enzinck, Griekenland (Greece). Delft, 1956. pp. 160 sqq.

CHAPTER THREE

INDUSTRY

In our oldest records, the poetry of Homer and Hesiod, we search in vain for an image of the ways in which the farmers and cattle-breeders made their own tools and other necessary resources for their subsistence and their labour (the degree of home-industry which Bücher [1] puts at the beginning of economical development). In the society which the two authors describe, also in the more primitive society of the latter, some crafts separated themselves from the agricultural work and developed into independent trades: the blacksmith (*chalkeus*), the potter (*kerameus*), the leatherworker (*skytotomos*), and the woodworker (*tektōn*) exercise a craft of their own, and no more merely as workmen of the lord, but partly also as independent craftsmen who work outside the so-called self-sufficient household [2]. We find examples of the two forms of craftsmanship which Bücher distinguishes at this first degree of the independent craft: the goldsmith who is summoned to appear with his tools in Nestor's house from whom he then receives his precious material [3], occurs as a "Störarbeiter" (labourer working in the house of his employer) next to his colleague who has a smithy in the town as a "Heimwerker" (labourer at home); for the rest iron is also worked at the farm: as a prize Achilles promises a piece of iron so big that neither shepherd nor farmer need to go to town to lay in a provision of it for five years [4]. The poor female spinner who earns scanty wages for her children is perhaps an example that a degree of "Lohnwerk" (labour for wages) was also found here and there [5].

A general term for craft did not yet exist; the name *demiourgos* by which the man is indicated who works for the community and not for one single man is used for the craftsman as well as for the diviner, the minstrel and the physician; later it will remain the title of a

---

[1] Bücher pp. 92 sqq.
[2] Hom., Il. V, 59; VII, 221; XII, 294 sqq.; XV, 441; XVI, 483; XVII, 389; XVIII, 601; Od. III, 425 and 432; V, 249 sqq.; XVI, 56; XVII, 384; XXI, 43.
[3] Hom., Od. III, 436 sqq.
[4] Hom., Il. XXIII, 833.
[5] Hom., Il. XII, 433 sqq.

functionary in many a Greek state [6]. It goes without saying that the farmers try to supply their own needs as much as possible—Hesiod recommends this even—, but for the iron of his plough he invokes the help of "Athena's servant" [7]. We see that some occupations get separated from agricultural work and become independent crafts (in Bücher's terminology the phenomenon of the "Produktionsteilung" (division of production [8]); specialism has yet made little progress: the smith makes ploughs as well as ornaments; the same woodworker makes a sill, a bow and a ship [9]; he is probably only called a cart-wright when he is doing this work. Traces are still to be found of the circumstance, which fits in this society with little differentiation, that the trade of the father passes on to the son.

Another fact is still worth noticing: nowhere in these oldest periods are slaves mentioned as craftsmen.

In the days preceding the 8th century most products of craftsman-ship were manufactured by local craftsmen everywhere in Greece. Only in the coast-towns which were never completely out of touch with the world across the sea and the east in particular some foreign products of great value were always imported for the wealthy citizens. This local supply of products of craftsmanship remained the rule also in the following centuries. The colonization from the middle of the 8th till the middle of the 6th century, by which the territory inhabited by Greeks expanded considerably, caused, however, a breach in this local supply. But now as before the manufacture and the working of raw materials for export, though growing continually, was confined to the precious products, especially those which belong to industrial art as fine kinds of wool or garments made of it, marble and bronze for sculpture or adornment, and earthenware valued for some reason or other. Objects for daily use are still made on the spot.

Some towns become famous on account of the excellent quality of certain goods; the surroundings of Miletus furnish highly valued wool and woollen garments. From the middle of the 7th till the middle of the 6th century the pottery of Corinth was very much in vogue in the whole Greek world and without it, from the coasts of the Black Sea to Carthage and Etruria; in the next century, however, people prefer

[6] Hesych. s.v. dèmiourgos; Thuc., V, 47; Polyb., XXIV, 5. Cf. Pauly-Wissowa-Kroll, R. E. s.v. Dèmiourgos; C. M. van den Oudenrijn, Demiourgos. Thesis Utrecht 1951, pp. 102 sqq.

[7] Hes., Erg. 428.

[8] Bücher pp. 307 and 309.

[9] Hom., Il. IV, 485 and 110; V, 249 sqq.; Od. XVIII, 384.

the pottery from Attica [10]. But the wide distribution of these products proves least of all the existence of large work-shops in the countries involved: the manufacture of china-ware in China and carpets in Persia, products sold and used in much wider regions later on clearly prove that a production in small trades or even at home can go hand in hand with it. We cannot even assume for certain that the Milesian garments were woven on the spot. Polycrates from Samos imported Milesian sheep [11]. At present we know that also in the middle of the 3rd century a Greek land-owner kept Milesian sheep in his estate near Memphis; it proves that the sheep themselves were also exported more or less regularly; this will certainly have been the case with the wool.

In the centuries of colonization a number of technical inventions coincide with the expansion of industry, an expansion, provoked by the needs of trade. These inventions again enhanced the importance of the craft: people learnt to solder iron in Chios; they learnt to cast bronze in Samos [12].

The increase of the number of people who found their livelihood in practising a craft is also proved by the list of means of subsistence which Solon enumerates in one of his poems [13]: some crafts are brought on a level with agriculture, in former times the only one in existence. For the rest we cannot conclude that the number of trades compared to those mentioned in the oldest poetry has increased; the division of labour has developed little further; the sculptor himself cuts the stone which he is going to carve and paint, bronze images are cast by the same man who builds ships. The cases recorded are not scarce where, as of old, the son assisted his father in his craft and succeeded him [14].

For this part of economic life also our knowledge becomes a little less vague in the 5th and 4th cent., especially in Attica. We shall now first put together the facts handed down to us by authors and inscriptions, then we can examine how far the economic development of industry has proceeded, more in particular whether and to what degree capitalism must be mentioned here. For this investigation, naturally,

[10] Cf. Francotte, L'industrie dans la Grèce ancienne I, pp. 62 sqq.

[11] Athen., XII, 450 d. Cf. Aul. Gell., N.A. XVII, 34; Theocr., XV, 125. Cf. also Daremberg-Saglio s.v. Lana.

[12] M. Collignon, Histoire de la sculpture grecque I. Paris 1892, pp. 153 sqq.

[13] Solon, I, 43 sqq.

[14] Paus., I, 8, 4; VI, 19, 8; IX, 12, 4; Plut., Vita X or. VII, 39; Plin., N.H. XXXV, 108; 110; 111; 123; 137; Harpocrat. s.v. Parrhasios; Suidas s.v. Polygnotos and Apelles; Plato, Prot. 16; cf. Rep. V, 467 a. Cf. Collignon, Histoire I, p. 230 and Loewy, Inschriften griech. Bildhauer, No. 1.

only those crafts are to be considered which have flourished. As such we find the building trade, the manufacture of pottery and textures, metalworking and the labour in quarries and mines. Now already we must draw the reader's attention to the fact that most crafstmen were retailtraders.

The *building-trade,* such in opposition to modern times, does not owe its significance to the necessity of providing the growing mass of the population with houses. To begin with, a regular and large increase as modern times have shown us, was unknown in the Western part of the old world, consequently also in Greece. And for the rest the greater part of the population were satisfied with exceedingly simple dwellings [15]. The Southerner passes the greater part of the day, sometimes also of the night, in the open. The craftsman performs his work partly out of doors [16]. The whole public life is enacted here: lawsuits, assemblies of the people, performances, competitions, sacrifices and other festivals. Hence the Greeks dispensed with many conveniences in their homes: the houses were airily built of woodwork and clay dried in the sun. In Plataeae the citizens once intended to surprise the Thebans, when the latter had occupied their town; in order to do so unperceived they decided to dig through the common walls of the houses to meet each other in this way [17]. The thief applied the same tactics to penetrate into a house; our burglar is called "the man who digs through a wall"[18]. When at the beginning of the Peloponnesian war the Attic farmers were obliged to leave their fields and had to betake themselves to the city, they did not only bring their children, women and movables, but also the woodwork of their houses [19]. In the country or in the town some rich people may have possessed houses more firmly built but their construction was also left to the cooperation of some "tektones" [20].

The large and precious buildings which were raised were almost exclusively temples; furthermore only a few other public establishments can be mentioned as arsenals and boat-sheds. Not before the 4th century monumental buildings as stone theatres are erected here and there for the assemblies of the people or the municipality. For

[15] Cf. p. 8.
[16] Cf. Schol. ad Hes., Erg. 493. Moreover representations on Greek vases.
[17] Thuc., II, 3, 3.
[18] Aristoph., Nub. 1327; Ran. 773; Plut. 204; Plato, Leg. 831 e; Rep. 344 b; Ameips., I, 670, 24 (K).
[19] Thuc., II, 14; VII, 27, 5.
[20] Cf. p. 8, 46.

the performances of Sophocles' or Aristophanes' pieces in the 5th century the flatforms for the spectators were always raised in wood. Through inscriptions we are pretty accurately informed of the manner in which temple-building was accomplished [21].

When the assembly of the people had decided to erect a temple, it appointed at the same time a building committee who was charged with the execution of this resolution; this committee was considered as an official board, so like any other citizen charged with a trade or profession they received no pay, and after the expiration of their activities the board had to render an account of them; such a function, however, lasted sometimes longer than a year. The supervision as in all matters of monetary expense remained with the Council. Besides a scribe, an architect (*architektōn*) was assigned to this committee as an expert who was probably also chosen in the assembly and who was naturally many years in function. Unlike the other members of the board, he did not occupy a post. He was often summoned from elsewhere, so he need not be a citizen and he received a salary.

The committee, chosen by the people, enlightened by the architect, designs the plans, the specifications and the conditions for the execution. They are published, often by inscriptions on stone plates. We possess an inscription in which the conditions and specifications for the manufacture and raising of these stone plates are published. It proves—which equally applies to the execution of the building itself —that the work is let out and performed in small lots: once for instance the manufacture of thirteen tiles and their deposition beside the thirteen tiles already present on the southern along-side of the temple between the cella- wall and the columns. So there are a great many contractors (*ergōnai, ergolaboi*) [22], but only a small part of the whole work was assigned to each of them [23]. Moreover, in the great majority of the cases known to us the material was provided by the customer, that is to say the people, represented by the building committee; they had the necessary stone cut and transported from the quarries to the work; so the contractor did not want any money for

[21] C.I.A. I, 324 and 325; II, 834; Michel, Recueil, 584 and 591. Guiraud, La main-d'oeuvre industrielle dans l'ancienne Grèce, pp. 183 sqq.; Huch, Die Organisation der öffentlichen Arbeit im griechischen Altertum. Thesis Leipzig 1903; Choisy, Etudes sur l'architecture grecque. Paris 1894; Fabricius, De architectura graeca commentationes epigraphicae. Berlin 1882; Jevons, Work and Wages in Athens. Journal of Hell. Stud. XV, pp. 239 sqq.

[22] Banker-guarantee of an ergonès: Ditt. Syll.² 6018 (Epidaurus).

[23] Cf. note 21.

the purchase of the building-material. Besides, the payment of the contractor is arranged in such a way that every time at the beginning of a precisely circurscribed detail of the work he receives the money due to him and agreed upon. A certain part, for instance a tenth, however, was deducted and was paid after the delivery and approbation of the whole work, undertaken by him.

When building the enormous temples there is therefore no question of capitalistic working. In the 5th century Athens executed them still partly under her direct management, but she gradually more and more adopts the system of letting out in contract, may be because the supervision of the people was easier then; the contractors are private craftsmen who work side by side with their labourers. In the accounts of the Erechtheum [24] the same man figures once as a contractor, another time as a casual labourer working for wages. They have no capital and do not require it, the less so because they have no regular workmen either: for each separate work they choose some fellow-labourers (*synergoi, synergazomenoi*).

Some particulars about the labour-conditions must still be mentioned, especially because they are of importance for our knowledge of the social and intellectual life of the time. The work at the temples, the buildings and their ornaments is done for piece-wages and day-wages without our being able to perceive why now the one means of payment, then the other is applied. Piece-wages are generally paid for the smallest items, e.g. the working of a pane in the ceiling; for the building of the Erechtheum the following wages were paid for sculpture: 60 drachms were paid for the cutting of a normal figure, e.g. a grown-up man, a mule, a horse or a chariot; 30 drachms for a van, 20 drachms for a child. It follows that the quality of the work was not taken into account.

We may observe the same with regard to day-wages: no difference is made between skilled and unskilled labour; carpenters receive the same wages as their assistants; even the architect receives nothing more [25]. The fact that skilled and unskilled labour was paid at the same rate is unconceivable to modern conceptions and so scholars have wanted to eliminate this equality of labour-appreciation as far as it is expressed in wages, by the supposition that the architect will have received a separate reward for the designing of the plan. But this

[24] C.I.A. I, 324. Cf. 321 and 325. Huch, Die Organisation p. 59.
[25] H. Francotte, L'industrie I, pp. 316 sqq.

supposition, of which there is no single indication in our records, does not reckon with the general phenomenon that at a certain degree of the social and intellectual development no difference is made between manual labour and head-work. During many centuries the physician receives the same amount of money as the craftsman in Greece [26]. In the Middle Ages and even later on conditions were not different. The architects of our cathedrals and towers were craftsmen and were treated and estimated as such.

It is a remarkable feature that the minority of the masons whom we learn to know from Athenian inscriptions was formed by citizens; the others were slaves and aliens [27]. When building the temple in Epidaurus [28] only one of the master-masons was a native of Athens, the others came from abroad as is shown by the fact that they received a remuneration for travelling-expenses. When erecting the large buildings the cities would be absolutely short of necessary local craftsmen, it seems that they were more often in want of workmen than of work.

It appears from preserved accounts that slaves doing the same work received the same pay as the free labourer, which is also socially significant. It indicates that their position will not have differed much from that of their free colleagues at least for those slaves who were capable of exercising a craft.

Another craft which must have procured a livelihood to a great many people in Antiquity was *pottery-making*. Earthen-ware of all kinds was used in much greater quantities proportionally than nowadays; wood in Greece was scarce and precious; boxes and barrels were not objects of daily use, metal also was little used in daily life for plates and dishes. Dry and wet goods which one wanted to preserve were kept in earthen jars of which large quantities were required because they were liable to break and had to be replaced more often than our wooden or metal casks and tins. The custom to place precious vases on and in the graves of the deceased will also have contributed to a considerable demand. As a rule the local production will have supplied greater part of the enormous needs; red clay suitable for the manufacture of earthenware is found almost every-

---

[26] When Hippocrates uses the word dèmiourgos, it is mostly a physician, and he might also have written iètros, which was mostly used. But also artisans in general he calls dèmiourgoi; the ordinary physician belongs to them (Hipp., De arte XIV, 26; Praeceptiones XXXI, 6 (ed. I. L. Heiberg). Cf. Van den Oudenrijn, Demiourgos pp. 132 and 138).

[27] C. I. A. 324, col. I, 56-57.

[28] Michel, Recueil 584.

where in Greece, and in every district the potters will have provided their fellow-citizens when they were not able to supply for themselves. But besides this local production the making of earthenware for export must have taken a high flight in some towns in early days. We must first clear away a misunderstanding in order to rightly judge this business; archeology is accustomed to speak of Greek vases, a term adopted from the Italian word for plates and dishes, "*vasi*". This word is apt to give the idea of ornamental vases; for the greater part, however, the Greek vases were certainly not ornamental. The Greeks were no lovers of art in the modern sense of the word and neither were they collectors; they did not know what it was to manufacture objects, merely for an aesthetic gratification, at least not in their golden age. The vases mainly were objects for daily use; they were exported with or on account of the contents which chiefly consisted of "the two liquids most agreeable to the human body" as a Roman author [29] remarks, "wine to be taken internally and oil to be applied externally". The Greek and especially the Athenian vases were used for the transport of these wares which the Etrurians brought from Attica in exchange for the bronze, which they took there; afterwards the wealthy Etrurian families charmed by the beautiful adornments will have ordered complete sets for their festivities and religious ceremonies: amphoras, craters, lecythi, oenochoës, hydrias, and the various kinds of cups [30]: in a world where especially those kinds of products were imported from abroad which gratified the higher class people, the faculty to produce beauty so innate to the Greek [31], was much more significant to economical life than nowadays. Above [32] we have already referred to the earthenware required for the export of salted fish.

Now, what were the labour-conditions which enabled the potters to turn out such an extensive production of earthenware? We have already [33] drawn the attention to the fact that the large turnover of

[29] Plin., N. H. XIV, 150.

[30] Pottier, Le commerce des vases attiques au VI siècle. Rev. Arch. III (1904), pp. 45 sqq.

[31] H. Bolkestein, De waardering der Griekse kunst door haar tijdgenoten (The Appreciation of Greek Art by its Contemporaries. Tijdschrift voor Geschiedenis XLIII (1928) pp. 113 sqq. Cf., however, A. W. Byvanck, Les beaux-arts au temps de Platon. Amsterdam 1955. Seeing works of art gave pleasure (Her., II, 137. Cf. Seneca, Ep. 115, 8). The people that employed its word for "just proportions" also for "ornament", that saw "rythm", where we only perceive "shape", cannot have been lacking in natural sense of beauty (Her., V, 58; Xen., Comm. III, 10, 10; Alexis, II, 317, 59 K.).

[32] P. 40.

[33] P. 44.

a product did not include a large-scale industry, at any rate there is
no trace to be found of its existence. The craft requires one or more
men capable of planning and executing the shape and the design of
the product and for the rest assistants for the kneading of the clay,
the preparation of the paint and the managing of the oven. But the
division of labour is still simple; here too the distinction between
intellectual and manual labour is unknown. The potter is often the
man who plans the design and executes it, but it also happens that this
designing has become a special job; some potters are assisted by more
than one painter [34], who, however, work also for other masters and
have no permanent situation.

For the prosecution of his trade the potter needed a room for the
pottery and one for the adornment, beside the pottery an oven in the
open air and a shed for the materials; the pottery will have served at
the same time as a show-room; more than 12 or 15 labourers will
seldom or never have been united in one workshop. It is evident that
thus a large-scale industry is out of the question. Undoubtedly the
master was an entrepreneur who paid wages to labourers, free men
and slaves [35]; but he needed no large capital neither for the payment
of wages, nor for the defrayment and the upkeep of the stock, the
workshop, the utensils and materials. It is likely that a great number
of them will have known a certain degree of prosperity, called *ploutos*
by the Greeks [36], producers as they were of a product much in demand,
at least in times when trade was not handicapped too much.

The fact that in this craft goods were produced, partly destined for
export, gives rise to the question what relation existed between the
masters of a workshop and the merchants who conveyed their products
to the foreign customer. Our records give us no direct answer to this
question, but in general the power of the merchant is the greater the
more primitive commerce is. For the merchant alone is cognizant of
the distant market and not the producer. So we may suppose that many
a potter was dependent on the trader in so far as the latter was
established in his city. Was the relation indeed such as normal in
home-industry where the trader-entrepreneur, (the "Verleger" in

---

[34] The potter signed "epoièsen", the painter "egrapsen". Cf. A. N. Zadoks-
Josephus Jitta, De antieke cultuur in beeld (Pictorial Ancient Culture) p. 77.

[35] Francotte, L'industrie I, pp. 68 sqq. Cf. p. 76 (ho Skythos egraphsen, ho
Lydos egraphsen).

[36] Cf. J. Hemelrijk, Penia en Ploutos. Thesis Utrecht 1925 and J. J. van Maanen,
Penia en Ploutos in de periode van Alexander. Thesis Utrecht 1931.

Bücher's terminology) [37] fixed the production of the craft? There are no data extant allowing us to make a conjecture.

As regards the men employed in pottery making, the same may be remarked as in the building-trade: in Athens a great number of them are aliens, among them also slaves, as the city often could not cope with the need of skilled labourers. On a vase adorned with the picture of the potter's workshop we also find an image of a woman among the persons working there [38], so it is probable that in this craft women were also used though we do not know to what extent. The supposition that the woman is the proprietress of the business, because she sits on a raised platform, is little in keeping with the subordinate legal status of woman, at least in Athens; it was a.o. prohibited for a woman to make engagements in which the involved sum of money amounted to more than the value of a medimne (11 gallons) of barley [39]. Under these circumstances it will hardly have been possible for a woman to work a trade.

Of the great iron and steel, coal and textile world-industries, governing economic life in modern times, only the last, be it on a much smaller scale, was of some importance outside the home and the small workshop [40]. But here we must not forget that the wants to be satisfied in ancient Greece were much more trifling than those in modern European society. The *textile industry* had mainly in view the providing of clothing and the great mass of the population was contented with the simplest garments imaginable thanks to the beautiful climat. As a rule people wore as underwear and upper garments simple pieces of cloth, both made of wool [41]. They wrapped them round the body and fastened them with a pin on each shoulder. In the country people lived still closer to nature, there they were dressed in goat-skins [42]. Almost everywhere the unfertile soil produced enough grass for the sheep to graze upon, so wool could be gained and spun in every district. The weaving of a simple square piece of cloth could be done by any woman, and the making of garments not

[37] Bücher, pp. 92 sqq.
[38] Daremberg-Saglio, Dict. II², p. 1127, fig. 304.
[39] Hermann-Talheim, Die griechische Rechtsaltertümer p. 8. Cf. Guiraud, La propriété pp. 148 sqq.
[40] Pollux, I, 80: eriourgia, eriourgeion as well a place as a trade; talasiourgia, talasiourgikos domos part of the house. Cf. Blümner, Technologie I² pp. 108, 110, 121, 164, 171.
[41] Cf. p. 8, 3.
[42] Aristoph., Eccl. 724; Lys. 1151; Poll., VII, 68.

subject to fashion did not require any special dexterity. We can now easily explain that almost all the garments were made on the spot and, thanks to slavery, as a rule at home, in contrast with the clothes of modern times, where the material for the cheapest cotton blouse comes from abroad. It can only be cut by skilled seamstresses, owing to the ever changing fashions.

The more precious tissues worn by the more wealthy and during religious ceremonies were an exception. Everything made of linen belonged to this class of clothing, for linen clothes were only worn by the upper classes. Mainly imported from Egypt [43], the material was, however, shaped by women in Greece, for instance in the island of Amorgos [44]. This happened equally with the tissues of finer and more precious wool, Lydia and the *hinterland* of Milete were renowned for it [45]. It is more note-worthy though, that one single town is named for its manufacture on a large scale of work-blouses, worn especially by slaves (*exōmides*); Xenophon [46] assures us that in Megara the greater part of the inhabitants lived on the making of these blouses, but no more than any other author in antiquity is he strong in scientific exactitude when discussing economic or social phenomena; so we need not take his communication literally. In the meantime what he says is not without importance, even when looking at it with some reserve; it proves together with many other data, when applying the standard of Bücher's tri-merous scheme to ancient economic development [47], that the degree of *Stadtwirtschaft* self-sufficient town-economy was already greatly exceeded here and there. But this scheme, though it has rendered and is still rendering great services, hardly characterizes the development of economic life in Antiquity. It distinguished itself absolutely from the economic life in the Middle-Ages, because it was enacted along the coast of an easily navigable sea [48], consequently ensued in early times already traffic between distant regions, provided they were situated on the sea. So here a

---

[43] Her., II, 105; Poll., VII, 71.

[44] Aristoph., Lys. 150 and 735; Ran. 364; Eq. 130; Aesch., I, 97; Poll., VII, 57; Harpocrat. s. v. Amorgidia; [Plato], Ep. XII, 363a.

[45] Athen., XII, 519 b; Eustath., Comm ad Dionys. Per. 823; Plut., Alcib. 23.

[46] Xen., Comm. II, 7, 6. Cf. Hesych. s. v. Exōmis. Poll., IV, 118; VII, 159; Aristoph., Lys. 661. Other instances of towns with specialties: weapons of Rhodos (Diod., XX, 84), swords of Chalcis (Athen., XIV, 627 b), shields of Boeotia (Poll., I, 149), krateres of Argos (Her., IV, 152), woollen fabrics of Miletus (Schol. ad Aristoph., Ran. 542. Cf. Pausan., VII, 21, 7).

[47] Bücher pp. 116 sqq.

[48] Cf. Xen., Hell. II, 1, 17.

"Volkswirtschaft" (national economy) became possible which by the scanty needs of the mass of the people, however, only influenced some crafts, especially in the interior; the traffic in precious products, needed only in small quantities, was of little significance; the export of blouses from Megara was an exception, impossible to be explained for want of data. The fact that a certain town specialized in the manufacture of a certain product (the weapons of Rhodus, the swords of Chalcis, the shields of Boeotia, the craters of Argos were famous in Antiquity) gives no indication at all of the standard of economic development as a whole. The example of the Middle Ages, also knowing this specialization of certain towns, warns us against excessive conclusions in this respect.

While all or at least nearly all the men worked in the above-mentioned branches of industry, the building-trade and pottery-making, the women naturally played a part in the making of woven material and clothing. Spinning was exclusively the work of women, weaving in the main too, as also probably dyeing [49]. The carding and the washing of the wool was on the whole left to the men, while only men performed the work of fulling [50].

From this enumeration it is evident that in this craft all the work from spinning to dyeing was not done by the same hands: a certain distribution of the work was accomplished here. Impossible, though, to speak with certitude of the nature of this distribution. We do not know in particular whether those who performed these various labours were united, wholly or in part, in one craft, in one workshop, under common guidance. We may fairly assume that most weaving and such like work was done at home: the purchase of slaves facilitated the expansion of work at home. From the earliest times female slaves were employed for these occupations [51]. It must often have happened that the produce of their labour, in so far as it was not wanted in the house itself, was sold in the market, especially to those who were too poor to supply their needs by means of slave-work. In a society as existing in Greece where slavery was widespread, there will have been no fixed limits between the production for home-consumption (*"Eigenproduktion"*) and production for the market (*"Kundenproduktion"*); it depended on the surplus, especially whether this surplus was obtained intentionally or by chance.

[49] Poll., VII, 169 (cf. VII, 721; Schol. ad Theocr., XV, 80; Paus., VII, 21, 14; C. I. A. II, 1434; Plato, Rep. V, 455 c.
[50] Herfst, Le travail p. 20.
[51] Schol. ad Hom., Il. VI, 491; Od. VI, 305; Il. VI, 324.

It is not impossible or improbable that in Greece weaving-workshops existed here and there, in which a greater number of men or women were united under the supervision of one entrepreneur; not impossible because an independent craft is not incompatible with the general standard of economic development; not improbable because it occurred in some other crafts. But not a single example has been handed down to us which makes the existence of such a workshop-craft absolutely certain.

For this craft we do not know the relation between the labour of free men and slaves. The use of the latter, especially women-slaves, may be deduced from the general situation which formed a transition from home-consumption to market-consumption and may be supported by some examples. Slave-work will have been the rule, wherever workshop-crafts existed. But undoubtedly a number of free men, whether or not assisted by slaves, will have found a livelihood in the making of cloth and garments. Among them many aliens (*xenoi,* cf. the mediaeval guests) will have found a place as in so many other crafts in Athens.

There was one craft, however, where the production for home-consumption was excluded from the beginning: *the winning of ore and stone from mines and quarries.* We are only somewhat familiar with the working of the silvermines in the Laurium district of Attica. The ground, containing veins of ore, was State-property at first wholly, in the 4th century perhaps only in part. The State rented out concessions to citizens as well as to foreigners [52] by means of the same magistrates who also farmed out demesnes of the State or who let public works out in contract, in large plots or in small ones [53]: we hear of a man who only kept one slave at Laurium from whom he received the slave-rent (*apophora*) [54], and of an other who "toiled and worked" there with his own body [55]. But Nicias, the well-known party-leader in the Peloponnesian war, let out 1000 slaves to a concessionaire Sosias from Thrace for whom he received one obol net apiece and a day [56]. This considerable difference as to the size of the rented-out concessions may be connected with the different possibilities

---

[52] Xen., Vect. IV, 12. Cp. p. 2, 7.

[53] Aesch., I, 101; Dem., XXXVII, 4; C. I. G. 162 and 163; Harpocrat. s. v. diagraphè; Suidas s. v. agraphou metallou dikè.

[54] Andocides, I, 38.

[55] Dem., XLII, 20; Xen., Vect. IV, 10; I. G. II, 3, 32.

[56] Xen., Vect. IV, 14; Plut., Nic. 4; Lys., XIX, 47. Cf. J. H. Thiel, Xenophontos Poroi. Thesis Amsterdam, 1922 pp. 20 sqq.

of exploitation. Part of the ore could be gained at the immediate surface of the soil in the same way as marble was cut from the quarries; this was work for the individual. Where, on the contrary, the ore could only be dug from deep in the bottom by the sinking of extensive shafts, a wholesale exploitation under the supervision of one man was required.

Part of this district has been found in modern times and could be investigated as the Greeks left it after gradually giving up its working in the first centuries of our era. This, with the aid of the few descriptions of mines and mine-working in other regions of the old world [57], enables us to receive an impression of the working-conditions. The underground galleries, square, rectangular or in trapezium-shape, were 2 to 3½ feet high and about as wide, as narrow and low as possible in order to save work for the laying out and the maintenance [58]; the galleries were propped by wooden shores. So the miners had to work in a kneeling or recumbent position in galleries connected with each other, where ventilation could not but be extremely defective. They toiled in the dark passages by the glimmer of little lamps which marked at the same time the length of their shift. Work was continued without interruption night and day: this happened at least in the gold-mines on the border of Egypt, Arabia and Ethiopia which Diodorus describes [59]; women and children were also employed there.

In this trade we find human vitality sapped by night-shifts, heavy labour for women and children, such complete exhaustion as is quite unknown in the Old World and which is little in keeping with the nature of their precapitalistic society characterized as it is by not unlimited aspiration for gain; the supply of the necessities of life ruled production, and with regard to most goods needs were but small. This exception to the rule may be explained by the fact that here the production of gold and silver was at stake, the only materials of which one never had enough because they represent the exchange-value in its most concrete form.

Quite distinct from the mining-work as such, the underground winning of ore, is the manufacture of ore into metal. This took place in workshops above the ground which were, in contrast with the mines,

[57] Xen., Comm. III, 6, 12; Plin., N. H. XXXIV, 167; XXXIII, 98; Plut., Comp. Nic. et Crass. 1, 1.
[58] Theophr., De lap. 63.
[59] Diod., V, 38; III, 11-13; Theophr., Lap. 63; Ael., V. H. XII, 44; Apul., Met. IX, 12.

private property [60]. We know little more of their exploitation than
the fact that they often formed the more or less fortuitous part of an
Athenian's fortune, which phenomenon we shall discuss further on
more at lengths.

Little or nothing is known of the sawing of marble in the quarries
which were as a rule State-property. The right to cut stone there was
leased; it appears from inscriptions that here too tenants often were
aliens [61]. In the trade itself there is not a single circumstance to cause
a wholesale working and we are not acquainted with any example of it.

The labourers in the mines were, almost without exception, slaves;
on a previous page [62] we mentioned an Athenian who himself worked
in a silver-mine. Xenophon communicates that many of them grew old
in the mines [63]: they were craftsmen who earned their livelihood
there on their own account and independently; no example has been
recorded of free labourers working for wages for an entrepreneur in
the Attic silvermines. In Sicily prisoners of war were sometimes made
to work in the quarries [64]; from this circumstance, however, we may
not conclude with certainty that the State exploited them herself and
did not rent them out to entrepreneurs: we may presume that the
State put her prisoners of war at their disposal on payment. No trace
is to be found in Greece of State-exploitation of the mines; we shall
treat State-exploitation in general later on (chapter VI).

So far we have been dealing with the principal things which we
know of the larger crafts. Now we must still gauge the height which
economic development attained.

In the first place we must point out that it is advisable to avoid
carefully the much used word "factory" when speaking of the
workshops of Greek industry [65]. At least in an economic historical
treatise this word should be confined to the large workshops in which
human labour is replaced by machines. Now Greek and ancient society

---

[60] Ardaillon, p. 211.
[61] Thiel, Xenophontos Poroi p. 45 and the inscriptions quoted there.
[62] P. 54.
[63] Xen., Vect. IV, 10.
[64] Thuc., VII, 86.
[65] H. Bolkestein, "Fabrieken" en "Fabrikanten" in Griekenland ("Manufactories"
and "Manufacturers" in Greece). Tijdschrift voor Geschiedenis XXXVIII (1923),
pp. 5 sqq. A contestation of K. J. Beloch, Griechische Geschichte I (1893) p. 398;
Id., Die Grossindustrie im Altertum. Zeitschrift für Sozialwissensch. II (1899);
Ed. Meyer, Die wirtschaftliche Entwicklung des Altertums. Kleine Schriften pp. 43
and 116; Id., Gesch. des Altertums III (1901) § 303; R. Pöhlmann, Gesch. des
antiken Kommunismus und Sozialismus II, pp. 161 sqq.

as a whole were unacquainted with machinery; what she meant by it were complex wooden instruments serving for the removal of articles in bulk [66]; she did not use them as tools for production [67]; they never got further than a roughly wrought kind of water-mill mentioned in the Ist cent. B.C. [68]. The tools which Greek industry used were little more than utensils and it is exceedingly instructive for the knowledge of the economic development that one of the words indicating these tools in Greek (*epipla*) also means furniture [69]: it shows the little difference between the market production and the independent craft of the *"Eigenwirtschaft"* (production at home).

There is another circumstance which proves likewise the erroneous and non-historical use of the word "factory". The Greek word with which we are wont to render this meaning, *ergastèrion,* indicates repeatedly not a building or a room, but a group or gang of workmen [70]; the inheritance of the father of Demosthenes [71], the famous orator, comprises two *ergastèria,* consisting of a certain amount of cutlers and joiners. And where did these men work? In Demosthenes' house; the workshop is part of the living-room [72]. It will often have been difficult to distinguish the slaves' room from the workshop. Naturally *ergastèrion* also means the place where the work is done, a piece of mining-ground e.g. [73]. Thanks to the subtropical climate it was probably often situated in the open, on the premises of the house. We must further draw the attention to the fact that the word *ergastèrion* means as well workshop as showroom. (also the room where the doctor treats his patients for instance) which is perfectly comprehensible in the sphere of retail-trade [74].

So factories in the sense which we must give to this word in a historical treatise were lacking in Greece, but she had trades in which a not inconsiderable number of labourers, as far as we know always slaves, worked together in a workshop; once a number of 120 has been recorded, owned by the father of Lysias, the plea-writer [75], but

---

[66] Vitruv., De arch. X, 1, 1.

[67] By *mèchanopoios* the maker of a theatre-apparatus is indicated (Aristoph., Pax 174; Plato, Gorg. 512 b; Xen., Inst. Cyr. VI, 1, 22).

[68] Anthol. Pal. IX, 148. Cf. Strabo, XII, 556; Vitruv., De arch. X, 5.

[69] Poll., s. v. epipla; Xen., Oec. IX, 6-9; Lys., XII, 19.

[70] Dem., XXVII, 9 and 26.

[71] Dem., XXVII, 9-11.

[72] Dem., XXVII, 24, 25 and 27.

[73] Isaeus, III, 2; Dem., XXXV, 4.

[74] Cf. about ergastèria also Laum, Stiftungen in der griechischen und römischen Antike I, p. 136.

[75] XII, 19.

we do not know how many of them were employed in one trade. In order to determine further the standard of economic development we must raise the following question: How was the technical organization in these large workshops? Had it reached the stage which in modern times preceded the introduction of machinery?

In order to ascertain whether the answer in the affirmative repeatedly made tallies with reality, it is necessary to distinguish properly the degrees of development of the craft. This is only possible by making use of precisely defined terms. Therefore we must avoid the word labour-division, open to many explications, as Bücher has expounded in a convincing way [76]. We shall briefly resume here his scheme of this development in so far as it is of interest for the solution of the problem in hand. When some isolated crafts happen to disengage themselves from the original production Bücher calls this phenomenon *"Produktionsteilung"*, division of production [77], this splitting up of labour continues in some of these crafts; next to the trade of the blacksmith, which includes everything, the specialised trades of farrier, coppersmith, gold- and silversmith appear; besides the leather-dresser, the saddler and the shoemaker. Bücher chose for this phenomenon the name of *"Berufsspaltung"*, specialisation [78]. The coppersmith distinguishes himself from the blacksmith by confining himself to a certain kind of work; they agree in so far as both of them manufacture the whole product, they all perform the necessary work themselves.

A following degree of division of labour is of a different nature, and has much further reaching consequences; here the labour-process for the achievement of a product is analysed in separate movements, each of which is performed by another labourer. All the labourers who subsequently collaborate at the final stage are then united in one large workshop; the work formerly done by one man, by the artisan, is now distributed among a great number of them who together form the *"Gesamtarbeiter"*, the collective labourer. Each of them does his incomplete part of the whole. Bücher calls this *"Arbeitszerlegung"*, division of labour [79]; he is of opinion that it cannot be found before the 17th century.

We must now still pay attention to some differences between the

---

[76] Enstehung pp. 306 sqq.
[77] Bücher p. 309.
[78] Bücher p. 308.
[79] Bücher pp. 188 and 305 sqq.

splitting up of trades and crafts and the specialisation, by which one man works at one small task; while it is the main object of the latter to produce *better* products, to ameliorate the *quality,* the former has the tendency to *increase the quantity* of the products as, just the reverse, a strong increase in the necessities of life has been indispensable for its coming into existence. Further it has been this division of labour which compelled the labourer to perform mechanical and infinitely recurring actions to a small fraction of a product and in doing so took the joy out of craftsmanship.

Bearing these distinctions in mind, it is evident that a reference to the great amount of professions and crafts which the Greek world knew also, is not to the purpose for the problem which we are investigating; it is also irrelevant that for instance for the making of arms a great many categories of craftsmen had to step in as well as the local specialists of which examples have been given above.

A reference to a passage from Xenophon's *Cyropaedia* [80], is of greater importance, because it also seems to prove the division of labour, the only one which may be considered, indeed, as a proof and deserves therefore to be wholly quoted. The author praises the affability of his hero, the ideal monarch Cyrus. As one of the expressions of this affability, at the same time the means of securing the affection of many, he communicates his habit of surprising his friends now and again with the forwarding of some dish from his special kitchen. They not only appreciated it as a distinction but as much on account of the gratification of the palate and this, says Xenophon, is but natural [81].

"For just as all other arts are developed to superior excellence in large cities, in that same way the food at the king's palace is also elaborately prepared with superior excellence. For in small towns the same workman makes chairs and doors and plows and tables, and often this same artisan builds houses, and even so he is thankful if he can only find employment enough to support him. And it is, of course, impossible for a man of many trades to be proficient in all of them. In large cities, on the other hand, inasmuch as many people have demands to make upon each branch of industry, one trade alone, and very often even less than a whole trade, is enough to support a man: one man, for instance, makes shoes for men, and another for women; and there are places even where one man earns a living by

[80] Xen., Inst. Cyr. VIII, 2, 5.
[81] Transl. Walter Miller.

only stitching shoes, another by cutting them out, another by sewing the uppers together, while there is another who performs none of these operations but only assembles the parts. It follows, therefore, as a matter, of course, that he who denotes himself to a very highly specialized line of work is bound to do it in the best possible measure."

It is evident why this passage is quoted: on account of the sentence which says that the one cuts leather and cloth and the other sews shoes and garments. At first sight it really looks as if here we have to do with a case of "Arbeitszerlegung" (division of labour); a same product passes through more hands before being achieved. But the first thing to be noticed here is that these simple cases of division of labour, where the work of making a shoe or a shirt is divided among two persons, wholly belong to retail-trade. It will often have occurred that the small master left certain simple occupations to his assistant, either slave or freeman; they naturally do not prove anything about the existence of a manufacturing-period, in which numerous piece-workers may be found in one large workshop.

Further we must not forget that in the manufacture the result and the aim of the division of labour has been: *increase* of the production in compliance with the strongly increased needs, it intended producing *more* wares with the same quantity of labour and delivering them at *cheaper* prices in this way. In Xenophon's passage it is clear from the context and from the words in which he describes it that the author, showing himself entirely a disciple of Socrates here, had exclusively in mind *the improved quality* as a result of specialism.

So it appears from the only passage from which scholars have deduced the existence of a wide-spread division of work which developed further in modern times and put its mark on labour conditions, is of no value as a proof of this system. It is certain that the economic development in Greece did not progress further than in the simple workshop-business in which a certain amount of workmen, always slaves as far as we know, were together serving one man, their proprietor, though probably not even in the same branch of trade.

Here we must needs put the question what kind of man the proprietors of *ergastèria,* workshifts or workshops, were. We notice at once that the Greek language did not know a word resembling our factory-owner. It is still more significant that Aristotle in his *Politics* never mentions entrepreneurs in general or industrial entrepreneurs, viz. factory-owners in particular, when enumerating the different stations in life. He distinguishes four classes [82]: the farmers (*to geōrgikon*), the craftsmen (*to banauson*), the traders (*to agoraion*) and the non-possessors (*to thètikon*). He cannot have counted the workshop-masters among the *banausoi*, for only those men belong to it who earn their livelihood by manual labour and a wealthy man as Demosthenes' father will probably not have handled anything but weapons.

The crafts of the father, bearing the same name as his celebrated son the orator, have been revealed to us somewhat in detail through some pleas of the son [83] in a lawsuit with his guardians about the inheritance. As the only complete data they deserve to be examined a little more closely. We write down the whole inventory as Demosthenes, the son, records it:

The inheritance of Demosthenes senior

I. Interest-bearing items

    1. two *ergastèria,* viz.

        a. 32 or 33 knife- and swordcutters at a value of 500 to 600 drachms apiece from which he had a clear annual revenue of . . . . . . dr. 19,000

        b. 20 joiners given as a security for a loan of 4,000 dr., yielding a clear revenue of 1,200 dr. a year 4,000

    2. about 6,000 dr. invested at 12 % yielding a yearly interest of more than 700 dr. 6,000

    This was the interest-bearing part of the inheritance, the capital sum of . . . .

                                               dr. 29,000

II. Non-interest bearing items (*arga*)

    1. in goods: iron, ivory, frames of furniture, bought for . . . . dr. 8,000

        gall-nuts (used as a mordant), bronze, bought for 7,000

    2. a house 3,000

    3. furniture, mixing bowls, gold and garments, the array of the mother. 10,000

    4. cash 8,000

    This was the inheritance of the home . . . . . dr. 36,000

[82] Aristot., Pol. 1289 b, 33; 1290 b, 40; 1241 b, 19; 1319 a, 28; 1321 a, 15.
[83] Dem., XXVII, 9 sqq.

III. Invested money

    1. bottomry given to Xuthus . . . . dr.   7,000
    2. to the banker Pasion. 2.400
    3. to the banker Pylades   600
    4. to Demomeles   1,600
    5. various posts of 200 and 300 dr., together about   6,000

    Total of invested money   about dr. 17,000

A general total of more than dr. 82,000 (in reality dr. 82,600).

What does the composition of this fortune prove about the economical and social function of its possessor?

To begin with, it is noteworthy that Demosthenes senior kept two gangs of slaves who perform two entirely different trades in his home (this appears distinctly from other statements in the speech [84]; no post is mentioned in the inventory above for the workshop neither for the tools). These two trades, a cutlery and the furniture-works, could hardly be in any way connected with each other. This strange combination may be explained in some sort when paying attention to the circumstances under which Demosthenes has the twenty joiners at his disposal. A certain Moeriades had borrowed 4,000 drachms from him; as a pledge he ceded to his money-lender twenty joiners-slaves of whom he has the usufruct [85]. In this case he enjoys the proceeds of their labour. It follows that Demosthenes, though owning these twenty slaves, is certainly no entrepreneur and factory-owner; for he only happens to dispose of them in his quality of money-lender; when making money out of them it is no entrepreneur's profit, but interest. Moeriades might have given him a wholly different security for the money raised, e.g. by leaving him the rent of the house as interest. At any moment these slaves and with them one of the traders may disappear from Demosthenes' house viz. as soon as Moeriades wants to settle his accounts.

It is no more certain that Demosthenes could be considered as an entrepreneur with regard to the cutler's shift. In the inventory only the money invested in slaves is put under "interest-bearing"; items which we are wont to call the materials, the ivory, the iron etc. come under the same rubric as the house, the furniture, ornaments and cash,

[84] Dem., XXVII, 24, 25 and 27.
[85] Dem., XXVII, 9 sqq. and 24 sqq. Cf. LIII, 10 and XXXVII, 4.

considered as non productive property (*arga*). This exclusion of materials [86], of a house (with workshop) and furniture (with utensils) is accentuated still more by the fact that not only in the inventory, but regularly throughout the speech the working-profit is merely calculated according to the proceeds of the work of the slaves in proportion to the price of their acquisition, c.q. their estimated value. The 32 cutlers yield 3,000 dr. a year: when sixteen of them are sold, the remaining sixteen produce 1,500 dr. [87]. Of all the elements which we are accustomed to take together as working-capital, only the slaves are considered as productive and the working-profit is only calculated according to their labour: these facts may easily be explained when assuming that Demosthenes senior did not work the cutlery himself as an entrepreneur, with his slaves, but left the performance of this trade with the whole pecuniary responsibility to a third party from whom he only obtained a fixed amount a slave annually or weekly. This way of making money out of slavery was not unknown in Greece (it is described more in detail in the next chapter); in this case Demosthenes did not act as an entrepreneur in his quality of owner of the slaves' cutlery, but as money-investor. This may also explain why there is no question at all of other elements customary in a working-account, for instance interest of the capital laid out in the workshop and its outfit, the cost for the keeping up, the depreciation of it, and the like. In the meantime such a primitive working-account is not wholly impossible in an exploitation at one's own risk, when keeping in view and admitting that it is only imaginable when industry is but slightly developed, for then labour is by far the principal factor in a trade and the working-capital hardly plays a rôle.

Even when assuming that Demosthenes himself conducted the cutlers' craft, it is still difficult to consider him as an industrial entrepreneur. A man who did not embark 23 % of his fortune in a trade, as a simple calculation in the data of his inheritance shows us, and invested on the other hand upwards of 33 %, so 1/3 of it, at interest, cannot be counted as such, the more so because he was wont to sell the wares, mentioned in his inheritance and which are indicated not very exactly as materials; in this way he asserts himself a merchant.

This last fact has induced scholars to compare Greek trade with the development of industry in the Middle-Ages, where at least very often the entrepreneur of the workshop originated from the merchant

[86] Dem., XXVII, 32.
[87] Dem., XXVII, 18.

who was first the leader or the master of a home-industry. As in the Middle-Ages home-industry emanated from the exporters of finished products, in Greece the origin of slave-work in industry, in particular the possession of an *ergastèrion* in one's own exploitation, is supposed to the found in the work of the merchants who imported the materials. Demosthenes' case is but a very feeble support for this supposition. It appears from his inheritance that at the moment of his death at most 18 % of his fortune was sunk in articles of commerce; on account of this we are not allowed to consider him as an importer. And this objection may be called conclusive when we bear in mind that in general the existence of a social status of importers is absolutely unproved in Greece of the 4th century.

A status of industrial entrepreneurs was also lacking. The variety of Demosthenes' fortune was certainly no exception. The inheritance of another Athenian of the 4th century, described in brief [88], consisted of a house, two plots of land, nine or ten leather-workers, among whom the working-manager of the gang (here no separate building used as a workshop is mentioned), one female worker of fine tissues, one embroiderer, then two other pieces of land and two mining-districts. Leocrates, another wealthy man in Athens [89] was an owner of slaves, metalworkers (whom he sold with his house and all, when temporarily abroad!). He was moreover, a shareholder in the lease of the import and export-duties and set himself up as a merchant at the same time. Nicias, though he let out 1000 slaves as miners to somebody else [90], cannot be characterized for that reason as an industrial; no more those rich Athenian citizens who with their money took part in the reclaiming of a piece of mining-ground, owned by Epicrates [91]. For this matter, it is not impossible that for the working of mines some entrepreneurs were employed who restricted themselves exclusively to this trade as is possibly the case with the above-mentioned Sosias [92], who was no Athenian, a fact certainly worth noticing. An example of a capital sunk entirely or nearly so in a craft is unknown to us.

From our knowledge of the facts handed down to us we must conclude that the Athenians possessing a fortune of some importance, acquired, it does not matter how, were accustomed to make it bear

[88] Aeschin., I, 97.
[89] Lycurg., c. Leocr. 58.
[90] Cf. p. 54, 56.
[91] A. Boeckh, Die Staatshaushaltung II, p. 115[x], note 798.
[92] P. 54.

interest in many ways. Hesiod already advised not to put all one's eggs in one basket! [93] In so far as they were no landowners and obtained interest from the ground, they bought slaves, whose exploitation, however, offered many difficulties; they invested part of their money in small commercial enterprises, especially in the form of "bottomry" (we shall treat this subject more at length further on) or they lent out their money at interest, either directly to the man who wanted it or indirectly by means of a money-trader ("banker"). We shall see below that the unproductive loans predominate [94]. As a rule, they do all this without making a profession of any of these occupations; they are principally capital-investors, living upon the interest of their money. It is not impossible that one person managed merely one rather considerable trade, though no example of it is known to us, but among the rich this was an exception. In general the trades requiring capital were still little differentiated, the limits between money-lender and money-trader, money-lender and merchant, money-lender and entrepreneur of a workshop-craft and between these crafts and professions were not yet sharply defined. Under these circumstances it is obvious that a social status of factory-owners, in the sense which we give to this word, was absolutely lacking, even apart from the absence of machinery and factories.

The necessity to ascertain how far Greek industry was developed economically made it desirable to discuss more at large the data acquainting us with the larger trades in which some tens of labourers were employed. In the meantime with a view to a right conception of the conditions of the trade as a whole and the social position of the persons involved, we must be fully aware of the fact that these large trades belonged to the exceptions. Greek society had hardly outgrown the phase of retail-trade, also in the domain of industry, even in the not numerous trades which worked for export as pottery e.g.. Beside the small farmer, freeholder or tenant (and the retail-trader at home or wandering about on the sea, see chapter V) the small craftsman who performed his trade alone or with the assistance of one or more slaves, was the normal type of the citizen, at least in the economically most developed city of Greece. The assembly of the people, says Xenophon [95], consists of fullers, leather-workers, joiners, blacksmiths, farmers and traders who sell their wares on the open sea or

[93] Hes., Erg. 687 sqq.
[94] P. 132.
[95] Xen., Comm. III, 7, 6. Cf. Aelian., V. H. II, 1 and Plato, Prot. 319c.

in the market. As, on the one hand, a status of entrepreneurs was
not to be found, the status of wage-labourers did not exist either;
in the not numerous larger trades the work was done by slaves whose
livelihood formed their wages according to Aristotle's statement [96].
A bright light is thrown on this condition by the remarkable fact that
the Greek language does know the words employer (*ergodotès*) and
employee (*ergolabos*), but quite different in their meaning from the
present one. The man who charges a craftsman with the making of
a pair of shoes or a garment or with the building of a house, whether
or not let out in contract, is called an employer (*ergodotès*); the
word seldom occurs [97], we find it a.o. in the above [98] mentioned
passage in the Cyropaedia and is best rendered with our word
"customer". With the word *ergolabos,* employee, less rare in our
records, they indicate a person who accepts and performs a work
consigned to him, as a rule after subscription [99]. Phidias e.g. is called
the *ergolabos* of the renowned Athena's statue [100]. The likewise
remarkable fact that the word for wage-earner (*misthophoros*)
generally means mercenary [101] (we shall discuss this more at large
in chapter VI) points also to the absence of a *class* of wage-earners.
It goes without saying that there were also poor people who let out
their energy in all sorts of trades: in agriculture, in crafts, at the
harbours, especially as unskilled labourers (they were called *misthōtoi*); so they were wage-earners, but their number was not great and
besides they were never used in large concerns. For a class-war as
the modern economical development has shown between entrepreneurs-
employers and wage-earners-employees the conditions were absolutely
lacking in Greek society.

We know little of the circumstances under which the mass of the
craftsmen lived; their lives formed the normal existence of the town

[96] [Aristot.], Oec. I, 5, 3.
[97] Poll., VII, 182.
[98] P. 59.
[99] Poll., VII, 200.
[100] Xen., Comm. III, 1, 2; Plut., Per. 31; Cim. 4; Schol. ad Aristoph., Pax 506;
Dem., XVIII, 122. Cicero, Orator 5 speaks of sculptors as opifices. Strabo calls
Phidias and Praxiteles technitai (VII, 353; IX, 410). Zeno of Citium writes sligh-
tingly about temples as the "work of architects and artisans" (Von Arnim, Stoic. vet.
fr. I, 264 and 265). Posidonius, the Stoic from the second century B. C. no more
includes painters and sculptors among the votaries of artes liberales than wrestlers
(Sen., Ep. 88). Cf. Bolkestein, De waardeering der Grieksche kunst door haar tijd-
genooten (The Appreciation of Greek Art by its Contemporaries). Tijdschrift voor
Geschiedenis 43 (1928), pp. 113 sqq.
[101] Plato, Thaeet. 165 d.

and did not provide any material for the *belles lettres,* at least not before the comedy of the 4th century of which little has been preserved. The stones with inscriptions concerning matters of State and cult, as a rule, do not mention their crafts and of the thousands of the extant painted vases only some tens represent scenes of daily life.

The home contained at the same time the workshop which was also used as magazine in so far as the goods on sale were not exposed in the open. The houses were open on the street-side, so easily accessible to the public [102]. In this manner they offered ample opportunity for gossip and exchange of thoughts in a world where coffee-houses were lacking and a modest amount of working hours sufficed to supply the needs of the worker himself and of the population in general. The perfume-shops were most in demand for a chat [103], generally speaking the workshops in the neighbourhood of the market [104]; Socrates could be sure to get a hearing there.

We get the impression that society in Greece during the 5th and the 4th cent., in so far as it was not shaken by war or party-contests, was economically evenly balanced, that is to say that the needs and the supply were equal; the differences as well as the alterations in it were very slight. The craftsmen naturally knew mutual jealousy. "The potter sulks at the potter, the carpenter at the carpenter, the beggar is jealous of the beggar and the minstrel of the minstrel" proclaims Hesiod already [105], and this will always have remained so. Greek life is full of rivalry which finds its culminating point in matches: matches of sculptors and potters, of physicians and minstrels; but this rivalry expresses itself especially in the endeavours to ameliorate the quality of a work or piece of workmanship, natural in the independent craft. Competition resulting in and aiming at a more rapid and cheaper delivery and thus obtaining higher profits was not stimulated by a mostly regular sale and limited needs.

Another consequence of the domination of small trade in this stable world was the absence of unemployment, a notion for which the Greek language had no equivalent, no more than for competition. Xenophon makes somewhere [106] the hypothesis that bronze- or iron-workers or farmers should be obliged to give up their trade, if it did

---

[102] Schol. ad Hes., Erg. 493.
[103] Aristoph., Eq. 1375-1376.
[104] Dem., XXI, 22; Lys., XXIII, 3; XXIV, 20; Athen., XIII, 581 d. Daremberg-Saglio II, p. 1092, fig. 2969.
[105] Hes., Erg. 23 sqq.
[106] Xen., Vect. IV, 4 sqq.

not pay any more. The case that in a certain trade the number of available skilled labourers was too large for the supply of the needs will not often have presented itself, except temporarily in time of war. Unemployment too as a regular social phenomenon is connected with whole-sale trade and violent fluctuations in production. So it was that it only occurred on a somewhat large scale in the only real whole-sale trade: war, since enlisted forces waged it. The discharge of mercenaries caused unemployment, to be compared in a certain degree to the corresponding phenomenon in modern industry [107].

As is conceivable in a world where a craft was only rarely performed in large workshops and without the division of labour which enables also the employment frail hands and feeble arms, the labour of women and children was very limited. Even in craft where the women's part in the work will undoubtedly have been greatest, in the manufacturing of cloth and garments, her presence in large workshops is not recorded [108]. The woman's workshop was her home where she sometimes assisted her husband in his craft or where [109], as a widow, she had to support herself by manual labour [110]: in a world of war as the Greek world undoubtedly was, many wives will have lost their husbands when young. Others will have had to provide their families with food and clothes. Her task was most onerous in the houses of the poor where the wife and the children had to perform the work of the missing slave.

A very great part of the women who had to earn their own livilihood was forced to sell their bodies. *Ergazesthai,* to work, used of women, denotes the profession of the prostitute [111] and *ergastèrion,* workshop, indicates, as well as the more general word *oikèma,* house, a brothel [112]. The majority of these *hetairai* was formed by slaves who were exploited by their owners. With a view to the fact that prostitution was taken for granted in Greek life and that disregard for the individual is a natural consequence of slavery the profession of brothel-keeper was generally not treated with contempt. The number of free women-citizens living by themselves and earning their living as a *hetaira* will not have been large, at least not in the centuries discussed

---

[107] Hence Isocrates' plan to colonize Asia Minor from Cilicia to Sinope (VII, 24; V, 120).

[108] Cf. Xen., Comm. II, 7.

[109] Xen., Oec. VII sqq.; Plato, Meno 71 c; Leg. VII, 806 a.

[110] Dem., LVII, 35 and 45; Aristoph., Thesm. 446 sqq.

[111] Dem., LIX, 20; Pol., XII, 13, 2; Plut., Timol. 14; Athen., XIII, 572.

[112] Dem., IL, 67; Alciphr., III, 27.

here, when Athens was still prosperous and the family-duties were
still taken seriously, also towards poor female relations. In the 4th
century, however, after the continuous wars which ravaged Greece and
which, together with the never-ending faction-discord, uprooted
thousands of men, the families of the citizens will also have had their
share in this profession. Yet it is obvious that besides the female slaves
the free aliens and the freed women formed the largest contingent.

Examples of child labour except as helps of their parents which
from all times has been the rule among the labouring-classes, are
hardly known to us., though slavery must have stimulated it. If marriages between slaves and the begetting of children was allowed, the
owner will not have fed useless mouths a long time without making
the most of them later on. On a vase-painting which is usually
considered as a scene from mining-labour but which represents more
probably a loam-pit, a boy figures as an assistant [113]. One case is
recorded to us of an Athenian who was condemned to death because
he had made a free boy from abroad work in his mill [114]; the heavy
punishment proves, however, that the transgression consisted in the
treatment of a free man as a slave. Child exploitation as such will not
have been aimed at and the culprit would never have been prosecuted,
if the victim had been a slave.

Among the labour-conditions existing in the mines and probably
only in the mines, the continuous working by day and night has also
been mentioned [115]; in no other trade the need and the spur to it will
have existed except for the production of gold and silver, the ex-
change-material par excellence. Not as a part of the continu-labour,
but in stead of day-work, night-labour will have occurred now and
again; we know for certain that this happened in the mill and in the
bakery [116], the cool of the night will have been the principal reason,
as a discarding of clothes by labourers in other crafts may be explained
by the natural heat of the sun.

Finally a negative phenomenon indispensable for the knowledge of
Greek society: the lack of any organization of the persons working
in a craft. Before the 4th century there is in general no trace to be
found of unions of private persons (this in contrast with parts of the
State's community which the Greeks considered as unions too), except

[113] Francotte, La main-d'oeuvre p. 204.
[114] Dinarch., I, 23.
[115] P. 55-56, also, however, p. 38, note 184.
[116] Athen., IV, 168 a and 172 d.

the clubs of the aristocracy, which may be found in the end of the
5th century in Athens partly formed for the sake of social intercourse,
partly with a political view. The oldest of these unions were established
round a local sanctuary in whose service they put themselves, or they
were formed by aliens who wanted to make the practice of their cult
secure in a foreign country [117]. The union of citizens into a political
society (in Attica *dèmos, phylè* and *polis*) sufficed for every need and
left no room for organizations with special aims. It was not necessary
to become a member of a guild to be able to exercise all one's rights
as was the case in the Middle-Ages; in the democracies as they existed
almost everywhere in Greece in the 4th century every free-born citizen
was independent of his function in economic and social life. In the
same way, unions of members of a same craft were lacking in these
times [118]. Not before the significance of the political organizations
had weakened with and after Alexander (not the least so because
thousands of them were established abroad) the moment is ripe for
the union of private persons, also of members of the same craft.

So corporations which may be compared to mediaeval guilds were
lacking and consequently also the whole organization of the craft, of
masters, mates and apprentices, attendant with it. The countless rules
and prescriptions connected with the craft were also unknown. In the
coercive state such as many are wrongly prone to see in the Greek
State [119], economic life was absolutely unchecked; the fact that in all
the crafts the number of aliens was very great is very instructive.
Undoubtedly the Greek craftsman will have had the feeling of self-
esteem known to every capable workman in an independent retail-
trade, but his political rights will have filled him with still more
pride, because he could exercise them in every assembly of the people
equal to the most respectable citizen, this in distinction from his fellow
"guests" (*metics*) [120]. It may have been this circumstance too which
widened their horizon beyond their workshop and showroom.

It is a wide-spread idea [121] that the Greeks regarded manual labour

---

[117] Aristot., Eth. Nic. 1159 b, 19.

[118] Cf. Zimmern p. 270: We must beware of calling these associations "gilds"
in the mediaeval sense of the word: They exercised no control over their members;
everyone at Athens was free to exercise craft or calling that he chose." Cf. Endenburg, Koinoonia pp. 4 sqq.

[119] K. R. Popper, The open Society and its Ennemies. London 1925. I The Spell
of Plato[3]. London 1949.

[120] Cf. Xen., Comm. III, 7, 6.

[121] This conception is founded on utterances by Xenophon (note 122), Plato, Leg.

as degrading such in contrast with modern society which is said to have been influenced in this direction by Christianity. It is a fact that many statements of Greek authors to this purport may be quoted. One of the most eloquent evidences in which this criticism in described most in detail is drawn from Xenophon [122]; it runs as follows: "The so-called "banausic occupations"—nearly all manual labour was meant by it [123]—"are in bad odour and are very much despised in the world. And with justice. For they spoil the bodies of those working in this way, because they are compelled to sit still and stay at home, even near the fire. And when the body weakens, the spirit weakens still more. Moreover this labour occupies a man so much that he cannot devote himself to his friends and to the State. Such men must needs be bad friends and bad defenders of their country. Hence it is forbidden in some regions especially in those where war is in esteem to meddle with any "banausic" labour. The best occupations are agriculture and war" [124]. Similar judgments could also be quoted from Plato [125] and Aristotle [126].

In order to ascertain the significance of such statements for the knowledge of Greek social life we must first circumscribe the problem which gives rise to these sentences. For we cannot speak of a general judgment which a whole people pronounced upon a certain numerous social status in its midst (in this case the status of the craftsmen); with respect to social problems an unanimous judgment is impossible in a society with various classes. A social class is judged differently by a man belonging to the same class and by one belonging to a lower or better class. Now we must not forget that the quoted and similar passages are pronounced by intellectuals who, moreover, belong to the proprietors-class. A class of intellectuals without property who could maintain themselves by mental work was hardly known in the 4th century. So it goes without saying that these intellectuals, at the same time proprietors, looked down upon craftsmen and their equals [127]. This would be characteristic, if it had ever been different in later times. In order to settle this and to decide whether one class feels

V, 741 e, Rep. IX, 590 e; VI, 495 d, Her., II, 164-167; Aristot., Pol. 1258 b, 37; Aristot., Eth. Nic. 1124 b, 31.

[122] Xen., Oec. IV, 2; VI, 5. Cf. Comm. IV, 2, 22.

[123] Poll., I, 50; Plato, Rep. VI, 495 d; Aristot., Pol. 1258 b, 37.

[124] Dem., I, 27.

[125] Plato, Rep. VI, 495 d. Cf. Charmid. 163 b.

[126] Aristot., Pol. I, 4, 21; VII, 8, 233. Cf. Dionys. Hal., Ant. Rom. III, 28.

[127] Cf. Aristot., Pol. V, 2, 1.

itself superior to an other, we must not rely upon statements but on
behaviour and pay special attention to the latter. Particularly the answer
to two questions may elucidate this problem. What professions does
one esteem admissible to one's son in a certain class? With whom
does one allow one's daughter to be married? Paying attention to these
criterions we shall come to the conclusion that the judgment of proprietors and intellectuals about craftsmen in later centuries and also at
present did not differ much from the Greek's judgment. The real
question which arises is rather this: how can we explain that this
disregard was pronounced so openly in the Greek world while nowadays the problem is suppressed or replaced by statements that there
is nobility in toil?

There is another distinction which we must keep in view when
judging this problem for fear of jumping to a wrong conclusion. At
no time and with no people manual labour as such has been regarded
as degrading, not even by the wealthiest people, but only this kind of
manual labour which the non-moneyed class has to perform in order
to earn their livelihood and which therefore leads to all sorts of social
dependence or intellectual limitedness. From the fact that in the
Homeric poems monarchs also put their hands to the plough [128], in
contrast with Plato's and Aristotle's statements [129] later on it has
been inferred abusively that a strong reversal in the opinion about
manual labour has taken place. For even nowadays the land-owner
will not consider it beneath his dignity occasionally to tackle the most
humble job himself without damaging his social position which is
determined by his origin and property.

The opinion that the people in Greece who looked down upon
manual labour would have made an exception for agriculture, as for
instance Xenophon in the above quoted passage is not exact either
and may be explained by the flabby way of formulation in such cases.
When one author calls the trade of the farmer, to *geōrgein,* respectable, semnon [130], e.g. and another, on the contrary, designates his
work as slave-work [131], there is no contrast in the judgment of the
same status; in the first case one thinks of the man who possesses the
soil and in the last of him who cultivates it with his own hands. In a
state like Sparta the tilling of the soil was no more permitted to the
propertied citizen than the performance of a craft.

[128] Hom., Il. VI, 313; Od. XXIII, 180 sqq.; XIII, 365; V, 243; XV, 320.
[129] P. 70, 121.
[130] Dem., I, 27.
[131] Aristot., Pol. 1328 b, 4.

The huge mass of the Greek and also of the Athenian population (we only dispose of data about the last) living in close contact with retail-trade [132], performed manual labour themselves and did certainly not disdain it. In aristocratic states, regions as Sparta and Thessaly [133], where the land-owners secured their revenues by their lance and made the others work, the latter have naturally known and shown their disdain; the men of their class elsewhere will undoubtedly have done the same. Here we must draw the attention to the fact that the circle in which such ideas were applauded will have extended beyond this narrow group of men, in so far as always and everywhere the view of the wealthy and civilized classes is partly copied by the poor, though this influence will have been less wide-spread than in modern times owing to the lack of anything to be compared to our press.

There is another circumstance which may have produced the same effect. Not so much on account of the theoretical consideration [134] which may present itself to the mind of the privileged class that a citizen must have leisure to participate in public life, in assemblies, council or court of justice, but on account of the actual situation which enabled the Athenian republic to remunerate each political duty [135]. Thus citizens who otherwise would have earned their living by manual labour could support themselves in this way and lost the habit of working. So it is possible (we know little or nothing about the way of thinking in these circles) that with this democratic exploitation of political power the practice of idling convinced the multitude of the inferiority of labour. We may assume also that the presence of the numerous slaves who performed a good deal of handwork and who were despised on account of their slavery, contributed to this disdain of the non-working class for the free men who did the same work as the slaves under the same conditions and at the same wages; on the other hand the cooperation in a craft of the non-propertied citizens and the slaves will have aroused a feeling of comradeship excluding a disregard of the slaves by the working citizens [136].

[132] Cf. Xen., Comm. III, 7, 6.
[133] Aristot., Ath. Pol. II, Xen., Lac. Pol. VII, 1-2 (Sparta); Aristot., Fr. ed. Rose p. 386 (Thespiae); Xen., Oec. IV, 3; Aristot., Pol. III, 3, 4 (Thebes); Pol. II, 4, 13 and Plut., Qu. Gr. 29 (Epidamnus).
[134] Xen., Oec. IV, 2.
[135] Greenidge, A Handbook pp. 163 sqq.
[136] Jesus of Nasareth was a carpenter (Marcus, VI, 3), Paul was a packing-case maker (Acts XVIII, 3, cf. I Cor. 26 sqq.) In these circles the opinion on manual labour—also with the Greeks—has always been different. With the Christians—as contrasted with the Greeks—it was at first these circles that gave their opinion upon this labour in literature, which has become Holy Writ through Christianity.

CHAPTER FOUR

SLAVERY

In the preceding pages we mentioned slaves and their occupations many times summarily, but slavery was of such fundamental significance for the economic, social and moral life of the Greeks that we must now take a keener look at this phenomenon.

The Greeks of historical times were aware of the fact (dramatists [1] and historians [2] have stated it) that their ancestors had no slaves in their employ; they knew it, not from reminiscences or traditions but undoubtedly by observation of the conditions in the remote parts of the country, where the number of slaves will have been very slight. At the earliest degree of social development, known from contemporary writings, we meet already with slaves, in the farmer's world of Boeotia in the 8th century B.C. described in Hesiod's poems [3]. We learn, however, little more than the fact of their existence. We may deduce the farmer's ideas from the advice to procure oneself a labourer without a family, a maid-servant, not burdened by a suckling and a dog with sharp teeth [4]; it does not, however, inform us about the slaves' treatment.

We know much more of the more developed society, which forms the background of Homer's imaginative world, though it has been described by a poet and in different phases.

We discover here violence as the principal source of slavery; war and plunder not to be distinguished from each other [5] in these centuries at all and hardly in historical times, brought slaves along with them [6]; sometimes a slave is mentioned who was a slave by birth [7]. The number of male slaves, at least, is not great. The extent and the arrangement of the traders, especially the crafts, was

---

[1] Athen., VI, 263 b and 267 e (Pherecrates, Cratinus, Crates).
[2] Her., VI, 137; Athen., VI, 265 b.
[3] Hes., Erg. 500, 571, 595, 764.
[4] Hes., Erg. 600 sqq.
[5] Instructive is the expedition of Sparta against Elis (Xen., Hell. III, 2, 21 sqq.). On the prosperity of Elis: Polyb., IV, 73, 6.
[6] Her., I, 66; III, 39; Thuc., III, 86 sqq.; C. I. G. II, 2263.
[7] Plato, Meno 82 b; Polyb., II, 3; Eustath. ad Hom.. Od. II, 290, 1445, 51.

still so little developed that a man produced hardly more than was necessary for his maintenance. So the labour of a slave hardly surpassed the cost of his living; at this degree of development the vanquished are killed as a rule [8]. Homer's heroes acted according to this rule [9]. If a man was kept alive, it was owing to his ransom [10]. The women and children were also carried off as booty, as well as the movables [11]. It is in accordance with these facts that the Iliad mentions slaves only a few times [12]; they are naturally mentioned more often in the Odyssey where the normal life in one's own property is described [13]. But, as to the numbers related there now and again, we may as well relegate them to the realm of fancy.

The occupations of the male slaves partly consisted of work within the household as the preparing of meals [14], the carving of meat [15], the cutting of wood [16]; partly of work in the fields and in the orchards [17]; in the "Hauswirtschaft" (self sufficient family-economy) these two kinds of work naturally coincide. There are no data extant about the labour in the crafts. The much more numerous female slaves found their tasks in household-duties; with the mistress they ground flour and baked bread [18], they spun and wove [19], but they also received their masters for sexual intercourse [20]. The poet strikingly characterizes their merits, when saying that "they are beautiful and skilled in womanly occupations, that they attend the loom and share their master's bed" [21]. There is no example of a womanslave working

[8] Her., VII, 156; Thuc., I, 98; III, 36 and 68; V, 3 and 32; VII, 85; Xen., Hell. I, 6, 14; Polyb., II, 58, 9; Diod., XVI, 34; XVII, 14; Paus., VII, 16, 8; Dem., XIX, 305 sqq.; Plut., Comp. Pel. and Marc. 1.

[9] Hom., Il. I, 366 sqq.; II, 689; X, 373; XI, 589; Od. VIII, 523; IX, 40 sqq.; XIV, 264 sqq.

[10] Hom., Il. VI, 46; VIII, 378; XI, 313; I, 13 and 111. In much later times eranoi were formed in order to ransom captives (Dem., LIII, 6-10; LVII, 18).

[11] Hom., Il. XXIV, 725 sqq.; VI, 425 sqq.

[12] Hom., Il. XIX, 333.

[13] Hom., Od. XVI, 140 and 305; IV, 42.

[14] Hom., Od. I, 109 sqq. and 146.

[15] Hom., Od. I, 141.

[16] Hom., Od. XX, 161.

[17] Cf. J. Hasebroek, Griechische Wirtschafts- und Gesellschaftsgeschichte pp. 10 sqq. and 14 sqq.

[18] Hom., Od. VII, 103; XX, 107.

[19] Hom., Il. VI, 324 and 491; Od. I, 358; VI, 307.

[20] Hom., Il. IX, 664 sqq.; XVIII, 28; XIX, 301; Od. XX, 7 and 12; XXII, 37 and 445; Il. V, 70; XI, 101 sqq.; XIII, 173; Od. IV, 11 and 12; XIV, 202.

[21] Hom., Il. I, 31; IX, 128 sqq.

in the fields. As in later Greek the word for workman (*ergatès*) will especially indicate the field-labourer [22], so the workshop of the women (*ergastèrion*) becomes the brothel[23]. If, may be, the blacksmith was the first craftsman who performed a trade of his own outside the *oikos*, prostitution was the earliest independent trade for a woman, and remained so throughout Antiquity.

The slave forms part of the family and the family-property [24]; both are indicated in Greek with *oikos*, house. The words expressing his position also refer to it: *oikeus* and *oiketès* are certainly connected with *oikos*, *dmoes* with an other word which also means house (*domos*), *doulos* perhaps too. He is called and is an inmate of the family; admitted in the circle of the patriarchal family, he will generally have been treated properly; he is sometimes mentioned in one breath with the children; his position will not have been very different from that of the day-labourer [25]. It sometimes happens that he is allowed to possess some property acquired by his own means [26]. No trace is yet to be found of manumission. For the rest, the poet has clearly seen the detrimental consequences connected with this institution, notwithstanding the tolerable treatment. Slavery is unworthy: "as soon as the master neglects to enforce obedience, the slaves are no longer inclined the work decently. Half a man's manliness is taken from him, when the gods enslave him." [27]

All conditions were lacking for the extension of slavery in the oldest agrarian society where the fertility of the soil was small and where little or no need of agricultural products was felt outside the *oikos*. This possibility presented itself only in some parts of the Greek world working for the market next to the production for home-consumption and particularly there where craft had become independent, loose from the *oikos*. This happened especially in those regions where products were manufactured, unknown elsewhere or where they distinguished themselves by a superior quality, while expansion of labour in a craft stood a good chance in districts with clever craftsmen. Of

---

[22] Athen., VI, 267 c; Hesych., s. v. ergeitai and herkètai.

[23] Dem., IL, 67; Alciphr., III, 27.

[24] Hom., Il. XV, 498; Od. I, 251; IV, 318; VII, 314; VI, 181; oikou misthōsis: p. 152.

[25] Eumaeus bought a slave himself (Hom., Od. XIV, 449 sqq.); Dolios, in the service of Laertes, has a wife and grown-up sons (Od. XXIV, 387); Eurycleia was treated by Laertes as his own wife (Od. I, 431, cf. IX, 207).

[26] Hom., Od., XIV, 449 sqq.

[27] Hom., Od. XVII, 322-323.

the Greek country the western coast of Asia minor fulfilled these conditions best: the *hinterland* of Miletus produced splendid wool and by means of the cochineal (*kokkos*) a beautiful and firm dye [28], so the women's room where the house-wife conducted the work of the *dmōai* could gradually change into the workshop where production for the market was the principal purpose. Tradition will have it that Chios, always renowned for its excellent [29] wine, invented the soldering of metals; the vicinity of the East, technically likewise further developed, will have made its influence felt here. The interior of Asia-Minor, identical with Asia as to its climate, flora and fauna and differing from its coasts, wholly belonging to the Mediterranean world, was inhabited by a population backward in civilization and ruled by tyrants [30]. Throughout Antiquity it supplied the enormous demands of the slave-market: the availability of a great mass of economically and intellectually backward men is one of the most important and favourable conditions for slavery in more civilized countries. So it will not have been much beside the truth when Theopompus, an historian from the 4th century B.C., a native of Chios, proclaims [31] that his city was the first town to import men from foreign regions in order to buy and use them, that is to say that his city started providing itself on a large scale with the labour-forces necessary for its workshops.

As little as we know of the economical conditions in general, so little are we acquainted with the development of slavery in particular during the 6th century. Not before Athens in the 5th century became the leading state in Greece's economic and intellectual life, we are capable of obtaining some knowledge about slavery from the writings of those times and from preserved documents.

As everywhere where this institution exists one of its sources is naturally the birth from slaves. Whatever validity may have been granted to the cohabitation of a slave and a female slave, (the juridical arrangement does not seem to have been the same in all Greek states) such unions will naturally have taken place and regularly so. Xenephon's model-farmer separated the men's room from the women's

---

[28] Cf. p. 52, 45.

[29] Strabo, VII, 317; Plin., N. H. XIV, 96 sqq.

[30] According to Herodotus (V, 6) the Thracians sold their children as slaves.

[31] Athen., VI, 265 b. Cf. 266 f. Important centres for the slave-trade were moreover: Ephesus (Her., VIII, 105) and Pagasae in Thessaly (Aristoph., Plut. 521 with schol.). In the first century B.C. 10000 slaves a day were sometimes sold on Delos (Strabo, XIV, 668).

apartments to prevent sexual intercourse without his consent, "for
though the good slaves are wont to become more affectionate when
one allows them to beget children, the evil ones become still more
unwilling by such connections" [32]. So he advocates natural selection
by which the owner will profit. It is also recommended elsewhere [33]
to allow the slaves to procreate children in order to win their affection. Yet the number of home-born slaves will not have contributed
much to the keeping-up of slavery [34]. The breeding of slaves can never
have taken place on a large scale because it was not economical as
long as the supply was not excessively difficult and costly, for such
a breeding does not only include the upkeep of the woman but also
the cost for the rearing of the children, two categories of slaves for
whom no or little employ was to be found. The work of the female-
slaves confined itself especially to the performance of domestic services, from these women most *oikogeneis* will have been born. A large
industry employing women did not exist, as we have seen above [35].
No more did we find a trace of trades in which children could be
exploited in great numbers. It appears from preserved records that
the number of home-born freedmen in proportion to the whole was
very high (217) of a total of 841). This is not astonishing, for it
was exactly this category which was the first to receive consideration
for manumission; and certainly when it was meant as a favour and
a reward.

The principal means of supplying the market with slaves were war
and plunder which often could not be distinguished. The booty was
sold in the market. Xenophon lets his ideal monarch say [36]: "It is an
eternal law among all men that the live and dead stock belong to
the victors when a town is captured in war-time"; and the Socrates
of the same author declares the making of enemies into slaves just
and right [37]. The history of the 5th and 4th centuries gives many
applications of this conception. Under the most unfavourable circumstances of a raid through unknown and inhospitable districts the Greek

[32] Xen., Oec. IX, 5.

[33] Hom., Od. XIV, 62 sqq.; XXI, 214 sqq.; XVII, 212: XVIII, 322; [Aristot.],
Oec. I, 5; Plut., Amat. IV, 751.

[34] Stob. LXII, 48. Guiraud, La main-d'oeuvre p. 94 thinks, on the strength of data
concerning the release (52,5 % of the number of the freedman was "born in the
house"), that the percentage wàs considerable, but he forgets that this category was
often privileged (Schol. ad Aristoph., Eq. 2. Cf. also Soph., Oed. Rex 1123).

[35] Pp. 51 sqq.

[36] Xen., Inst. Cyr. VII, 5, 73.

[37] Xen., Comm. II, 2, 2.

mercenary-army yet found an opportunity of kidnapping so many slaves that their number became an impediment for their march. In a moment of danger they had to relinquish them again [38]. Nevertheless a little later an important amount of money could be distributed as the proceeds of this slave-booty [39]. And not only barbarians underwent this fate.

But cases as the capture of Thebes by Alexander which gave him an opportunity of selling 30,000 prisoners of war, Greeks [40] were exceptions; the majority of them were probably sold outside Greece. When prisoners were taken in the battle, an exchange of mutual live booty often followed, sometimes a ransom was paid [41]. The pirates in the Greek waters were also principally interested in the ransom to be paid, as appears from our records [42]; they did not count in vain on the attachment of the victims relations and the Greek sense of comradeship and zeal to deserve well of their co-citizens. Finally the few cases in which a citizen, male or female, was condemned to slavery by law [43] cannot possibly have carried weight. It follows that the number of slaves of Greek nationality in Greece cannot have been large, though Plato's [44] and Arristotle's [45] wish that only barbarians should be slaves will not have been fulfilled.

Needless to say, however, that the latter formed the great majority among them, a circumstance which has been of great influence on the opinion about slavery and its lawfulness. Almost all the districts and nations within the Greek trading-sphere, especially those from the East and the North, were obliged to deliver over sons and daughters for Greek slavery: Mysia, Lydia, Caria, Lycia, Bithynia, Phrygia, Paphlagonia, Cappadocia, Armenia, Syria, Phoenicia, also Jews (cf. Joel, about 400 B.C.; 3, 4: "Yea and what have ye to do with me, O Tyre and Zidon, and all the coasts of Palestine? (the land of the

---

[38] Xen., An. IV, 1, 12-14.

[39] Xen., An. V, 3, 4-6.

[40] Diod., XVII, 14.

[41] Thuc., V, 3; Dem., LVII, 18; LIII, 6 sqq.; Diod., XIV, 111; C. I. A. II, 193. Cf. Bull. de Corr. Hell. XVII, p. 108.

[42] C. I. G. II, 2263; Thuc., II, 94; Xen., Hell. V, 1, 22; III, 2, 26. In Athens even existed associations whose object it was to support the ransoming of prisoners of war. Cf. p. 75, 10.

[43] Plut., Sol. 15 and 23; Dem., XIX, 255; LIII, 11; XXV, 65. Diod., I, 79; Lys., XII, 98; Isocr. XIV, 48; Ael., V. H. II, 7; Harpocr. s. v. v. apostasiou and metoikion.

[44] Plato, Rep. V, 569 c.

[45] Aristot., Pol. I, 1, 5; I, 2, 16-18. Cf. also Xen., Hell. I, 6, 14-15; Plut., Comp. Pel. et Marc. 1.

slave-traders.) The children also of Judah and the children of Jerusa-
lem have ye sold unto the Grecians."); further Egyptians, Libyans
and Arabs: Thrace, Macedonia, the Getae, Sarmatae and Scyths, Illyria;
finally also Italy [46]. Little or nothing has been recorded about the
manner in which these human chattels were obtained; they will often
have been either prisoners of war, sold as booty, or subjects of some
tyrants who dealt in this ware [47]. Some tribes are said to have sold
their children for export [48]; in many districts raids will have been
held in order to kidnap men [49]. The slave-dealers (*andrapodokapèloi,
sōmatemporoi, andrapodōnai*) saw to it that they were transported to
the markets [50]; the principal ones were situated at the outskirts of
the Greek world: Ephesus [51], Chios[52], the ports on the Black Sea [53],
Pagasae [54] in Thessaly. Furthermore the big fairs [55] held round
famous sanctuaries or at the market [56] offered splendid opportunities
for the sale of men [57]. The slaves offered for sale were placed on
an elevation where they might be seen properly [58]; the persons interested had the right to make them walk or to have them undressed
in order to ascertain their validity by handling them; the trader who
concealed a defect laid himself open to punishment [59]. Below [60] we
shall still discuss more at length the significance of slavery for ancient
commerce. But now already we want to draw the attention to the
moral consequences of slavery, because and as long as the slave is a
form of merchandise, the idea that he is a man like oneself can never

---

[46] These nationalities we learn to know in the Delphian inscriptions, dealing with
the selling of slaves to the deity. Inscriptions recueillies à Delphes par C. Wescher et
P. Foucart. Paris 1864. Further Athen., I, 27 f; III, 108 e; Xen., An. IV, 8, 4;
Dem., LIX, 35; Phil. III, 31; Stob., XLIII, 95; Polyb., IV, 38, 4; Strabo, VII, 304;
Poll., VIII, 132. Cf. Westermann, pp. 34 sqq.

[47] Hor., Ep. I, 6, 39. Cf. Philostr., Vita Apoll. VIII, 7, 42.

[48] Her., V, 6.

[49] Strabo, XI, 495 sqq. Cf. C. I. G. 2263 c.

[50] Paus., X, 32, 15. Cf. Zenob., V, 36; Poll., III, 126; Diod., XV, 7.

[51] Her., VIII, 105. Cf. Plato, Prot. 314 c.

[52] Athen., VI, 265 b. Cf. 266 sqq.

[53] Ezechiel, XXVII, 13; Strabo, XI, 493; Dem., XXXIV, 10; Philostr., V. Apoll.
VIII, 7, 42.

[54] Aristoph., Plut. 521; Athen., I, 227 sqq.; Eustath. ad Hom., Od. I, 262 sqq.,
1416, 25.

[55] Aristoph., Eq. 43. Cf. Alciphr., III, 38.

[56] Hesych. s. v. kyklos; Poll., VII, 11; III, 78 and 216.

[57] Paus., X, 32, 5; Zenob., V, 36.

[58] Poll., VIII, 11. Cf. Lucian., Biōn Pr. passim.

[59] Lucian., B. P. 6; Eun. 12; Harpocrat. s. v. kykloi.

[60] P. 83.

find acceptance with the public. Furthermore slavery cannot possibly exist without slave-trade because it can never maintain itself sufficiently by procreation, and this fact alone condems slavery ignominious.

If we want to ascertain for what occupations the slaves were used we must take into account the circumstance mentioned before that it was not easy to draw the line between domestic work, such as the servants perform nowadays, and trade-work; there will have been many transitions from home-consumption to market-sale, so there was often little difference between the servants-room and the workshop especially in the middle class, the largest of the existing classes. It is certain, though, that the number of slaves, males and females, used exclusively as household-slaves was not great, in accordance with the fact that the very rich people who lived in great style were not numerous and the outward luxury had not yet reached a high degree of development [61]. Athens of the 4th century was an insignificant provincial town, compared to Imperial Rome.

In a g r i c u l t u r e the slaves were undoubtedly employed to a large extent, though the conditions for work on a large scale were lacking. For in those parts of Greece where the big land-owners prevailed, in Laconia, Messenia, and Thessaly, no trace is to be found of a labour-system corresponding with the work in the tropical plantations as in Carthage and Italy later on. The ground was cultivated in small lots by serfs [62]; they, however, will undoubtedly have owned slaves. In Attica small farming was prevalent; the farmer did most of the work himself, the more so because corn-growing as well as the cultivation of olives and grapes required much care, incompatible with slave-work as the experience of all times has taught us; all the same slaves were not lacking here either. In the medium-sized properties, as Xenophon's Ischomachus owned, conditions were somewhat different. The absent landlord who had his abode in the city had a working-manager, *epitropos,* who was charged with the supervision of the ordinary labourers, slaves and freemen, *ergatai* [63]; the first group will have been the largest. Generally speaking, one gets the impression from the authors that at least in Attica slave-work dom-

---

[61] [Aristot.], Oec. I, 6; Poll., X, 28; Eur., Hec. 363; Plato, Prot. 314 c (cf. Philebus 62 c); Athen., I, 3e; Dem., XXI, 158; XXXVI, 45. They charged it to Meidias as bragging that he sauntered in the market-place with three or four slaves.

[62] Guiraud, La propriété pp. 228 sqq.; H. Francotte, L'industrie II, pp. 296 sqq.

[63] Xen., Oec. XII, 2 sqq.

inated [64]. In the interior of Greece where trade was slack, slavery
was reduced to the smallest proportions; from the conditions there
the Greek poets and historians will have deduced the original state
of slavery, as we remarked in the beginning of this chapter. The use
of slaves whom the owner must support throughout the year is nowhere economical for season-work; it is more profitable to engage day-
labourers, slaves if you like, but owned by others for the busy times [65].
We shall again discuss this form of slave-exploitation further on [66].
It appears that female slaves were seldom used for field-work; among
the more than 1000 cases of manumission known from inscriptions
the female labourer does not find a place [67].

Slavery played a much more important part in i n d u s t r y. In
most of the small crafts the master was assisted by one or more slaves.
In the building trade they were even more numerous than the free
wage-labourers. For that matter, they received the same pay as the
free masons [68]. In the larger workshops only slaves were used as
labourers; whole batches of them were employed in the silvermines
at Laurium; numbers of 500, 600 had 1000 slaves belonging to one
proprietor and are mentioned as being leased out for work in the
mines [69], Xenophon [70] proposes even to set 10,000 men to work in
order to gain revenues through Government-exploitation, indeed a
Utopian scheme indeed! When the Spartans in the last part of the
Peloponnesian war occupied a small town in Attica, 20,000 of them,
coming undoubtedly for the greater part from the mining-district,
went over to the enemy [71]. It is probable that in some workshop-
trades, for instance in those in which the manufacture of woollen
cloth and garments took place, female labourers were exploited; an
example, however, has not been recorded.

In t r a d e also slaves held a place. On the ships (and Greek trade

----

[64] Plut., Per. 16; Xen., Oec. I, 6; IX, 11 sqq.; VIII, 22; X, 10; Comm. I, 5, 2;
Aristoph., Eq. 947 sqq.; Vesp. 613; Diog. Laert., II, 8, 74; Poll., III, 126; X, 28;
Athen., IV, 171 a; Theophr., Char. XVIII; [Aristot.], Oec. I, 6, 1345 a; Plato,
Prot. 314 c; Phileb. 62 c; Athen., I, 3 c; Lucian., B. P. 7; Thuc., II, 78; Her., III,
150; Xen., Inst. Cyr. VIII, 5, 3 and 8, 20; Plato., Gorg. 517 d.

[65] Schol. ad Thuc., I, 141.

[66] P. 84.

[67] Cf. Guiraud, La main-d'oeuvre, pp. 139 sqq.

[68] Guiraud, La main-d'oeuvre, pp. 181 sqq.

[69] Xen., Vect. IV, 15 and 16; Andoc., I, 38; Hyp., II, 1, 2. Cf. also Thiel,
Xenophontis Poroi pp. 20-21.

[70] Xen., Vect. IV, 17.

[71] Thuc., VII, 27; Xen., Vect. IV, 25.

existed only by means of navigation) part of the crew was formed
by slaves [72]. "There are two kinds of slaves," says a pamphlet coming
forth from Aristotle's school [73], "the overseer and the workman." In
agriculture, industry and trade both categories are found: the prosperous husbandman who lives in the city and "farms with his supervision," [74] leaves the daily management of his farm to a slave-over-
seer. The same author indicates the conditions which a man must
fulfil in order to be entrusted with such a confidential post [75]. The
supervision and sometimes also the exploitation of a workshop was
often performed by an overseer (*hegemōn tou ergastèriou*) [76]. And
merchants sometimes established a slave in the cities where they carried
on business to take care of their interests. They naturally had a more
independent position; they likewise often appointed a slave as a skipper and made him trade for them [77].

Bisides the private persons *the State* made use of slaves for many
of its occupations; they were in its service as workmen or as officials [78]. The former were not numerous, which is not astonishing
when we realize that the Greek State had little concern with economical
life as the public services were still very little developed. Athens
occupied slaves at her mint [79], furthermore a few others for the
mending of roads and for the making of official buildings [80]. The
officials were of much more importance; in Athens, the police who
had to maintain order during the sittings of the court and in the
assemblies was composed of Scythian slaves [81]. Every proud, independent citizen had to submit himself to their instructions [82]. Moreover
the whole staff of officials charged with clerical work and the exe-

---

[72] Dem., XXXIII, 8.
[73] [Aristot.], Oec. V, 1.
[74] Xen., Oec. V, 4.
[75] Xen., Oec. XX, 16-17.
[76] J. Hasebroek, Staat und Handel im alten Griechenland p. 77.
[77] Cf. Westermann, pp. 22-23 (misthophorounta sōmata, chōris oikountes).
[78] Aristot., Ath. Pol. 54.
[79] Schol. ad Aristoph., Vesp. 1007.
[80] C. I. A. II, 834 b (add.), col. II, 1, 31; IV, 2, 834 b, col. I, 1, 44. In the
Athenian nave were also many slaves working as rowers (Dem., IV, 36; Harpocr.,
Pollux, Suidas s. v. chōris oikountes. As a particularity it is mentioned that the
rowers of the state ship Parhalos were freedmen (Thuc., VIII, 73). A great number
of slaves was considered to be necessary for a state powerfull at sea (Xen., Vect. IV,
42; Athen. Pol. I, 11).
[81] Poll., VIII, 131; IX, 10; Photius s. v. toxotai; Schol. ad Aristoph., Ach. 54;
Harpocrat. s. v. dèmosios.
[82] Cf. Plato, Prot. 319 c.

cution of decrees consisted of slaves [83]; as the Greek State did not know permanent officials and invested every year other inexperienced laymen with authority, we need not wonder that a good deal of State-government was left to slaves who formed in this way the only durable element in the administration.

It goes without saying that no place was allotted to women in this last category of State-slaves. Female slaves, and a little number of free women, besides working at home and in industry prostituted themselves in order to subsist; their workshop was the brothel.

The owners of male and female slaves made that part of their property pay in three manners: by hiring them out to third parties, by l e a v i n g   t h e i r   e x p l o i t a t i o n   t o   t h e   s l a v e s   t h e m-s e l v e s (in return the slaves had to pay a fixed amount of money; in both cases the proprietor is only living on the interest of his money) or he can exploit them in his own trade: only in this form of slave-exploitation the owner may be considered as an entrepreneur in the modern sense of the word [84].

The   h i r i n g   o u t   o f   s l a v e s took place in many forms and for all sorts of purposes. Individuals were available as cooks, flutists, household- or entertainment-slaves [85]. In Athens applicants could find them as a rule in fixed places of the city, e.g. near the temple of the Dioscur [86]. They were called hirelings, *misthōtoi*; for this matter free men offering their services in the same way were also indicated by this name. Slaves were hired but whole-sale as unskilled labourers, especially for labour involving risk of life in the silvermines of Attica. Nicias the well-known leader of the aristocratic party in the first and the second phase of the Peloponnesian war, hired out a thousand men for this purpose [87]. The word used in Greek for this hiring out means at the same time: to invest money; this may be an indication that we must consider it as a form of interest and not as profit of an entrepreneur.

When a slave-owner left it to the slaves themselves to find employ for their energy the second form of exploitation deserves our consideration. In one of Demosthenes' speeches [88] the orator tells us once that slaves were hired out by their master, but also that they offered

[83] Dem., VIII, 47; XXII, 70; Schol. ad II, 19; C. I. A. II, 737.

[84] Boeckh, Die Staatshaushaltung I³, pp. 90 sqq.

[85] Posidippus fr. 12 (K.); Theophr., Char. XI and XXII; Eupolis fr. 159 (K.).

[86] Guiraud, La main-d'oeuvre, p. 130.

[87] Xen., Vect. IV, 14 sqq.

[88] Dem., LIII, 1. Cf. 19 sqq.

themselves to reap the harvest or to pick fruit. For these occupations, however, the payment was due to the master. Here we can plainly see that it was alluring for a slave-owner to withdraw himself from the risk which slave-keeping always involved (he must support them also when they did no work and were unproductive) by shifting this charge on to the slave's own shoulders. He leaves it to him to earn his livelihood but stipulates a fixed daily payment [89]. No distinction is made between the words for the sum of money which he receives from his slave or in the first case from the person who engaged him; beside the real word for slave-rent, *apophora* [90], the general indication *misthos* is used which is generally translated by wages. We draw the attention to the fact that this form of exploitation is one of the many indications of the economically unsound conditions, clinging to slavery, because it has the tendency to heed only one's own interests.

It is different when the exploitation of a slave is not left to himself individually but when a gang of slaves is charged with the collective performance of a trade under the guidance of one of them who was held wholly and financially responsible to the owner. However, we do not know any particulars about such a business. We do not know who provided the tools, the workshop and in general the working-capital, whether a third person furnished it or if it was borrowed from the owner. Our data do not allow us to solve these questions. No more do we know whether this form of slave-exploitation existed also in agriculture, in other words whether there were slaves who acted as agents for the farmers.

Finally it also happens that the owner makes his slaves either carry on a business on his own acount and at his own risk or that he sets them to work in large numbers in his own business. Again the transition from the first stage to the latter is imperceptible; the master can force his slave to keep a little shop and cash himself a fixed rent for house and trade or he can hold the business in his own hands. In this case the slave has to make count and reckoning regularly as happened to a slave who kept a perfume-shop, *myropolion*; together with the barber's shop it was one of the retail-trades most frequently mentioned and best patronized in the Greek world.) As we have seen above [91], examples are also

---

[89] Stob., XCV, 21; Isaeus, VIII, 35; [Xen.], Ath. Pol. I, 17; Plato, Leg. VII. 806 e.

[90] Ammonius s.v.. Cf. Andocides, Myst. 35; [Xen.], Ath. Pol. I, 11; Theophr., Char. XXX; Artemidorus, I, 31 and 76; III, 41; Stob., V. 67; Diog. Laert., VII, 5, 169.

[91] Pp. 61-62.

known of a great number of slaves combined in one workshop. Most
of them, though, were employed as assistants in the workshops of
small masters. Here we are also at large about the particulars in practice. Did these slaves always receive food, clothes and accomodation
in kind from their master? Or did they receive fixed wages by which
they had to support themselves? Where they obliged in the last case
to bring their own tools or did the owner-entrepreneur furnish them?
In reality there will probably have been a rich variety of all kinds
of usages.

It will have happened in all categories that slaves did not live with
their master but that they had their work and lodging out: for these
slaves a special word was used: *chōris oikountes* (those living sepa-
rately [92]); we do not wonder that this term also indicated freedmen, once we know under what conditions they were manumitted
(cf. p. 99).

What picture can we form of the condition of the slaves and their
treatment, both apart from their juridical position? Modern investigators have answered the question in many different ways. Formerly [93] this condition was depicted as very unfavourable, whereas
at this moment the opinion prevails that it will have differed little
from the position of the wage-labourer in the 19th century, even that
the slaves were better off in many ways [94]. They refer to a pamphlet
written by an anonymous aristocrat from the last quarter of the 5th
century whose words deserve to be fully quoted. He writes [95]:

"An extra amount of licence is granted to slaves and resident aliens
at Athens, where a blow is illegal and a slave will not step aside to
let you pass him in the street. I will explain the reason of this peculiar
custom. Supposing it were legal for a slave to be beaten by a citizen,
it would frequently happen that an Athenian might be mistaken for a

[92] Dem., IV, 36. Cf. Ciccotti-Paton, Le déclin p. 144; Francotte, La main-d'oeuvre
p. 133.

[93] H. Wallon, Histoire de l'esclavage.

[94] Ed. Meyer, Die Sklaverei im Altertum. Kleine Schriften I, pp. 188: Wenn die
Hörigkeit der aristokratischen Epoche des Altertums, der homerischen Zeit, den
Wirtschaftsverhältnissen des christlichen Mittelalters entspricht, so steht die Sklaverei
der folgenden Epoche mit der freien Arbeit der Neuzeit auf gleicher Linie, sie ist
aus denselben Momenten erwachsen wie diese. Dies zu zeigen ist die Aufgabe des
zweiten Teils unserer Untersuchung.

On the other hand Max Weber, Die sozialen Gründe des Untergangs der antiken
Kultur. Gesammelte Aufsätze zur Sozial- und Wirtschaftsgeschichte, p. 291: Ein
heutiger Proletarier und ein antiker Sklave verständen sich so wenig, wie ein Euro-
päer und ein Chinese.

[95] [Xen.], Ath. Pol. I, 10-12. Cf. Zimmern p. 384.

slave or an alien, and receive a beating, since an Athenian is not better
clothed than a slave or alien, nor in personal appearance is there any
superiority. Or if the fact itself that slaves in Athens are allowed to
indulge in luxury, and indeed in some cases to live magnificently be
found astonishing, this too, it can be said, is done of set purpose.
When you have a naval power dependent upon wealth, we must per-
force be slaves to our slaves, in order that we may get in our slave-
rents and let the real slave go free. Where you have wealthy slaves
it ceases to be advantageous that my slave should stand in awe of you.
In Lacedaemon my slave stands in awe of you. But if your slave stands
in awe of me, there will be a risk of his giving away his own money to
avoid running a risk in his own person. It is for this reason then, that
we have established an equality between our slaves and free men."

Besides this statement, there is another general reason why the
slaves had to be well treated. It was the slave-keeper's interest to treat
his human property well because they represented a certain value and
unless they were well treated they were not willing to produce
profitable work. Statements are preserved from Xenophon [96] and
Aristotle [97] with his school in which they advise the holding out of
a prospect of freedom as a stimulus for hard work.

We must not attach too much weight to the passage of the sharp
opponent of Athenian democracy to whom the at least outward,
similarity of Athens' population was an abomination. The exaggeration of the partyman is too apparent. For the rest we can not deny
that in slavery itself as well as in the peculiar circumstances under
which it was carried on in Athens there was a tendency to kind treatment, at least of some categories of the slaves.

This does not apply in the least to the slaves working in the mines
of Laurium, the most southern district of Attica, which formed a
considerable part of the whole. Here the underground work was done
under the miserable circumstances described above [98]. Even without
direct particulars about the life of these wretched men we may be
sure that in the course of the centuries many thousands of them met
death there in the most horrid way.

The owners did not deal in such a barbarous manner with the other
slaves; the second category, the plantation-slaves were unknown in
Greece.

[96] Xen., Oec. III, 4.
[97] [Aristot.], Oec. I, 5. Cf. Plato, Leg. VI, 777 c and d.
[98] P. 55.

Part of the State-slaves who performed the work of our clerks, belonged to the better situated ones; they probably had fixed hours of attendance. After these they were free to act as they liked [99]. They lived without the daily supervision of an exacting master. They had an official dwelling at their disposal [100], the superiors received wages besides their direct maintenance which explains the fact that some of them could attain a certain degree of well-being [101].

All the slaves, moreover, who exercised a trade or craft outside the home of their master naturally enjoyed more pleasant independence; likewise those who only had to pay a fixed amount of money to their master and were allowed to keep the surplus of their earnings [102]. So there was no reason for them to complain of their economical position; they had indeed a motive for working hard and their labour often conduced to pretty favourable material circumstances. The slave-captain of whom we read [103] that he was capable of advancing money will not have belonged to the exceptions.

Further the male and female slaves who had daily and direct intercourse with their masters will not have been treated badly,—for this is the rule in relations where there is but little distance materially and intellectually between the employer and the employee —, the numerous assistants in the smaller crafts and the household-slaves who differed but little from the former worked under such circumstances; undoubtedly there will often have existed a feeling of mutual affection between the home-born slaves and their masters [104].

In contrast with these undeniable facts we must also note some others from which it becomes apparent that part of the slaves felt a gnawing discontent and a deep rancour against their condition.

The strongest proofs of it are the never ending attempts to escape and the need of measures against it [105]. Some land-owners made their

[99] These state slaves were called dèmosioi (Aesch., I, 54; Aristot., Pol. IV, 12, 144, 19; Plato, Leg. IX, 872 b; Dem., XXII, 70; Poll., VIII, 71; Harpocrat. s. v.
[100] Aesch., I, 59. Cf. schol. ad Aristoph., Ach. 54.
[101] Aesch., I, 54.
[102] Inscriptions recueillies à Delphes 202 and 263. Cf. [Xen.], Ath. Pol. I, 11.
[103] Dem., XXXIV, 6, cf. 28, 29, 41.
[104] Athen., IV, 149 d.
[105] The master of a run-away slave gave the latter's personal description and offered a reward (Xen., Comm. II, 10, 2; Her., IV, 9). Here appears to be the beginning of insurance against running away (loss of profits) [Aristot.], Oec. II, 2, 34. Instances of escapes on a large scale: Athen., VI, 265 e sqq.; 267 a; XIII, 572 e. This was only possible for great numbers of slaves performing the same kind of work and speaking the same language (Cf. Plat., Leg. VI, 777 c; [Aristot.], Oec. 1344 b, 18).

slaves work in chains, tactics which were sure to provoke running away according to Xenophon [106]. Those who had tried to do so got a brand on their foreheads [107]. But notwithstanding all these measures, escape and efforts to catch the run-aways, *drapetai*, were the order of the day; there were men who made a trade of this work, *drapetag-ōgoi* [108]. States concluded treaties in which they pledged themselves mutually to extradite slaves [109]; especially in days of great commotion, large masses of slaves succeeded in escaping from the country of their bondage; during the Decelean war more than 20,000 slaves from Athens went over to the enemy [110]. In order to prevent such mass escapes which involved certain deliberations and arrangements, Plato warns against the bringing together of many slaves speaking the same language in one trade [111]. It was, indeed, especially the circumstance that the slaves consisted as a rule of absolutely dissimilar types of different nations speaking various languages which rendered a forcible and unanimous resistance impossible, although they might have imposed the superiority of their number.

Further there are still many incidental statements to be quoted, which all indicate that masters and slaves were continuously living on war-footing. In one of Xenophon's pamphlets [112] a tyrant describes the unrest of his life, in peculiar how he is inferior to the ordinary citizens who are supported by their country, "for the citizens protect each other without a promised reward from slaves and criminals". Slaves ad criminals are here brought on one level in so far as they are both enemies of society. One of Euripides' figures says [113]: "Slaves respecting the social status of their masters incur the violent hatred of their equals." "So many slaves so many enemies," was a proverb later on [114].

Whence that ever smouldering rancour and discontent? This ques-

---

[106] Xen., Comm. II, 1, 16; Oec. III, 4; Plut., Comp. Nic. and Crass. 1. Cf. Theophr., Char. 18.

[107] Schol. ad Aesch., II, 79; Lucian., Timon 17.

[108] On the prosecution of run-away slaves: Dem., LIII, 6; LIX, 9; Plato, Prot. 310 e; Xen., Comm. II, 10, 1; Lucian., Fug. 27; Dio Chrys., X, 4; VII, 123. Letronne, Journal des savants 1833, p. 329.

[109] Thuc., IV, 118 sqq., cf. I, 139. Die Mysterieninschriften von Andania. Abh. der k. Gesellschaft der Wissenschaften zu Göttingen VIII, p. 217.

[110] Thuc., VII, 27, 5.

[111] Plato, Leg. VI, 777 c.

[112] Xen., Hiero IV, 3. Cf. Plato, Rep. IX, 578 e; Leg. VI, 756 e; Aristoph., Ran., 745 sqq.; Lysias, VII, 35; Athen., III, 62.

[113] Fr. 50 Nauck². Cf. Eur., El. 632-633.

[114] Sen., Ep. 47, 5. Cf. Festus, p. 261 a.

tion must needs be put, though we must not forget that only part of the slaves will have fostered these feelings. We must not look for an explanation in political lawlessness and social slighting which did not allow their admittance to the assembly and shut them out from the wrestling-schools of the free young men; for this does not distinguish them from the mass of labourers of the 19th century. Here, however, slaves had an advantage over them because they will have felt this lawlessness and slighting, less as an injustice, because they were to a large extent aliens and no compatriots. Neither will their position under Civil Law have aroused their discontent and hatred, nor the circumstance that they were chattles and no men in the eye of the law. For many of them this was a mere theory and in reality the manner of living of many a slave in Athens will have differed little from the life of the free craftsmen or day-labourers [115], to the vexation of the born aristocrat [116]. For law and public opinion protected him from the excesses of his master's arbitrariness. When thinking of Aristotle's words: [117]: "a slave's pay is his food," the fact has been pointed out not injustly that the numerous labourers who lived in the 19th cent. under the truck-system were in reality also slaves notwithstanding their juridical liberty. The ancient slaves will often have been treated better and with more care than the labourers in the industry of the 19th century, because their loss or devaluation was to the disadvantage of their owner while the latter can be replaced without any cost for the entrepreneur. But those who have come to the conclusion, especially on account of the last consideration, that the majority of the slaves received a fair treatment because it was in tne employer's interest, forget that a good treatment does not always guarantee contentedness with one's fate. Above we have seen (p. 78) that an increase of slaves did not occur on a large scale and that import from abroad supplied the needs as a rule. It follows t h a t o n c e t h e g r e a t m a j o r i t y o f s l a v e s k n e w l i b e r t y; to them Homer's word [118] may be applied that a man is bereft of half his manliness on the day on which he becomes a slave. In this way the reminiscence of lost freedom in their native land must have prevented, not only those slaves to whom life was a curse as in the mines, but also many a one whose material life was bearable, from

---

[115] Plato, Rep. VIII, 563 b; Dem., IX, 3; Plaut., Stich. 446; Plut., Garr. 18.
[116] [Xen.], Ath. Pol. I, 10.
[117] Aristot., Polit. I, 5, 3.
[118] Hom., Od. XVII, 322-323.

being contented with their fate and it must have stimulated their exasperation.

Because slavery is so absolutely at variance with everything considered good and just in the Western world it is of socio-historical interest how the, in many respects highly civilized Greeks, regarded it and in particular what men of genius thought about it. The circumstance that many a Greek slave was considered as an equal by his fellow-craftsmen in daily intercourse [119] cannot have prevented the owners and intellectuals from disdaining them: Exactly these classes of men form the public opinion. One can never regard the things which one buys for money, even if they are human beings, as one's fellow-men and as equals, the less so when the purchased labourers originated to a large extent from nations inferior in intellectual development, as was a rule in Greece; a circumstance of which we may never lose sight when explaining the contemptuous judgment of slaves. Slave was often synonymous with an uncivilized man from a distant and absolutely foreign nation. The metaphorical use in Greek of the word slave, *doulos,* and its derivation as well as of its contrast free, *eleutheros,* leaves no doubt about the general, unfavourable opinion. Another eloquent evidence of this fact is that in Athens and elsewhere as well no importance was attached to a slave's testimony, he was not deemed capable of speaking the truth when not compelled by torture [120], though Aristotle [121] with good psychological insight entertained doubts as to the efficacy of this means of coercion.

But did all the intellectual leaders of the people, the dramatists and philosophers, judge likewise about slavery and slaves?

Sophocles occupied himself very little with this problem in so far as we can conclude from his preserved works; yet we meet there, besides his statement that men are equals by nature [122], but that it is fate which renders them unequals (needless to say that he may not have thought of slaves here), an other expression that the body may be slave but that the spirit can nevertheless be free [123].

---

[119] No difference in dress: [Xen.], Ath. Pol. I, 10; Aristoph., Vesp. 444. But the hairs and beards of the slaves were often short: Aristoph., Av. 911; Plato, Alc. 120 b; Lucian., Timon 22.

[120] Dem., XXIX, 5, 12, 40; Isocr., XVII, 13, 15, 16, 21, 27, 53, 54, 55. Cf. Dem., XXXIII, 18; Lysias, VII, 36. Bongenaar, Isocrates' Trapeziticus pp. 89, 90, 94, 98, 103, 110, 112. Antiphon, II, 2, 7; Isaeus, VIII, 12.

[121] Aristot., Rhet. I, 15, 1376 b, 31. Cf. Dem., XXVII, 14; Antiph., V, 31.

[122] Stob., LXII, 33.

[123] Westermann p. 24.

A good many statements from Euripides who here too will have been the pupil and fellow-combattant of the enlightened, the sophists, are recorded; they show clearly how much this problem was discussed in those circles. Repeatedly one of his figures assures us that the only thing dishonourable about a slave is his name [123a], for the rest he is not at all inferior to the philosopher, provided he is good. Another of his figures has it that the nobility of a man does not depend on his status [124]. The reflection repeated many times later on in many varieties is very significant too: we are all slaves in some respect, either slaves of money or of fate and no mortal man is free, we are all slaves of the gods [125].

The colonization had dispersed the Greeks in early times along the coasts of the Mediterranean and the Black Sea and brought them in contact with many nations. Hence the early birth of cosmopolitism of which the first traces are already to be found in the Greek world before Alexander the Great; with the coming into existence of the conception "man" in contrast with citizen of a certain state the notion grew that all men even slaves were equal. On the stage [126] people are taught that a slave is in no way inferior to a free man; nobody is born a slave; fate makes the body so; a state of slaves exists nowhere; he who is free to-day toils to-morrow in the mines or is for sale in the market.

It was unavoidable that the Greek philosophers, to whom the best regulation of state and society formed one of the most important problems (Greek has but one word for these two conceptions, *politeia,*) occupied themselves also with the place which the slave occupied in it. As a matter of fact Plato gives many instructions about it which intend securing him a just treatment. He demonstrates in his "Laws" [127] that this good treatment will consist in not committing any injustice towards slaves; he wants men to be even more on their guard against it towards them than towards their equals. The master must even make this a rule, not only for the sake of the slaves, but for his own sake in order to practise self-education. For there is nowhere a greater proof of the fact that a man loves justice thoroughly

[123a] Cf. J. Schmidt, Der Sklave bei Euripides. Jahresberichte der Fürsten- und Landesschule zu Grimma, 99, 1892.

[124] Stob., LXII, 38 and 39. Here comedy continued Euripides' work: Stob., LXII, 28 (Philemon). Cf. C. Langer, De servi persona apud Menandrum. Thesis Bonn, 1919.

[125] Eur., Orest. 418 and 488; Hecub. 864. Eurip. on slaves: 48, 49, 50, 31, 57, 85, 86, 216, 217, 218, 313, 511, 529, 831, 1019 (Nauck).

[126] Meinecke, Fr. Com. Gr. III, 162 (Anaxandrides); IV, 47 (Philemon).

[127] Plato, Leg. VI, 777.

and hates wrong than from his behaviour towards those to whom he may do injustice with impunity. On the other hand he professes that a clear distinction between master and slave must continue to exist. The master's word must be law to the slave, familiarity destroys the master's authority and makes service more difficult for the slave.

So Plato recognizes the institution (not a word is breathed about its seemliness) and without relinquishing the distance between slave and master, he prescribes a good and just treatment which will make the slave more useful and docile and which will enable the master to show and strengthen his moral. The instructions as well as the motives themselves, the moral interest of the master, show a remarkable resemblance regarding slavery to the opinions [128] the Stoa later on and of Christianity [129] with their also purely individualistic view of the problem.

The institution itself is no problem to Plato [130]. Not so with Aristotle [131] who faces the question of its lawfulness in point of principle. Somebody from Gorgias' school had taught: "The gods made all men free, nature made nobody a slave" [132] and this statement had met with a wide response on the scene. Aristotle quotes this saying in order to dispute it: "according to some", he says, the power of the master is unnatural. By virtue of a human institution one man is supposed to be free and an other a slave, by nature there is no distinction; because it is based on force, the whole relation between master and slave is said to be unjust." But then he gives his radical defence of slavery, which may be summarized as follows:

In every community there are men intellectually capable of the maintaining of this community. An other part, however, is only capable to do so by bodily power. The former are by nature the rulers, the latter the slaves. Now such a relation as between mind and body exists between husband and wife, between master and slave. By nature everybody is a slave who has only so little intelligence that he is merely able to understand the thoughts of others but is not capable of developing his own thoughts: he is born to obey others. The barbarians are like that; they are born slaves; to them it is not only necessary but also better to be slaves. Slavery is useful for the slaves themselves

---

[128] E. J. Jonkers, De l'influence du Christianisme sur la législation relative à l'esclavage dans l'Antiquité. Mnemosyne ser. III, Vol. I, pp. 241 sqq.

[129] Cf. note 128 and p. 92.

[130] That the lawfulness of slavery was disputed appears from Aristot., Pol. 1253 b, 20. Presumably this only refers to those conquered in war (1255 a, 6 sqq. Cf. also Plato, Rep. 469 c.

[131] Aristot., Pol. I, 1 and 2, 1255 a. Cf. VII, 6, 229 and Stob., LXXXV, 15.

for the above-mentioned reason; therefore it is just. The relation between slave and master as between the one who serves and the one who commands is established by nature; and as the slave is only an implement and the implement by its nature the property of somebody else, it is likewise natural that the slave is the property of his master.

When we read such strikingly weak arguments from an exceedingly sharp-witted and versatile man as Aristotle undoubtedly was, it is once more apparent how much slavery was considered as indispensable and natural by those who made use of it and profited by it. As a proof how difficult it is for logic to overthrow the barriers of personal interest even if announced under the scientific name of racial theory: many of us, at least, are inclined to consider every defense of a domination by the rulers as natural and in the interest of the suppressed. But whence the conviction that slavery is indispensable and natural?

Scholars [133] have often been inclined to explain the existence of slavery in Greece by their disregard of manual labour which they are supposed to have shunned and left to others. In so far as this disdain of work existed, it was more a consequence of slavery than a cause of it. But, as we have demonstrated above [134], the opinion about the general disregard of labour in Greece is based on an erroneous point of view. It did exist among the wealthy and intellectuals, but by this phenomenon Greek society hardly distinguishes itself from that of other countries and later times. The great majority of the people earned their living with the sweat of their brow, and when the little and non-possessing class did not know the love of labour which is nowadays often wrongly considered as a natural virtue of man, we must see this phenomenon not as a peculiarity of a certain nation, but as a normal characteristic of a society where the production was exclusively a means of supplying the needs. The making of profit aiming at an increase of the production and, which on the other hand, would raise the needs dominated only the few and public opinion disapproved it.

The reason why slavery was unavoidable is rather to be found in the circumstance that Greece as an economically and politically highly developed country was situated in the midst of economically and politically backward regions. A large number of men lived there whose

[132] Schol. ad Aristot., Rhet. I, 13.
[133] See the literature in J. J. Koopmans, De servitute antiqua et religione Christiana. Thesis Amsterdam (V. U., Liberated University) 1920, pp. 65 sqq.
[134] Pp. 71-72.

working-power was little valued in their own country on account of the low standard of production. They lived either under tyrants who could sell their subjects at will, or in small communities which were unable to protect their members sufficiently from being kidnapped. Greece could by its relatively higher development of agriculture, craft and trade make use of cheap workmen and by its greater riches and stronger armament it could afford to buy them. These conditions gave birth to slavery, and as long as these conditions remained unaltered there could be no question of a modification in their position and the opinions about slavery.

Slavery was considered so normal in the world of reality and fancy that the question about its efficiency with as result an inquiry into its advantages and disadvantages never arose. It could not arise, because the indispensable means of comparison, a society in which all manual labour was done for wages by free men was not to be found in Antiquity. On the other hand it is easier for us to pass a historical judgment because we are cognizant of so many forms of labour in the course of history.

In order to do so we must first of all ascertain the significance of slavery for *economic* development.

In the beginning the farmer and his next of kin were self-sufficient in Greece too [135]. Together they built their dwelling and storage-place and manufactured the necessary wood and earthenware. With the growing needs in a country which by its easy traffic could not but come into contact with all sorts of foreign produce, this self-sufficiency would have given way more and more to the purchase of the desired objects, if it had not been possible to increase the working-power of the house by the introduction of the cheap labour of slaves. In this way, as a first result for economic life, slavery has seriously impeded the production for free commerce, for the market.

In an other manner it has checked considerably not the form of production but production itself. It goes without saying that food, clothes, and still more the housing for the great majority of the slaves was confined to a minimum [136]; it was not in the masters' interest to give them more than their maintenance [137]. Thus follows that only the

---

[135] Cf. also J. Hasebroek, Griechische Wirtschafts- und Gesellschaftsgeschichte pp. 9 sqq.

[136] Clothes: Aristoph., Eccl. 427; Vesp. 444; Lys. 1151; Poll. VII, 68; Hesych. s. v. v. katōnakè and heteromaschalos chitōn; Photius s. v. heteromaschalos chitōn. Food: [Aristot.], Oec. I, 5; Hesych. s. v. choinikes. Cf. Her., VII, 187; Thuc., IV, 16.

[137] [Aristot.], Oec. I, 5; Hesych. s. v. choinikes; Athen., III, 98 e; VI, 272 b.

first needs were supplied of a considerable part, in some districts of half of the population. It was a situation to be compared with the present if our labourers would have hardly any purchasing-power, while it is after all the want of cotton and not of silk, of potatoes and not of asparagus which claims a greater production and necessitates it. As slavery eliminates the mass of its victims as consumers, it cannot but harm *economic* development.

It has been said that the slaves in Antiquity played the part of machinery in modern times. The similarity, however, is but superficial, and in many respects the slave is inferior to machinery. Even when only paying attention to economic development. First of all it is true that a considerable part of the working-capital is invested in either category, but the difference is that, when the work comes to a standstill, the slave, like the machine, does not bring in the interest of the capital invested for his purchase, but that he, unlike machinery, requires his food, even when his working-power is not made use of. This difficulty must have made itself felt much more in a world in which there was no question of a ready market and so of an uninterrupted production, on account of the manifold wars and in general the unsafety of traffic. In another respect the slave-owner's risk is much greater than the risk of the entrepreneur who has invested money in machinery. The death-rate of the slaves must have been high, considering the unfavourable circumstances under which they lived in material and moral respects, and it will have been less calculable than the wear and tear of our machines. We have seen [137a], moreover, how strongly they desired to escape. It was impossible to wholly prevent this; the supervision would have been too costly. Finally the fluctuations in their market-price were usually great because the offer increased considerably after every war. Through all these circumstances an important item for a durable, wholesale trade was lacking: the possibility of a cost-estimation.

The risk of losing interest of the capital invested in slaves was the greater according to their respective quality and value, that is to say it was greater for slaves, skilled in a certain craft. In the 4th century an unskilled slave could be bought for 100 to 200 drachms, the price of a skilled labourer, on the contrary, was 500 and more drachms [137b];

Cf. Her., VII, 187; Thuc., IV, 16; Aristoph., Plut. 253; Pax 1249; Dem., XXXV, 32; Plut., Comp. Aristid. et Cat. 4.

[137a] P. 89.

[137b] Xen., Comm. II, 5, 2; Vect. IV, 23; Inscriptiones Delphicae 125, 270, 273, 40. Cf. Westermann, p. 14.

according to Xenophon [138] one talent was once paid for an overseer in the mines. The endeavours to buy slave-craftsmen on a large scale or unskilled slaves in order to bestow some cost on their training for a craft can never have been widespread. This too was a drag on the establishment of large trades; no wonder that they were but seldom found. Nothing is known to us of a large workshop with free labourers, while on the other hand it could not but follow that the crafts requiring skill remained to a large extent in the hands of independent free men.

An other explanation of this phenomenon is to be found in the circumstance, corroborated by the experience of every slave-keeping society, that a large part of the slaves, naturally without interest, care, and attention for their work are only fit for rough and unskilled work which may also be done without the above-mentioned qualities.

Lastly we must once more point out that the advantage of slave-labour lay mainly in the small cost of maintenance and the low price of the purchase. If there was a rise in the prices on account of less import and if one was therefore obliged to breed one's own slaves, the cost of exploitation increased in such a degree that slave-keeping hardly became remunerative, because in a society where the technique of industry was little developed work for women and children was lacking. These circumstances, however, did not occur in the 5th and 4th centuries.

And herewith the principal consequences of slavery for the economic development have been indicated. They are hardly different from the effects which they in had on s o c i a l life.

In passing we have already remarked [139] that free labour was not supplanted by it. It is even highly probable that this work did not suffer seriously from the slaves' competition. The available data make the impression that the two kinds of labour were kept in equilibrium, at least in the period which is treated in this booklet; at any rate no trace is to be found that free labour opposed slave-work or even complained of it. The opportunity so to do was certainly not lacking; in Athens e.g. the assembly consisted for a large part of craftsmen, if we may believe one of Xenophon's statements [140]. The farmers, who had their work or dwelling outside the city, will merely have asserted their rights as elsewhere in the few cases that vital interests were at

[138] Xen., Comm. II, 5, 2.
[139] Pp. 32, 33 and 54.
[140] Xen., Comm. III, 7, 6.

stake. These craftsmen as the poorer class people did not hesitate to make use of their political rights to force the owners to give "free gifts" to the people. When large buildings were let out in contract by the State, there is no proof that they ever demanded free citizens to be the first to be employed. On the contrary, we know that in the building of the temples citizens, aliens, and slaves were used, all receiving the same pay [141]. It seems that there was sooner a deficiency than a surplus of free labourers.

Slavery has also played an important part in a wholly different domain of social development: the growth of the population. Only a small quantity of the great number of slaves contracted a marriage, legally or otherwise [142]; consequently the birth-rate of the slavish population was exceedingly low. Now, generally speaking, the birth-rate of the labourer is high and the natality of a whole nation is increased by it, whereas in Greece the slaves, forming a considerable part of the total of its inhabitants, were nearly barren. It follows that under these circumstances the increase of the population (one of the conditions for the increase of the needs and thereby for the expansion of production) was checked. In order to realize the significance of this problem, it suffices to imagine how at present the population of France would fare,—a country showing much resemblance to Attica on account of its prevailing small farming—if it possessed instead of the miners rich in children in the Northern departments the barren slaves from the Laurium district.

In Greek society where retail-trade predominated, also in industry, all conditions were, naturally, lacking for a movement to be compared to the labour-movement of the 19th century. On the other hand the total absence of this movement sets even the supposition of an important development of industry at nought. Moreover an organization which might have led to a successful revolt could not but miscarry in those cases where a great mass of slaves worked in one trade (in mining, and here and there in agriculture) on account of their different nationalities; consequently of the differences in language and mental attitude through which a feeling of solidarity, which may be aroused by a common fate, could never be felt. The action of the slaves had to restrict itself to impotent bursts of fury and their resistance could only express itself by escaping.

---

[141] Cf. Francotte, L'industrie II, pp. 150 sqq.

[142] In Xen., Oec. IX, 5 the male slaves live in the andronitis and the female ones in the gynaeconitis. Cf. Dem., XLVII, 56.

As almost everywhere where slavery has existed it was accompanied in Greece also by a phenomenon, showing clearly once more how much its nature is incompatible with a higher degree of economic development: the *manumission of slaves* [143].

As far as we know, this did not happen before the 5th century. The absence of data in earlier times, however, may be incidental; yet we may assume, by reason of general considerations, that it was only then that manumission did not confine itself to a few isolated cases. First of all manumission may be awarded by virtue of a decree of the people by the government, because it was in the interest of the State. It was granted as a reward either for the denouncing of a crime as sacrilege or high treason [144] or for a service rendered in a battle for their master's country. In this case the masters are indemnified by the State [145]. This form of manumission, however, is of no avail for our knowledge of economic life. This is different when private persons decided to manumit their own slaves.

Directly we know little or nothing of the extent of this custom in the 5th and 4th centuries B.C.. The forms in which the manumission took place (consecration or mock-sale to a deity [146]) are not to the purpose here. The motives for a manumission, however, are not unknown to us, thanks to some statements of authors. In some peculiar cases they will undoubtedly have been due to purely human feelings as gratitude e.g. for an important service. But as a rule considerations of an other nature prevailed. Xenophon [147] demonstrated that slaves more than freemen want auspicious prospects to induce them to work willingly. In his "Politics" Aristotle [148] promises to explain somewhere, how slaves must be treated and why the price of freedom must be offered to a slave; these arguments, however, are nowhere to be found in this work. We meet with them, though, in a pamphlet under his name and which originates from his school: *Oeconomica* [149]. Hints are given to enhance the slave's working-power and then he says a.o. "It is righteous and profitable" (it is not often so ingenuously

---

[143] Cf. A. Calderini, La manumissione e la condizione dei liberti in Grecia. Milano 1908.

[144] Lysias, V, 5; VII, 16; Plato, Leg. XI, 914 a.

[145] Aristoph., Ran. 33, 192, 693; Diod., XVII, 11; Dio Chrys., XV, 21.

[146] Aesch., III, 41; Dion. Hal., Is. 4. P. Foucart, De l'affranchissement des esclaves par forme de vente à une divinité. Comptes rendues des séances de l'Académie des Inscriptions. 1863 pp. 129-155.

[147] Xen., Oec. V, 16.

[148] Aristot., Pol. VII, 9, 237.

[149] [Aristot.], Oec. I, 5.

admitted that a thing which is profitable is felt at the same time as righteous!) "that liberty should be held out to a slave as a reward, for then, when their serving-time is limited, slaves are willing to work hard."

The motive is distinctly mentioned here: the interest of the master. We have indicated above how this often induced him to give his slave an opportunity of working independently. In this manner the slave differed socially little from the free craftsman, shopkeeper or merchant. The strongest stimulus, however, to induce a slave to work steadily and profitably was the prospect of his liberty some day. We may conclude from the phenomenon of manumission that slavery is incompatible with careful and persistent work. But, at the same time, we may deduce from economic motives to what cases and to what crafts it will have been mainly restricted: the prospect of manumission will have been held out in those occupations where particular zeal and exertion, promising larger revenues to the master, were not to be excited by mere compulsion; it will hardly ever have occurred to unskilled labourers, in the mines e.g. where the overseer's stick must have been the only spur. Furthermore it follows that the freedmen, when judging man at least after his economically useful qualities, formed the pick of the slaves and were the most laborious among the population. It is not incidental that besides the so-called "guest" (metic) the freedmen (who in Greece constitutionally occupied the place of metics [150] in contrast to Rome where the freedmen were citizens with fewer rights) [151] played an important part in trade; the best-known and wealthiest money-traders of the 4th century belonged to them [152].

Coming from distant and less civilized countries they cannot have had much influence upon the intellectual civilization of the Greeks. In so far as they came from districts whose customs diverged not too much from Greek habits, the daily intercourse with the Greeks and the presence of numerous outlanders must have disturbed the uniformity of thought and feeling, inherent to every people, and must have weakened natural tradition, this the more so because the merchants were accustomed to accompany their goods everywhere and so came into contact with men of various conditions [153].

---

[150] Harpocrat. s. v. metoikion; Photius s. v. isotelès.

[151] P. F. Girard—F. Senn, Manuel élémentaire de droit romain[8]. Paris 1929, pp. 130 sqq.

[152] Dem., XXXIV, 6; XXXV, 32; C. I. G. I, 894 and 859. Cf. 87.

[153] Pp. 111-112.

Marriages of free men and slaves were out of the question and will have been an exception; also with freedmen and aliens in the golden age, considering the well-known pride of the Greek citizen. So slavery cannot have influenced the anthropological composition of the population, nothwithstanding the institution of manumission.

A review of the significance of slavery in Greek society would be incomplete if we did not briefly indicate its consequences for *moral* development also.

To begin with: the moral standard of the slaves will not have been high; natives often from uncivilized districts, uprooted from their natural surroundings, living among other uprooted men with again other habits amidst a foreign civilization, they missed the indispensable support of national community or comradeship which are the criteria of most men's behaviour and judgment. As a rule they only had in common the hatred of their masters and the contempt or disdain which they experienced from them. Hatred and contempt have no other than an immoral effect on those classes of men who cannot get rid of these feelings by an unanimous opposition or by a struggle to rise above the circumstances, but who must bear everything patiently or chafing with rage. Particularly the sexual life of the slave to whom a regular sexual intercourse was impossible in a so-called marriage must have been dissolute and unnatural [154].

But slavery often was a cause of demoralization for the masters also. We have already seen [155] that slavery will die out without a regular supply of fresh human material from abroad. Slavery is condemned to disappear without *slavetrade.* The slaves in so far as they were not captured in war had to be purchased, to be stowed in ships by slave-raiders, transported and exposed for sale in the market. It is unimaginable that slave-hunting, slave-shipping, and slave-markets could ever go hand in hand with the respect due to fellow-men. The bestialities of the 17th and 18th century-slave- trade are too well-known: the colleagues of Mr. Legree in Antiquity cannot have been much more humane. The majority of the slave-owners will not have been brutes, but they bought live stock, and they cannot have treated them as equals, these "bodies" paid for as the Greeks often wrote [156] and which they procured themselves together with cattle. They called

---

[154] Hom., Od. XVII, 322-323; Xen., Hiero IV, 3; Sen., Ep. 47: Totidem hostes esse quot servos. Xen., Oec. IX, 5; Dem., XLVII, 56.

[155] Pp. 77 sqq.

[156] Dem., XX, 76.

them, probably in contrast to the quadrupeds, hominipeds (*andra-poda*) [157]. (Our Dutch forefathers counted with "pieces" from India!)

These views will undoubtedly have influenced the relations between the free men and the female merchandise. We have mentioned above [157a] that the Attic society in which a great many men were wont to marry late, offered a favourable soil for prostitution. It is impossible to ascertain whether it was wider-spread than in our modern world, but it is remarkable that it was not only generally tolerated, but accepted even by the Athenian philosophers [158]. In these centuries no trace is to be found of the conception that a man, when not married, has to refrain from sexual intercourse. Undoubtedly slavery must also have contributed to this part of Greek moral, though shocking in our sight. By far the greater part of the prostitutes were female slaves, in this manner it may be explained that men considered them more as mer-chandise than as women. The disdain of the slaves in general may have contributed to the fact that the women-citizens who did not recognize the slaves as their equals, did not feel hurt too much by the intercourse of men with the slaves [159].

Slavery has had so much influence on a great number of social and moral relations that it is well-nigh impossible to realize its enormous significance completely. A few examples may illustrate how it affected sundry aspects of ancient life.

Greek society where in agriculture, industry and trade small proper-ty and retail-trade prevailed, did not know much distance between rich and poor, at least not during the centuries discussed here. The Greeks attached a somewhat different meaning to these adjectives than we are wont to do [160]; the great differences characterizing Eastern society were certainly lacking here. Moreover, the little or non-posses-sors, by force of the Assembly in which they had the majority, had an ample opportunity to compel the wealthy to support them in times of need, when there was a shortage of grain e.g. This explains that the State neither interfered with public relief nor that private charity was

---

[157] Xen., An. IV, 1, 12; Hom., Il. VII, 475.

[157a] P. 27.

[158] Cf. N. Geurts, Het huwelijk bij de Griekse en Romeinse moralisten (Marriage in the Greek and Roman Moralists). Thesis Utrecht 1928 (with a summary in German).

[159] H. Licht, Sittengeschichte Griechenlands II, Chapter 4 (pp. 45 sqq.): Die Prostitution. In the Homeric society that could be different. Laertes for instance did not touch the beautiful Euryclea for fear of his wife's wrath (Hom., Od. I, 429 sqq.).

[160] J. Hemelrijk, Penia en Ploutos. Thesis Utrecht 1925 and J. J. van Maanen Penia en Ploutos in the Period of Alexander. Thesis Utrecht 1931.

often practised or praised and taught as an important virtue [161].
Slavery will also have influenced this negative phenomenon, for
exactly the class or people which elsewhere numbers most poor men,
consisted of slaves in Greece and the upkeep of the slaves was naturally
the masters business: the notion to tend alms to an unknown beggar
was lacking, while on the other hand the assistance of a friend or
relation was considered as one of the greatest duties.

Finally we must still mention a wholly different habit of life. From
our records we get the impression that in Athens a large part of the
mothers left the nursing of their babies to paid nurses [162], a remarkable phenomenon with a young and healthy nation. The circumstance that the presence of female slaves with whom pregnancy and
the giving of birth to children will have been no exception formed
an extremely tentative and cheap means of shifting the burden of
nursing children to their shoulders.

From the above it is apparent that slavery has been one of those
institutions, though considered inevitable for centuries, which have
hardly had any but detrimental consequences in every domain, a proof
besides many others of the inexactitude of that historism which admits
that the course of history is not only necessary, but also good.

[161] H. Bolkestein, Wohltätigkeit und Armenpflege im vorchristlichen Altertum.
Utrecht 1939.
[162] Dem., LVII, 45; Aristoph., Thesm. 446 sqq.

CHAPTER FIVE

TRADE AND MONEY-TRAFFIC

In a region as inhabited by the Greek tribes with its extensive coast and hundreds of bays and situated on an easily navigable sea, so closely covered with islands that there was hardly any place not within sight of land, the traffic by sea with foreign countries and with each other must already have existed in early times. Excavations in Crete from the beginning of the bronze era, so after about 3000, B. C. brought forth Egyptian objects; from the same time dates earthenware, found in islands in the Aegean Sea with representations of vessels of a shape different from the Egyptian ones, and which makes it probable that in these parts of the world an independent ship-building came into existence. A good number of finds have given us some notion of the nature of the international and other traffic during the Creto-Mycenean period [1]. In the following pages, however, we shall only occupy ourselves with trade of which already in classical times written data are available.

Homeric poetry does not yet know a word for trade. It uses the general word *prèxis*, action [2], enterprise, in the sense in which it also knows *prèktères,* dealers, entrepreneurs [3]. Trade is not yet a wholly independent and purely economic profession. On the one hand it is not yet to be distinguished from piracy [4]; the goddess Athena presents herself as Mentes, a Taphian merchant, exchanged bronze against iron [5], but the Taphians are elsewhere called pirates [6]. On the other hand, the development of bartering from the exchange of presents, an apparent previous stage everywhere, has left distinct traces. The base of the often exceedingly large presents is reciprocity. Foreign "trade" between wealthy persons was carried on in the form of exchange; in this way they became "guest-friends" [7].

---

[1] Cf. A. Köster, Schiffahrt und Handelsverkehr des östlichen Mittelmeeres im 3. und 2. Jahrtausend v. Chr. Leipzig 1924 (Beihefte zum "Alten Orient", Heft 1).

[2] Hom., Od. III, 72 and 82; IX, 253.

[3] Hom., Od. VIII, 162.

[4] Thuc., I, 5 and 7; Hom., Od. IV, 77 sqq.; cf. IV, 90. IX, 40 sqq.; XI, 401 sqq.

[5] Hom., Od., I, 185.

[6] Hom., Od. XV, 427; XVI, 426. Cf. Apollod., II, 4, 5. Strabo, 456 and 459.

[7] Hom., Il. VII, 473; XXIII, 745. Bücher p. 62. Hom., Il. VI, 234 sqq.; Od.

An important part of sea-traffic is passive and is exercised by the Phoenicians [8]. They chiefly bring slaves and valuable articles: worked metals, weapons, jewelry, furniture and precious tissues, which they exchange against foodstuffs, wood, cattle, and minerals [9]. Greek navigators are mentioned nowhere directly, but when talking of *tektones,* shipwrights are generally meant by it [10]. However, even without this indication it is certain that navigation was also practised by the Greeks.

Cattle is still often medium of exchange and standard of value [11]; the Greeks before Troy procure themselves wine for copper, iron, hides, and slaves [12]. The latter are mentioned more than once as an article of commerce [13]; but the precious metals also served this purpose, a special weight, a *talanton* passed current for it [14]. For the rest the words, used later on for buying [15] and selling, have still the sense of exchange.

No trace is to be found of a local trade and market; the scales mentioned once in a comparison are those of a female spinner, not those of a saleswoman [16].

It is curious to see that the farmer-poet Hesiod, living in the centre of Boeotia and who, according to his own avowal, saw the sea only once when crossing from Aulis to Euboea [17], inserted in his poem about agriculture an episode about navigation and traffic, always identical with the Greek. As may be expected from one not expert in these matters, hardly any news can be obtained from it, but a single item

---

XXI, 13-15; XXIV, 283; IV, 600 and 615; XIII, 41, 137, 203, 363; XIV, 286; Il. IX, 266 sqq.; Thuc., II, 97, 3 and 4; Eur., El. 359.

[8] Hom., Il. XXIII, 477; Od. XV, 415 and 473; XIII, 272; Thuc., I, 8; Her., III, 107, cf. 111 and 136; Athen., IV, 173 b.

[9] Hom., Od. XIV, 287 sqq.; XV, 403 sqq.; XIII, 277; XXIII, 745. Peoples and towns carrying on trade: Thuc., I, 13 (Corinth); Eur., Iph. in Aul. 284 (Taphians), cf. Suidas s. v. Taphios; Hom., Od. XIII, 256; XIV, 199. and, 245 sqq. XVI, 62; XIX, 172 (Cretans); Od. XIV, 35 (Thesprotans); Od. XX, 283; cf. Od. XXIV, 211, 366, 389 (Sicilians mentioned as slave-dealers); Il. XXI, 40; XXIII, 747; XXIV, 753 (The islands of Lemnos, Imbros and Samos mentioned as selling-places of slaves); Il. VII, 467 (Wine furnished from Lemnos); Il. IX, 72; Od. IX, 196; Il. XI, 639; Od. X, 235 (Wine from Thracia and Pramna).

[10] Hom., Od. IX, 126, cf. Il. V, 59 and XIII, 390; XV, 411; XVI, 483.

[11] Hom., Il. XVIII, 593; Od. I, 430.

[12] Hom., Il. VII, 474.

[13] Hom., Od. XV, 414 sqq.; XIV, 115 and 202; Il. VII, 474; XXI, 43, 78, 102, 114; XXII, 45; XXIV, 752 sqq.

[14] Hom., Od. IV, 129; Il. IX, 122.

[15] Hom., Od. I, 430; XV, 445.

[16] Hom., Il. XII, 434.

[17] Hes., Erg. 648-654.

deserves our attention. From the fact that this farmer occupies himself with this subject, but moreover from the advice given to haul the vessels ashore after the setting of the Pleiads, (that is to say in November [18], his description proves the small size of the ships), then to devote oneself to agriculture [19], to set sail again 50 days after the summer's solstitium, trusting oneself to Poseidon's good humour (if at least you have set your foolish heart on perilous navigation!) [20], from all this it is apparent that the poet thinks of men supporting themselves by turns through the plough and the oar. He does not seem to know a class of merchants devoting their lives to navigation. In his poem the word *emporia* occurs, the term which will indicate the trade by sea in general later on [21]. We do not wonder that the word *emporos* which means after its derivation and with Homer in general *traveller* [22] became commercial traveller in every-day language [23], the merchant who travels with his little boat from coast to coast and earns his livelihood in this way [24]. We see that here the dramatists also stick to epic language [25].

Hesiod does not mention retail trade either in the maket-place or elsewhere.

A result of the enormous colonization [26] carried on from the 8th to the middle of the 6th century was the huge expansion of the commercial domain exploited by the Greeks themselves. Greek settlements or cities came into existence on the coast of the Black Sea and on the sea-routes leading from Ionia and Greece towards it; in Sicily, in Southern Italy and the south of France (Massalia) and the north coast of Africa (Cyrene). The Greeks plied a brisk trade among these dispersed regions, partly with foodstuffs as oil, wine, and corn, partly with materials as timber, and metals, but especially with finished products, as a rule fancy-objects of great value. The first articles were transported in jars which were often wanted and bought for their

[18] Hes., Erg. 664 and 674. Cf. Dem., XXXIII, 23; Thuc., VI, 21, 2; Plato, Ep. 345 d; Pind., Is. II, 41; Xen., Ages. II, 31; Dem., LVI, 30.

[19] Hes., Erg. 622.

[20] Hes., Erg. 616 sqq. Cf. Dem., L, 17 and 19; XXXIII, 23; XXXV, 10-13; Bongenaar, Isocrates' Trapeziticus pp. 114-115.

[21] Hes., Erg. 644.

[22] Hom., Od. II, 319; XXIV, 300.

[23] Schol. ad Aristoph., Plut. 1155; Plato, Prot. 313 d; Polit. 290.

[24] Bücher I, p. 155 (Wanderhandel).

[25] Aesch., Choeph. 650; Soph., Oed. Col. 304 and 905; Eur., Alc. 100. Knorringa, Emporos, p. 30.

[26] H. P. Fairchild, The Causes of Emigration from Greece. Yale Review 1908.

intrinsical value; when the finding-places of these objects are known and their original provenance, it becomes possible to fix or at least to surmise the sea-routes, the decline and the rise of the harbours of exportation.

While still in the 6th century the most flourishing and thriving Greek cities were situated on the coast of Asia Minor of the Aegean Sea (most colonies were founded from this district), the centre of gravity of economical, political and intellectual life was removed to the Western part of this sea since the happy end of the Persian wars. Athens ruled the sea during the 5th century and even after the loss of its political supremacy it remained the centre of trade also in the 4th century.

What do we know about trade's development in these times and what about the forms in which it was carried on? These are the questions to which an answer will be given in the following pages.

The Greeks distinguished (as is obvious from the different words used) two kinds of traders: *emporoi* and *kapèloi,* terms translated as a rule by "whole-sale" and "retail-trader"; in reality these words indicated (definitions of these words have been handed down to us more than once) [27] respectively the man who wanders from one town to an other and in this way finds a market for his article and the merchant who is established in a town and sells his goods in the market or at home. So in itself the only difference between the two is that the *emporos* is a navigating merchant and that the *kapèlos* stays at home [28]. In this archipelago the *emporos* is as a rule a navigating merchant; the trade by land was of hardly any importance, as we shall see below [29]. This includes that the former will generally have had a larger turn-over, but it does not prove anything as to the existence of a real wholesale trade and a status of wholesale dealers.

To prove the existence of a wholesale trade it does not suffice to state that certain wares are transported across great distances, for then we should have ascertained its existence already in the earliest times, when we meet with amber e.g. from the Baltic in the countries of Southern Europe. A first condition to be fulfilled, if the term is to be applied at all, is a large and regular trade in certain goods. Did

[27] Schol. ad Aristoph., Plut. 1156; Plato, Soph. 223 c and 231 d; Politicus 260 c; Dem., XXV, 45; LVI, 7; Poll., VII, 12; Photius s.v.. Cf. also Hasebroek, Staat und Handel pp. 125 sqq.

[28] Knorringa, Emporos passim.

[29] P. 122.

the Greek world of the 5th and 4th centuries know such staple products? There existed only two kinds of these commercial goods, meant for daily use, so not exclusively precious goods of a peculiar quality, s l a v e s and c o r n; s a l t e d f i s h (though not in the same breath) may also be mentioned.

Above [30] we have at length discussed the extent and the significance of slavery, here we shall only draw the attention to the fact that the slaves did not only form one of the most important, but also one of the most precious and most lucrative articles of commerce: in the time of the Roman Empire its abolishment would deprive not only agriculture and industry, but also trade of one of its foundations [31]. They were precious goods which by way of exception could not be counted among the luxurious articles, but as Aristoteles expressed it once, belonged "to the first necessities of life" [32].

Considerable parts of Greece, in particular the coastal towns where the adjacent land was not very fertile, had recourse to the import or corn, by far the principal food of the population. This lack of corn necessitated a brisk trade in cereals; this indispensable food formed the normal freight of the tradingvessels, so much so that to the Greek the words "merchant" and "corn-dealer" were synonyms: Xenophon states with a characteristic ingenuity, proper to mankind, that the merchant is fond of grain [33]. In most cases of bottomry [34] known to us from Demosthenes' speeches [35], the cargo given as a security consisted of corn.

We have already [36] mentioned the transport of salted fish, especially from the Black Sea, but this national food was a less important article of commerce than the two preceding ones.

Some regions, moreover, were in need of the import of timber. Especially Attica could not nearly produce the quantities of wood, necessary for the building and the keeping-up of its large navy and merchant-fleet. Besides, the silver mines here made use of the indispensable props for underground mining. It goes without saying that iron was also imported, either as material or in the shape of finished products, but except for weapons it was but little in demand.

---

[30] Chapter IV.

[31] Cf. R. H. Barrow, Slavery in the Roman Empire. New York 1928; Ciccotti-Paton, Le déclin de l'esclavage pp. 357 sqq.

[32] [Aristot.], Oec. I, 5.

[33] Xen., Oec. XX, 27.

[34] P. 112.

[35] Dem., XXXII; XXXIV.

[36] P. 39.

Lastly the merchants dealt in olive-oil, but as the olive-tree was dispersed all over the Greek world, its trade was confined to the better brands (Attica's oil was most-renowned) [37] and to export to those districts, inhabited by Greeks, which did not produce oil themselves, as the countries round the Black Sea.

So the first condition for a real wholesale trade was lacking: the general need of commodities, much in request. The great mass and not only they, had but few material needs. Little was wanted for the accommodation of the house; furniture, requiring timber, curtains, carpets, and fancy-articles were but scantily used; little was also needed for the simple and hardly adorned clothing, little for the frugal meals, of the free population as well who did not know coffee, and tea, cocoa and sugar, colonial produce and exotic fruit. In so far as the merchant did not convey cereals, he was considered to earn his money by the sale of luxury articles. His cargo consisted of the goods described in the Revelations of St. John [38] about an Oriental merchant (as a matter of fact this description applies to the cargoes of all Antiquity): "the merchandise of gold and silver, and precious stones, and of pearls, and silk, and scarlet, and all thyine wood, and all manner of vessels of ivory, and all manner of vessels of most precious wood, and of brass, and iron, and marble. And cinnamon, and odours, and ointments, and frankincense, and wine, and oil, and fine flour, and wheat, and beasts, and sheep, and horses, and chariots, and slaves, and souls of men." The enumeration is long but in comparison with a list of goods of the present world traffic it proves the little extent of trade in ancient times.

This is also pointed out by another well known circumstance: in Greece it is always the merchant himself who buys, transports and sells the goods; during the time that the sea is navigable, the merchant is away on a voyage [39]. The stage of the "stehende Handel" (trade at home) which followed the "Wanderhandel" (wandering trade) in the later economical development of Europa was not to be found in Greece; neither trading-concerns from which a wholesale trade is directed nor shipping-companies; the few times that one man possesses more than one ship he is not necessarily a ship-owner or a chartering-broker.

---

[37] Plut., Sol. II, 24.
[38] XVIII, 12-13.
[39] Dem., XXXV, 20 and 33; Hesych. s. v. nauklèros and diopos; Suidas s.v. diopos; Harpocrat. s.v. diopenōn. The owner of the ship personally took part in the voyage, or made a proxy go.

Almost out of the question is that the *emporos* occupied himself exclusively with wholesale trade by the merefact that during one half of the year all traffic was stopped; for in winter the men did not venture out with their small vessels on a turbulent sea. But when navigating and roaming about from harbour to harbour [40] in order to look for a ready market he could never count upon the selling of his wares to one or more persons [41]; no trace is to be found of an expedition of goods on commission; when making a port he himself had to march with a dish on which his samples of corn e.g. were displayed; he will repeatedly have made his profits by retail sale, the Greeks called it *kotylizein* [42] after the measure (*kotyle*) which contained little more than half a pint. Thucydides' statement [43] is instructive for the nature of their trade: he tells us that many *emporoi* had embarked with their goods on the powerful fleet which the Athenians had equipped to conquer Sicily in order to do business with the conquered island; many a soldier had even taken a supply with him with the same intention [44]. The *emporoi* were mainly pedlars who often wandered with their marchandise from town to town on a ship belonging to somebody else.

A good many statements point to this character of the *emporoi* as hardworking craftsmen. Isocrates [45] describes somewhere the golden age in Athens' history under Solon and Clisthenes when poor and rich lived side by side as the lamb and the lion in paradise: "the poor were far from envying the rich, they bestowed as much care upon the fortune of the rich as upon their own, because they understood that the riches of the wealthy meant welfare to them, and the wealthy did not neglect the more destitute, but being of the opinion that the want of co-citizens disgraced them, they succoured the needy. To the one they gave land to till against a moderate rent, they sent out others to *emporia* (factories), and procured money to some others to start a business with." And Xenophon [46] records that farmers happened to

---

[40] Dem., XXXIV, 8 sqq., LVI, 9; Xen., Oec. XX, 27; Hell. V, 1, 21; Poll., IX, 34 s.v. deigma; Aristoph., Eq. 978 with schol.; Plut., Dem. 23; Athen., XI, 499 e; Plato, Leg. VII, 788 c; Harpocrat. s.v. deigma.

[41] Dem., XXXV, 10 and 16; XXXIII, 5; LVI, 7; Xen., Oec. XX, 28; Poll., I, 95.

[42] Poll., VII, 195, cf. Bekker, Anecdota Gr. 46; Dem., XXXIV, 10 sqq. Bongenaar pp. 214 sqq.

[43] Thuc., VI, 44, 1, cf. [Aristot.], Oec. II, 1350 a, 25; Xen., Inst. Cyr. VI, 2, 38; Hell. I, 6, 37; Diod., XX, 84 and XIV, 79.

[44] Thuc., VI, 31, 5. Cf. VII, 13, 2 and 57, 10.

[45] Is., VII, 32.

[46] Xen., Vect. IV, 6.

give up agriculture when it was no longer remunerative in order to pass to *emporiai*, *kapèleiai* and *tokismoi* (money-lending by profession). From this it is apparent that *emporoi* are not considered at all as wholesale traders; they did not differ much from *kapèloi* as regards the extent of their trade and the amount of their revenues. These words are interchanged repeatedly: slave-traders are called *sōmatemporoi* as well as *andrapodokapèloi* [47]; the man who accompanied the armies in order to buy the booty and to dispose of it again, are called alternately *emporoi* and *kapèloi*, like those merchants who tried to sell slaves and cattle, clothes and jewelry at the fairs, kept on the occasion of the great temple-festivals.

Considering this state of affairs it is not astonishing that Plato [48] makes no difference between all these men. He speaks of those who wander about in the markets or from town to town, by sea and by land, exchanging money for other goods or money for money: money-changers, *emporoi*, *nauklèroi* and *kapèloi*. He treats them with the same disdain as the *dèmiourgoi*, craftsmen, in a remarkable and instructive contrast with Cicero [49] who more than two centuries later was to esteem retail trade beneath his dignity, "whole-sale trade, however, admissible because it brings goods from all parts of the world and distributes them among the people without higgling, especially when he who exercises it, retires finally from the harbour to the land and rehabilitates himself by buying landed property."

Aristotle [50], when enumerating the social statuses, mentions likewise the *agoraioi*, traders, side by side with the farmers and craftsmen; as little as he isolates the "manufacturers" from the craftsmen, he distinguishes *emporoi* from *kapèloi*; he has an equally unfavourable opinion about the two. Naturally there were *emporoi* who obtained a large capital: Herodotus [51] tells for instance that a merchant from Samos had drawn big profits from his trade with Tartessus in Spain, rich in silver. This Colaeus plied his ship himself and profited of exceedingly favourable circumstances; a comparison with the expedition of the Dutch to the Gold-coast in the 16th century is obvious. From the 4th century the name of Lampis has come down to us, an outlander established in Aegina who "of all the Greeks owned the

---

[47] Isaeus in Harpocration s.v.; Lucian., Adv. Iud. 24.

[48] Plato, Rep. 371 sqq. Van den Oudenrijn, Demiourgos pp. 124 sqq. (Demiourgos in Plato).

[49] Cic., De off. I, 42.

[50] Aristot., Pol. IV, 3.

[51] IV, 152.

biggest cargo-boats" [52]. There will have been more merchants like that. But the great majority of the *emporoi* of the 5th and 4th centuries were men who earned their livelihood by a life of hard and dangerous toil; a separate class of merchants did not exist.

Even the trade of the merchants in general was not distinctly separated from other professions, for there were many merchants who did not occupy themselves exclusively with trade; in this sphere we meet with the same phenomenon as we have noticed, when discussing industry. There were many occassional merchants, men who made their money profitable in all sorts of manners (who made it *energos,* as the Greeks called it) [53] a.o. by laying in a cargo mostly in association with others in order to sell it with profit somewhere else. They also who did nothing but lend money to *emporoi* considered their trade as a seatrade; they counted themselves among the *emporoi*, partly undoubtedly to participate in the advantages which the law conferred on them, a more rapid adjudication e.g. [54]

Properly speaking, this manner of trading belongs to money-trade. As it is however so closely connected with sea-trade and navigation, we shall discuss it here. The Greeks called it *nautikon daneion* [55]; in Roman jurisprudence it is translated by *foenus nauticum* [56]; this is akin to what is called bottomry in the Middle Ages and later on in our antiquated Commercial Code [57].

We may define bottomry as follows: when money was lent with the purpose of trading with it by sea, with, as a rule, a ship, a cargo or a freight as a security, on the understanding that this money, augmented by the interest or prime, agreed upon, should be paid back when the ship or the cargo reached its destination and that the risk of navigation through shipwreck, war or piracy was exclusively run by the moneylender [58].

On the one hand a private person, even though he named himself a merchant, could, by this form of loan, put out his money at interest

[52] Dem., XXXIV, 5; Stob., XXIX, 37.

[53] Isocr., VII, 35; Xen., Hiero XI, 4; Ditt., Syll.[3] 955; Dem., XXXVI, 5; XXXIV, 50. Cf. Bongenaar pp. 61 and 75. Dem., XXXVII, 6; XXXIII, 4; XXXVII, 53 and 54.

[54] Since the middle of the fourth century: Dem., VII, 12; XXXIII, 23. Boeckh, Die Staatshaushaltung p. 54.

[55] Cf. Daremberg-Saglio s.v. Foenus. Pauly-Wissowa-Kroll s.v. Eranos.

[56] Dig. XXII, 2; Cod. Just. IV, 33.

[57] Art. 569.

[58] Dem., XXXII, 14; XXXIII, 6; LVI, 3; XXXV, 10, 32, 52; XXXIV, 6.

with a fair chance of big profits (the prime varied between 20 and
30 %, this depended on the circumstance whether the money was
lent for a single or a return voyage) [59], on the other hand an *emporos*
who was always in need of cash, because bottomry was not sufficiently
developed, could procure himself the means for a business-trip. A
skipper might do the same to defray the expenses of the voyage: the
paying of wages to the sailors or, when they were slaves, as was
mostly the case, to supply them with food. If the ship or the cargo got
lost, the money-lender was the worse for his capital and interest; on
account of this great risk people were not allowed to invest capital of
orphans in this manner [60]. On the other hand the debtor is only
exempt from his obligations through losses suffered during the navigation itself, not for instance because he could not manage to sell his
wares advantageously. It is obvious that this stipulation often gave
rise to all sorts of frauds, as the scuttling of a ship in order to prevent
its return after having pocketed the profits and so to escape the obligation to pay. The money-lender often made an agent sail along with
the skipper in order to prevent fraud or sailed along himself [61]. This
measure, however, was not always effectual. Many unsavoury lawsuits,
resulting from a bottomry-agreement are known to us from pleas of
the 4th century [62].

The economical significance of Greek bottomry is multifarious. The
credit-system failing, money due to foreign business-friends could not
but be paid in cash; the amount of the sum to be despatched could
be forwarded in the shape of a loan on goods to be sent to the debtor's
dwelling-place. A merchant or private person (we have seen that a
line between the two can hardly be drawn) undertaking a voyage to
a distant town, might also make his money pay by investing it in the
form of a mortgage on the cargo or the ship with which he made the
voyage. The main point, however, is that it was the form of speculation
most in request for money-owners and that, furthermore, dealers,
emporoi as well as skippers, were enabled to do business without
possessing much working capital themselves.

For these traders the *nautikon daneion* is still of an other nature.
It is a form of insurance and will often have been concluded to this

[59] Dem., XXXV, 10; XXXIV, 23; L, 17 sqq.; Xen., Vect. III, 9; Athen., VII,
292 b.
[60] Lysias, fr. 265 (Sauppe). Cf. Lysias, XXXII, 25.
[61] Dem., LII, 20.
[62] Dem., XXXIV, 8 and 26.

intent; especially the money-loan under lien of the fare strongly bears this character. This insurance, however, is widely different from ours; for at present the sea-assuror answers for the risks of the voyage but he defrays only the damage done and does not pay before the catastrophe has taken place, while on the other hand with bottomry the money is advanced under the special obligation to give it back fully increased with a prime when no naval disaster takes place [63]. An element of insurance, though, is to be found in the fact that some one takes the risk of guarding objects of somebody else against a certain compensation. The other element of insurance, the distribution of a possible financial loss among different persons was found in the probably mutual pledging, as we have noticed in the leases in agriculture [64]. Below [65] we shall discuss the difference between the *nautikon daneion* and the mediaeval *commenda,* the precursor of our limited partnership.

Through the existence of an institution like the *nautikon daneion* the question is raised whether the Greeks knew the association of persons and the clubbing together in order to exercise a joint trade [66]; the answer to this question suggests a means to determine the degree of development of economical life.

At the beginning of this book [67], when treating the oldest property-relations in Greece we pointed out that there are perhaps some traces of family-possession to be found. Though we cannot be positive about it, we may be sure that in historical times, very often exactly in the centuries described, the inheritance, either only the immovables or the whole, remained undivided at the death of the father; the brothers administered it together and divided the proceeds. As a rule they remained together, that is to say they did not start a household of their own [68]. The explanation of this often recurring phenomenon is probably in most cases to be found in the fact that the capital left behind was too small when divided, to procure a living to each of the sons and their families. This involved that no partition took place and consequently that a marriage and the setting-up of a home were put off. From manumission-contracts it is evident that joint property,

---

[63] Dem., XXXIV, 28.

[64] P. 32.

[65] P. 120.

[66] Cf. P. J. T. Endenburg, Koinoonia en gemeenschap van zaken bij de Grieken in den klassieken tijd. Thesis Utrecht 1937.

[67] Pp. 12 sqq.

[68] Lys., XXXII, 4; XVIII, 21; Dem., XXXVI, 8 sqq.; XLIV, 9 sqq. and 18 sqq.

also of movables as slaves e.g., existed [69]; the proprietors were then mostly closely related to each other.

It is highly probable that other forms of joint property proceeded from this undivided property among brothers. At any rate it is remarkable that those who traded on joint account were often brothers [70]. When inquiring into the forms in which this community of interest occurred, we meet at once with a phenomenon very likely to give us a poor opinion of its development.

The Dutch Civil Code [71] in accordance with legislation in all modern civilized countries, knows two sorts of companies, the *private partnership* or *company* and the *legal personality*. A *partnership* exists when two or more persons have goods in common with a view to divide the profits made from them. A legal personality is an association which may be concluded to any purpose, not contrary to law or morals, as a rule not for the furtherance of the material interest of the members, but for the benefit of some religious, charitable or social association.

Neither Greek law nor Greek language knew this distinction. On the one hand the law did not distinguish state organisations (as *phylè, phratria, dèmos,* parts of the people or their domain) from civil land organisations. On the other hand they made no difference between those concluded to make profits together and the others kept together by a common cult or the wish of feasting together, all these organizations are included without distinction in the more general word *koinōnia,* communion, association, partnership [72]; in common parlance no difference was ever made between an association and a partnership. Hence that the works about Greek corporate life [73] leave a confused and little satisfactory impression: this would also be the case if one was to compile in one book the things which polder-corporations, religious communities, footballclubs, chambers of commerce, associations of ex-warriors and limited companies have in common. It is also remarkable that Aristotle [74] classed his theoretical views on *koinōnia* in his treatise about the *philia* (to be rendered imperfectly by friendship); *koinōnoi,* the members of a *koinōnia,* were on a more or less

---

[69] Calderini, La manomissione pp. 180 sqq.

[70] Dem. XXXIV; XXXV.

[71] Artt. 1655 and 1690.

[72] Endenburg passim.

[73] E. Ziebarth, Beiträge zur Geschichte des Seeraubs und Seehandels im alten Griechenland. Hamburg 1929; Id., Das gr. Vereinswesen. Leipzig 1896; F. Poland, Gesch. des gr. Vereinswesen. Leipzig 1909.

[74] Aristot., Eth. Nic. VIII, 1159 b, 25 sqq.

"friendly footing" according to their being brothers, comrades or merely *koinōnoi*.

When investigating in what domain of commercial life a communion in trade occurred, we see that it seldom happened in agriculture, except in the form of undivided *property*. While it was usual in Babylon e.g. for two or more persons to rent a plot of land together (a great many contracts with a sometimes rather complicated juridical construction have been preserved) [75], from the Greek world only one example is certainly known to us from an Attic inscription of the 4th century [76], in which, moreover, the two tenants are father and son. It is possible that here the usual form of mutual security rendered the common lease superfluous.

In industry we scarcely meet with an association of persons and capital for one trade [77]; the examples on record about the reclaiming of plots of mining-ground and the manufacture of the ore [78] would teach us little about the nature of the association, if they were not elucidated by examples in other trades. This also holds good with regard to the few cases from which the existence of partnerships in business is apparent, from the rent of taxes customary everywhere in Greece [79].

It probably occurred most in trade, at least examples there are best known to us. The items which we know of its pecularities and the circumstances under which it took place allow us to define its character and to ascertain from what needs it arose.

We must try to realize, when judging the cases handed down to us, the haziness of the terms used in Greek and beware of modern translations, as partner e.g., capable of rousing wholly wrong conceptions. We have already pointed out that a separate term did not arise for an association of persons intending to undertake a business together and to divide the profits; the general word *koinōnia* was not even used in this restricted sense. The word *koinōnos*, occurring very often

---

[75] F. X. Steinmetzer, Über den Grundbesitz in Babylonien zur Kassitenzeit nach den sogenannten Grenzsteinen dargestellt. Leipzig 1909 (Der alte Orient XIX, 1-2); W. Schwenzner, Das geschäftliche Leben im alten Babylonien nach den Verträgen und Briefen dargestellt. Leipzig 1916 (Der alte Orient XVI, 1); W. Eilers, Gesellschaftsformen im Altbabylonischen Recht. Leipzig 1931.

[76] Ditt., Syll.[3] 966.

[77] Dem., XXXVI, 13, 37 and 43.

[78] Xen., Vect. IV, 32; Dem., XXXVII and XLII; Hyperid., III, 32; C.I.A. II, 781 and 782. Endenburg pp. 187 sqq.

[79] Andoc., I, 133 sqq.; Lycurg., c. Leocr. 19, cf. 58; Plut., Alcib. V. Endenburg pp. 193 sqq.

though proportionally little in the sphere of business-life, indicates generally the comrade with whom one shares the sweets and bitters of life, with whom one works on joint account ("collaborator" or in a disapproving sense "accomplice") [80] or with whom one has a property in common, and also the man with whom one does business [81]. It never has a distinct juridical significance and every translation evoking this thought is inexact.

The following case drawn from one of Demosthenes' speeches [82] may give an impression of the nature of a trade-communion and the use of the term *koinōnos*: it is one of the many examples [83] handed down to us.

In the harbour of Athens lies a vessel from Marseilles, a certain Hegesistratus is at the same time skipper and proprietor. The ship is chartered by an outlander Protus dwelling in Athens who intends sailing with it to Syracuse in order to buy a cargo of corn and to sell it in Athens. He undertakes this business together with somebody else, Phertatus, who is called his *koinōnos* [84]. They do not buy the grain with their own money, they borrow it in the usual way through *nautikon daneion* of another person, Demon; but the latter does not furnish it from his own means, but associates himself with others too, unnamed persons who are again called *koinōnoi* [85]. But even now everything is not settled; Hegesistratus the skipper raises money apparently for the wages or the food of the crew, with his ship as a security. It does not appear from whom he borrows it; what we do see is that the money is again lent by more than one person. The ship sets sail enabled thereto by the money provided in this way; besides the captain and the merchant Protus there is still an agent of the money-lenders on board who has to guard their interests; as a matter of fact he frustrates, just in time, an attempt to scuttle the vessel on the homeward journey. Going ashore in Syracuse Protus buys the corn, which he intended buying, and under the pretext that the cargo belongs

---

[80] Aristot., Pol. 1252 b 31 (marriage); Eur., Herc. fur. 583; El. 600; Menander, Disceptantes 536; Antiphanes, Gemini 1 sqq. (K. II, p. 43, fr. 80: parasite); Plato, Ep. VIII, 333 b; Polit. 1260 a 40 (slave partner of the master); Xen., Inst. Cyr. VII, 5, 71; Soph., Trach. 730; Eur., Med. 1361; Ion 771; Aesch., Suppl. 339; Plato, Leg. VI, 783 e; Aristot., Top. 161 a 37; Plato, Rep. I, 333 a; Leg. XII, 969 c; Lach. 179 e.

[81] Dem., LVI, 1; Xen., Oec. VII, 13; Isocr. XII, 184.

[82] Dem., XXXII.

[83] Dem., XXXIV, XXXV, IL, LII, LVI; Lys., XII.

[84] Dem., XXXII, 17.

[85] Dem., XXXII, 21.

to him, Hegesistratus succeeds in raising money here again, with the
cargo as a pledge; now not only in his own name, but together with
a compatriot and accomplice on board, Zenothemis, who is therefore
again called his *koinōnos* and collaborator [86].

This case proves how often people clubbed together in order to
undertake a business but especially that only small sums of money and
most modest affairs were at stake. The money-owners did not form a
partnership because big enterprises which they wanted to start could
not be executed without it, nor from the need of large working-
capitals. But on the one hand, because this manner of investment was
the most speculative which offered a chance of a proportionally high
interest, and on the other because sea-trade was coupled with exceedingly high risks, so all the persons involved had to divide the ill
chances as much as possible. It is therefore not astonishing that a form
of working came into vogue, meeting these demands: they made use of
participation, the means frequently applied in the Middle-Ages. Any-
how it is apparent from a stipulation which the donor of a foundation
inserted among his conditions, that the money available had to be
invested in sums of 30 drachms [87], how very uncertain every investment was and how strongly the need was consequently felt to divide
the risks.

All this clubbing together in order to form a working-capital throws
once more a clear light upon the fact that the Greeks lived in a world
where retail trade predominated. What is testified of mediaeval trade
may also be applied to Greece in the 5th and 4th centuries B.C.: it
is characterized by retail trade and participation. The possession of
more than one ship in one hand was exceptional [88]; it will have
occurred more often that a trading-vessel had more than one proprietor, among whom the skipper figured as a rule, probably with other
members of the crew. It is true that the crew often consisted of
slaves [89], but as we have noticed before, they also often participated
in trade independently: a slave-captain is known to have lent money
to a merchant sailing on his boat [89a]. "Every sailor, from the captain
to the last cabin-boy, possessed a share in the ship and the profits;
furthermore the crew was composed of relations [90]. These patriarchal,

[86] Dem., XXXII, 7.
[87] Ditt. Syll.[3] 577.
[88] Dem., XXXII: Hegesistratus is owner and shipper.
[89] Dem., XXXV, 33: Hyblesius and Apollonides with ten slaves.
[89a] P. 88, 103.
[90] A. Struck, Zur Landeskunde von Griechenland (Angewandte Geographie IV,

mediaeval norms are still nowadays in use for the greater part of the sailing-boats." Navigation in the Greek waters in the 19th century is described to us in this way, in classical times it will not have been very different.

The same motive, the endeavour to divide the risks, prevailed also in the cases of participation known to us in other trades. As a matter of fact the proceeds of the rent of the, as a rule, indirect taxes were uncertain, the profits of a piece of newly-worked mining-ground were as precarious. Xenophon [91] declares with regard to this work; "that private persons may risk the working more safely by joining and by participating the risks": this holds also good for the other enterprises, in which it was usual to act in common. The large amount of money due for the rent of taxes yielding great profits as the harbour-dues in Athens may at most also have been a motive for participation.

When finally inquiring into the forms of judicature which the community of trade assumed, it is first of all apparent that the principle of the limited company, (where each of the partners is not liable to pay in more than the amount for which he participated, so that the creditor can never reclaim more than the deposited capital), remained foreign to the Greek world. It could not exist in a society with a preponderant retail trade and small needs of capital, because it proceeds from the endeavours to form great enterprises requiring an important capital. This fact is the more significant because every form of enterprise which kept business and private capital apart failed in Greece and with it an efficient means of assuring the durability of any trade because its existence becomes thereby independent of the fate of private fortunes. And these were exactly very precarious in the Greek world. The number of citizens capable of keeping their capital throughout life seems to have been not large [92]. Many a citizen experienced that the safety of his property was but small, partly owing to the insecurity of the traffic by sea [93], partly as a result of the fierce struggles in the state and the wars [94], both circumstances of a chiefly

Serie 4, Heft 1912, p. 156; cf. G. von Below, Probleme der Wirtschaftsgeschichte. 1920, p. 387.

[91] Xen., Vect. IV, 32.

[92] Xen., An. I, 1, 9 and 10; Dem., XLII, 3; XXXIII, 10; Hyperid., III, 32 sqq.

[93] P. 11.

[94] R. von Pöhlmann - F. Oertel, Geschichte der sozialen Frage I³, pp. 340 sqq. and 188.

political nature. These facts also are to be considered as very important impediments for the development of large enterprises, which needs must have the possibility of continuity.

It is remarkable that in the Greek world no trace is to be found of the precursor of the modern sleeping partnership, the mediaeval *commenda* [95] which was a regular form of trade in the old and the new Babylonian empire [96]. A *commenda* is a business run either by the man who procured (*commendat*) goods, money or the ship, or by the one who carries on a business oversea with the money supplied. The difference with the Greek *nautikon daneion* is that the *commenda* divides profits and losses in a fixed proportion; here, on the contrary, the money-lender receives a fixed amount as interest of the invested capital. It has been supposed that the word *aphormè* indicated the capital furnished by a sleeping-partner on behalf of common trade and with a view to distribute the profits. This supposition probably owed its origin to statements of ancient lexicographers [97] who described it a.o. as *enthèkè,* of which the mediaeval word *hentica* or *entica* is derived and which was used for a *commenda-share*. In reality *aphormè* has never meant more than small working-capital [98]; in the few cases handed down to us in which it was supplied by a money-lender, the latter received a fixed interest for it [99]: so there is no question of limited company conditions. No more could these conditions be proved between the moneytraders and their lenders nor between those who rented taxes and their moneylenders or guarantees. It is said of a man under whose name a piece of miningground was registered that the most wealthy persons in the state participated with him [100], but here it is neither clear in what relation they stood to the real exploiter.

The other form of partnership which economic life produced later on, for instance in the Middle Ages, the firm, did not occur either. If we forego the common name it is characterized by the definition that the partners are held responsible *per capita* towards others; the creditor of the firm may claim the whole amount of the debt from each of the partners who are responsible with their whole private fortune. Now the principle of the responsibility *per capita* was not unknown

---

[95] W. Silberschmidt, Die Commenda. Würtzburg 1884. III, 12 b.

[96] Cf. p. 116, 75.

[97] Suidas s.v.; Hesych. s.v.

[98] Xen., Comm. III, 7, 11-12; Isocr. VII, 32; XIX, 12; Lycurg., C. Leocr. V, 6; Aristot., Pol. VI, 5, 1320 a 39.

[99] Lys., Fr. 12.

[100] Hyperid., III, 35.

in Greece; neither the active responsibility where each of the creditors has the right to demand the acquittance of the whole debt, nor the passive one where each of the debtors can be dunned for the payment of the whole. One example of the former reponsibility has been handed down to us [101] and of the latter even more than one [102]. But the responsibility *per capita* never became the standing characteristic of a certain form of business communion, and firms and partners are therefore out of the question. The less so because the principal, real characteristic of this form of partnership, the long-standing relation between the partners was not to be found in Greece, a thing signifi-cant for the judgment of the economical standard.

So the result of this investigation is as follows: any form of partner-ship creating a durable, legally recognized or regular relation between men who did business on joint account did not develop in Greece [103]. The numerous cases in which two or more persons combined to form an enterprise concern that form of business corporation which in the Dutch Code of Mercantile Law is termed a "transaction on joint account" [104] that is to say proceedings concerning one single or more special transactions which do not require a written deed or other formalities and which lay no legal claim on other persons except on those of the partners with whom those other persons have dealt. Nowhere in the cases known to us the partnership as such is sued, but always one of the partners. The *dikai koinōnikai* which Aristotle[105] mentions once are no law-suits in which one of the parties is a *koinō-nia,* but they concern differences between the *koinōnoi,* partners, mu-tually. No trace is to be found of a notification or an annotation of partnerships concluded, as was usual for instance in Lübeck in the

[101] Dem., XXXV, 12. Cf. Dutch Civil Code art. 1314.

[102] Dem., LVI, 45; Ditt. Syll.[3] 955 (= Dareste, Haussoullier, Reinach, Inscrip-tions juridiques grecques I, p. 313, XIV A.).

[103] Endenburg pp. 161-162.

[104] Cf. P. H. Smits, Een critische beschouwing der handeling voor gemeene reke-ning. Bijdrage tot de studie der stille of zgn. „burgerlijke" maatschap (A Critical Dissertation of the Transaction for Joint Account. Contribution to the Study of the Silent or so-called "Non-trading" Partnership). Thesis Amsterdam 1924.

From the 1st of January 1935 Dutch Law does not know the transaction for joint account any more. The entire division art. 57 and 58 was cancelled, because, as it is said in the explanatory memorandum, there was nothing in the regulations of the art. 57 and 58, and what they ordained about the transaction for joint account is already implied in the regulations that the Civil Code gives for the partnership. Indeed the transaction for joint account was, as a rule, held to be company. M. Polak, Handboek voor het Nederlandsche handels- en faillissementsrecht I, 1935, p. 247.

[105] Ath. Pol. LII, 2.

beginning of the 14th century, as appears from the preserved register of the *societates* [106]. To the Greek state partnerships do not exist.

These simple forms of trade which were considerably more simple than in the late Middle Ages e.g. prove, that business itself was also done on a rather small scale, though it was carried on in extensive regions and brought large, but short lived capitals into being in special cases.

As opposed to the relatively great significance which sea-trade held in the Greek world, trade and traffic by land in general fall into the background [107]. We have already mentioned [108] the circumstances which were the cause that few roads fit for traffic were to be found in Greece. Whenever a monument of importance was to be built, one of the necessary preparations was the outlay of a road along which the materials could be transported. It is evident that the transport cost of heavy material must have been high. The transport of precious articles of no bulk was merely remunerative for the traffic by land and in a lesser degree also for sea-trade; loaded with these wares the merchants will have repaired to the fairs which were sometimes kept near the sanctuaries in the interior. Trade by land, at any rate, has practically been of no importance for economical life.

Needless to say that with growing trade, especially when it took place by sea, the Greeks felt the want of a steady means of exchange. Since the reliance on metal-money was enhanced by the stamp which the State impressed on it and made it in this way into coin [109], it was issued in all those parts of Greece which received and despatched goods from across their frontiers.

By no means everywhere in the same degree. In the interior, the extensive regions which took none or hardly any part in the trade by sea the ordinary bartering in kind will have continued [110]. In these districts the disappearance of money which accompanied the collapse of ancient society will hardly have brought any change in the mode of life of the inhabitants. But in the commercial towns the coins were considered not merely as a means of payment but also as an article

---

[106] J. Kohler, Niederländisches Handelsrecht in der Blütezeit der Freistaaten I.

[107] Unsafety of the country-roads: Her., VIII, 125 and 126; VI, 16. Cf. Aesch., Choeph. 1001 and Xen., Comm. II, 1, 15; [Xen.], Rep. Ath. II, 5.

[108] P. 10.

[109] This happened first on the coast of Asia Minor and its interior (Her., I, 94; Poll., IX, 83).

[110] Dem., LII, 3, 5 and 10; C.I.G. II, 2059; Strabo, XI, 502, 506 and 493; Poll., VII, 14.

on sale, undoubtedly too because a great variety was in currency on account of the multitude of little states existing. In his book "Ways and Means" quoted above Xenophon [111] enumerates among Athens' avantages the fact that her silver coins are of excellent quality; in this manner the foreign merchants, touching Athens' port and not wanting to ship goods for the return voyage, can as safely export money "which is a good load, for wherever they sell it they get back more than they paid for it." One of the most usual words for money, *chrèmata,* objects for daily use, has always kept its original meaning [112]; in some passages [113] we cannot make out whether money or goods are meant. And the circumstance that objects of art or precious metal as cups, dishes and such like were considered and treated at the same time as coinage, indicates that money was never counted exclusively as a medium of exchange in the same degree as nowadays.

In order to ascertain the standard of development of economical life it is indispensable to investigate the extents and forms of money-trade. Especially two closely related questions must be answered here: Was the credit system known besides the paying in cash in a degree worth mentioning? Did money trade develop into a separate and important profession? In the land inhabited by the Greeks a great many free, little, isolated states existed and their independence found expression in the right of which they mostly availed themselves, to issue a coinage of their own. In the inter-state trade the numerous coins had to be exchanged continually. It is evident that at least in the coastal towns this occupation, requiring a certain technical knowledge of the prevalent coins, became a profession, though it was seldom exercised alone as such, the profession of the moneychanger who earned his living by making some agio [114]. Their intervention and their knowledge were the more required because in times of need a good deal of states had recourse to a primitive means of increasing their circulating medium viz. the debasement of their coinage by a larger addition of cheaper materials by which the worth of the metal [115] (and as we have seen the metal coins were much more

---

[111] Xen., Vect. III, 2. Cf. V, 3. [Aristot.], Oec. 1346 b 25; Isocr., XVII, 40.

[112] Hom., Od. XIV, 92; XVI, 315; XIX, 284; Hes., Erg. 407; Solon, Fr. 2, 6; 3, 3; 12, 7; 14, 4; 22, 8; Pind., Isth. II, 11; Soph., Oed. Rex 542; Ditt., Syll.³ 92.

[113] Theognis, 276, 346; Democr., Fr. 40, 78, 219, 222, 279, 282, 286.

[114] Trade with foreign money no doubt constituted the most important part of the business of the trapezitai: Dem., XXXVI, 11; L, 30; XIX, 114; Isocr., XVII, 40; Poll., III, 84; VII, 170.

[115] Xen., Vect. III, 2. Cf. Thiel, Xenophontis Poroi. Aristoph., Ran. 720 sqq.;

treated as goods than nowadays) was no longer at par with its face-value. When considering moreover that metal money was the only money in use and that money-debasement could only achieve the desired result in inland trade in so far as the State could only force her own citizens to accept debased coins, we must conclude that the inter-state traffic cannot have been very brisk.

The above mentioned circumstance that it was necessary to arm oneself against the receipt of debased coinage was also the reason that people preferred to be paid in the presence of an expert. But the activity of those versed in money-matters did not confine itself to the function of checking (after the table, *trapeza,* on which they counted the money they were called *trapezitai* [116]). The airily built houses facilitated house-breaking [117], they offered but scanty safety to the money and valuables which hardly differed from money, when they consisted of precious metal, especially when the inhabitant could not guard and defend them himself. So it was inevitable that particularly the *emporoi,* whose business entailed long absences from home during the trading season, felt the necessity to confide their valuable posses-sione to the care of a reliable man. Demosthenes mentions some-where [118] a merchant who, before embarking, entrusted his business friend Phormion, a servant of the *trapezitès* Pasion with the safe-keeping of two chiselled dishes and other valuable objects. We read of the same Pasion that another travelling merchant, living in Heraclea, when going on a business-journey gave him his valuables on deposit, before his departure from Athens [119]. The fact that the *trapezitès* safeguarded valuables could not but induce the merchants to achieve their payments in his presence. The ordinary citizen, on the contrary, often stored his money in his house or hid it in the ground [120].

Now in what way did these payments at the *trapezitès* take place? Usually in the presence of the interested parties; the man who had to pay money as well as the one who was going to receive it, set out for the house of the *trapezitès* or for his table in the market, where the money due was paid down in cash. This was at least the rule. It

---

[Aristot.], Oec. II, passim; Dem., XXIV, 214; Plato, Leg. 742 a; Ditt. Syl³. 218; Polyb., XXII, 15. J. Hasebroek, Griechische Wirtschafts- und Gesellschaftsgeschichte pp. 284 sqq.

[116] Poll., III, 84 s.v. trapezitès. Cf. VIII, 170; Dem., XIX, 114; L, 30.
[117] Cf. p. 45.
[118] Cf. Hasebroek, Staat u. Handel, p. 90 and Michell, p. 341.
[119] Dem., LII.
[120] J. Hasebroek, Hermes 1920, pp. 143 sqq.; Thiel, Xen. Por., Excursus IX.

sometimes happened, however, too that the man to whom the money had been entrusted, paid in the absence of the depositor. The manner in which this happened is clearly described in one of Demosthenes' pleas: [121] "When a man deposits money with the instruction to pay it to a third party, all *trapezitai* are wont to write down the name of the depositor and the amount of money. Thereupon they write beside it: to be paid to such and such a person. And when the man to whom they must cash up, is personally known to them they merely note down to whom the money must be paid; but when they do not know him, they also write down the name of the man who is to introduce and legitimate him before he shall take delivery of the money." Here too only payment in cash is mentioned. No example has been handed down to us of a form of money-trade where the parties in question both deposited money at the same *trapezitès'* so that a settlement of the accounts could take place merely by a transfer in the books [122]. But even if such isolated cases were known they could not but be incidental and could certainly not be regarded as an example of a clearing because all conditions for it were lacking in Greek society.

We must bear this also in mind in the following case studied more than once especially by jurists, who have sometimes deduced the existence of the bill of exchange from it. It is drawn from one of Isocrates' pleas [123]. The speaker dwelling in Athens, originates from the Pontus-region; his father is still living there. "Seeing that Stratocles was about to sail for the Pontus and as I wanted to have a considerable sum of money to be transferred hence, I begged him to leave some of his money there on my behalf, and to take delivery from my father instead who owed money to me. I considered it namely as a great advantage that there was no need to expose my money to the risk involved in a voyage, especially so because the Lacedaemonians ruled the sea in those days. When Stratocles inquired who was going to restore the money in case my father was to refuse to carry my order into effect and I should not be there on his return, I introduced him personally to Pasion and the latter pledged himself to pay in that case the capital as well as the interest." Needless to put the question whether the letter which the speaker gave to Stratocles must be considered juridically as a bill of exchange or as a letter of credit, as happens nowadays. The existence of neither is proved by it, the only

[121] Dem., LII, 4.
[122] Cf. e.g. Dem., XXXXVII, 51, 66, 77. Bongenaar p. 43.
[123] Isocr., XVII, 35.

thing apparent is that somebody wants to profit from the very special and incidental circumstances to obviate the risk involved by the transporting of money, that another man is going to sail for Pontus and that the former has a father living there who owes him money. The hesitation of the merchant, who was only to be moved to act in this way by the pledge of a *trapezitès* and the fact that the letter is addressed to a father proves that we have here to deal with a very exceptional case, so that neither bills of exchange nor credit-letters were known.

We should have come to the same conclusion even without direct data, as well on account of our knowledge about the nature and the extent of traffic in general as of the political situation in those times. We have seen above [124] that the merchant himself, laying aside a single exception, transported his goods by sea and tried to find a market for them. A result of it was that all his payments were made in cash; delivery on credit was unknown and therefore all credit-letters superfluous. Furthermore traffic between distant places, hampered as it was by the unsafe condition at sea, caused by piracy and war [125], could not operate on credit also on account of the great number of independent little states since the guarantee of a somewhat reliable inter-state jurisdiction was lacking. Besides at any moment an outbreak of war or a "revolution" could give rise to a new distribution of land and to cancellation of mortgage-debts [126]; so this very relative value of private property could make all claims worthless. Therefore all guarantees were lacking for a more or less significant credit trade. All money-trade was carried on in cash; the amounts to be transferred across the frontiers had to be transported in cash by a person on board a ship together with other goods, even with the quick communications existing between Athens and the Pontus. Hence the fact that the coins in the inter-state trade partly kept the character of goods and were indicated with the same word [127]. And even this international ready money cannot possibly have encompassed a large domain by the irregular navigation and the little safety by sea.

The older form of credit-paper: a written promise to pay or an I.O.U. to order by which a person pledges himself to pay the sum mentioned in it also to order of the payee, this form of negotiable

---

[124] Pp. 106 sqq.

[125] Cf. E. Ziebarth, Beiträge zur Geschichte des Seeraubes und Seehandels im alten Griechenland. 1929.

[126] Bolkestein, Wohltätigkeit pp. 69 and 131.

[127] Cf. p. 123.

paper which existed in Babylonia in the days shortly after Hammu-
rabi [128] was still lacking in the 4th century. Only in later contracts
the clause occurs that the debt must be paid to the money-lender or
to the man who claims it in his name [129]. They never went so far as
to use paper, payable to bearer, promissory notes without a name,
going from hand to hand like coins.

We have seen that the *trapezitès,* the money-merchant, besides
assaying and exchanging coins, made payments for absent merchants
who entrusted him also with the safe-keeping of their valuables [130].
But herewith the *trapezitès* is not yet at the ends of his occupations.
He steps in as a mediator between money-lender and money-taker, that
is to say he borrows money for interest from a third person to lend
it out again against a higher interest [131]. In this respect he occupies
the place of our bankers and by this name he is often mentioned: we
speak of banking with the Greeks.

Above we have avoided this term on purpose because it is apt to
rouse images about the nature and the extent of money-trade which
do not come up to reality; particularly credit trade, meant here not
in the sense of selling on credit but of lending against interest, was
of such a modest nature that it excluded banking of any importance.
But before considering this closer we must first look at some other
circumstances which illustrate the character of the Greek "bankers".

The *trapezitès* does not only trade in money; but he is a pawnbroker
as well. This is not astonishing when we think of the little difference
made between money and valuables. We read of a person in need of
money who pawns a few heirlooms, cups and a gold wreath; another
pawns copper at the shop of nobody less than Pasion, the most famous
of all the *trapezitai* in the 4th century [132]. Now a pawnbroker may
perhaps be called a banker because he owns a bank, but this is really
too far-fetched.

It may have happened in Greece that the pawner was not able to
redeem his pawn, then it came into the possession of the *trapezitès.*
His business must have resembled a second-hand shop. But he did

[128] Cf. p. 97, 1. W. F. Leemans, The Old-Babylonian Merchant, His Business and
his Social Position (Studia et Documenta ad Iura Orientis pertinentia. Vol. III).
Leiden 1950.
[129] C. I. G. 1371.
[130] Cf. p. 124.
[131] Dem., LIII, 9; XXXVI, 11; Isocr., XVII, 7 and 38; Stob., XCVII, 31.
[132] Dem., LIII, 9; XLIX, 21; XXVII, 24; Athen., XI, 478 c; XIII, 585 a; Lys.,
VIII, 10.

not only sell these pawns; he also let them out on hire. It sometimes happens that a person who must receive a visitor of note borrows, besides money, carpets, furniture-covers and silverware again from the same Pasion [133]. Lysias [134] mentions an identical case.

We have seen that retail and wholesale-trade existed; also that there was not very much difference between the two and that consequently a status of merchants who made a profession exclusively of whole-sale trade did not exist. The same may be said concerning the money traders; some of them operated with considerable sums of money, but nobody restricted himself to these loans only. Truth to tell, the wealthiest among them in the 4th century, the aforesaid Pasion, who possessed about 40 talents [135], carried on such small business that he often is no more than a second-hand dealer. This is to be found everywhere in Antiquity. It enables us to see the extent of money-trade in its right proportions. We possess contracts of the well-known Babylonian banker Egibi [136] from the 6th century B.C. treating of two pairs of shoes or the working-up of sacrificial offal and in the late Roman era the *argentarii* accept also objects of precious metal as pawns [137].

The fact that the *trapezitès* does not occupy himself exclusively with money-trade corresponds with our remarks about the trades of merchant and workshop-master who were neither entirely such. Only half of Pasion's fortune was sunk in his money-trade; a little less was invested in land and finally a workshop of shields of which he may have become the owner incidentally appears on the inventory of his personal estate. It goes without saying that he does not carry on this workshop himself; he lets it out; to him it is a sort of investment [138]. We are not amazed, considering the close relation existing between money-traders and merchants, that many were both at the same time or alternately; we see that Phormion, Pasion's freedman and later on his successor to his money-trade, is named as an owner

---

[133] Dem., XXVIII, 18. The use of the object given in pawn was often substituted for the receipt of interest. Pactum antichreticum.

[134] Lys., VIII, 10.

[135] Dem., XXX, 10; XXXVI, 5; Lys., XIX, 40; XXIX, 2.

[136] S. Weingört, Das Haus Egibi. Cf. A. Ungnad, Das Haus Egibi. Archiv für Orientforschung XV, p. 57 and Dubberstein in Journal of Near Eastern Studies IV, 64. On the comparable "banking"-house Marashu cf. C. Cardascia, Marashu; W. F. Leemans, The Old-Babylonian Merchant, His Business and his Social Position. Leiden 1950.

[137] Cf. F. Lot, La fin du monde antique et le début du Moyen Âge. Paris 1927, pp. 89-90.

[138] Dem., XXXVI, 4. At the time when Phormio was still a commissioner of

of ships which are retained at Byzantium [138]; so he also took part in the corn-trade in the Pontus-region. It is remarkable that in one of the few cases where more than one vessel is mentioned in the possession of one man this man is not a merchant, *emporos,* or a ship-owner, *nauklèros.*

If we wish to gain a fair idea of the place which the *trapezitès* occupied in money-trade, we must not forget that in most of the relatively numerous examples of bottomry [139] known to us the money-lenders are no *trapezitai,* professional money-traders, but private men who often call themselves *emporoi* and are considered as such. They can lend money more or less regularly (this is called *daneizein,* to lend, or *tokizein,* to put out at interest, or *ergazesthai chrèmasi,* to trade with money) without being *trapezitès.* The principal difference between him and the private money-lender is that the latter invests his own money, be it often in combination with other private persons while the former lends out the money entrusted to him for this very purpose. In treating the question of the extent of the credit-system viz. the lending of money at interest, one of the most important ones for our knowledge of economical life and the standard of its development, it really hardly matters whether it originates with professional money-traders or occasional money-lenders.

Naturally there are but few direct data which can enlighten us on this subject. But the fact may help us that of several fortunes of which the total is known the ready money constitutes a disproportionally large part of the capital. At the death of Demosthenes' father 82,600 drachms were left of which 8,000 drachms, so about a tenth of the whole capital, was "situated at home" as the term went (the opposite is "the money given out of doors") [140]. It is certainly not less remarkable that not less than 10,000 drachms were tied up in cups, gold ware, garments and trinkets, a striking illustration of Xenophon's statement [141] that in prosperous times the women are keen on precious clothes and gold finery. An Athenian not known by name had 32,840 of the 92,840 drachms at home, so amply a third. Nicias is said to have had the greater part of his considerable fortune in cash [142] and of

Pasion's he apparently also was koinōnos of the merchant Timosthenes; as a trape-zitès Phormio also possesses ships of his own (Dem., XLV, 64). Cf. Michell, p. 336.

[139] The lending of money to a merchant or skipper with the cargo, ship or freight as a security: H. Knorringa, Emporos pp. 92 sqq.

[140] Cf. pp. 61 sqq.

[141] Xen., Vect. IV, 8.

[142] Cf. p. 64.

others we also know that they had much ready money at home, without our being able to fix its proportion to their entire fortune [143].

When furthermore taking into consideration that the greater part of the Greeks' fortunes were invested in landed property and had therefore to be left out of account when trying to ascertain the extent of credit, these ciphers do not make it probable that the monetary capital was rigorously put out at interest. We may draw this conclusion the more as the quoted ciphers only teach us something about the investment of fortunes considered large in Athens; it is likely that the fortunes of the large majority of the moderate or small owners bore still less interest.

This conclusion is strongly upheld by the well-known fact that throughout Antiquity the storing of coins or valuable objects was normal with bigger and smaller owners: there is no time when no examples are recorded of this hoarding, *katoruttein,* of a treasure, *thèsauros* [144]; "no fortress and no money are so difficult to be guarded as a woman" says one of Euripides' figures [145]. When Xenophon [146] expounds his plan of an exploitation on a large scale of the Attic silver-mines, he defends it o.a. by the remark that, in contrast with all other goods, silver is the only thing of which one never has enough, for "when men possess a great deal of it, they bury the part which they do not want and in this way they derive as much pleasure from it as if it was being used." The type of the miser so satisfactory for the stage whose passion is the secret pleasure of the hoarded treasure [147] is merely a product of this pre- or early capitalistic world in which the putting out of money at interest is still far from general and the scrupulous possessors eschew the risk of giving money out of doors.

From the 4th century a fragment of a treatise of the sophist Antiphon [148] has been preserved which informs us splendidly of the practice, and the conception about money-lending; therefore it deserves to be quoted in part. "There is a story telling us that a man saw somebody dig up a considerable sum of money. He asked him to lend part of it at interest, but the other refused, for he was suspicious by

[143] Cf. p. 64.

[144] Dem., XXVII, 57; XXVIII, 2; Andoc., I, 118. Bongenaar p. 257; Knorringa pp. 17 sqq.

[145] Eur., Fr. 320 (Nauck²).

[146] Xen., Vect. IV, 6.

[147] Aristoph., Ran. 363; Plaut., Aulularia.

[148] Fr. 57 (Diels).

nature and not inclined to help others; so he did it again somewhere
else. An other person who had heard of this, took the treasure away
and when the owner of the hidden money came back later on he did
not find it any more. Deeply afflicted by this loss which was the more
regrettable because he might have lent it to one who was in need of it,
which would have been safer and moreover would have yielded profit,
he disclosed his troubles to the man who had been willing to borrow
from him; he now acknowledged his mistake, and deeply regretted
that he had not acted in good will towards him for now he had lost
his money." Whereupon the disappointed man advised him to imagine
that the money was still hidden: it did not matter after all to a man
who did not use it whether it existed in reality and to the person who
does not use his brains, money is worthless.

From this anecdote we learn two things: on the one hand that the
storing of money was carried into practice, a fact which we knew; and
on the other that this behaviour was considered unwise by others. But
it is more significant that the lending of money is considered here as
a service and the refusal as hardheartedness. How much this conception tallies with reality is apparent from a number of pleas, treating
affairs about money-lending where a loan is considered as an act of
friendliness, *charis, philia,* and is even named to render a service,
charizesthai. If we bear this in mind we understand better that
Aristotle [149], when speaking of the different forms of community
a.o. trade-community, treats this subject in the chapter of his "Ethics",
in which he describes friendship. Besides we must not forget that
the Greek word for friendship covered a much wider range than ours,
it was also used for the people to whom we write "with kind regards".

What is to be learnt from this connection between lending money
and doing somebody a good turn? First of all that lending money
is not wholly considered as a business-transaction. The time in which
it, on the other hand, was done exclusively out of friendship is not
yet wholly past [150]. Whether we have to do with a money-transaction
or with an expression of friendliness is not determined by the fact if
interest is paid or not; one may oblige a person by lending him money
and receive interest all the same. A more essential difference is
whether one lends to somebody who is in need of money and who is

---

[149] Aristot., Eth. Nic. 1159 b 25 sqq.

[150] Lys., Fr. 39; cf. Bongenaar pp. 200 and 211; Dem., LII, 24; Hes., Erg. 371;
Poll., II, 152.

helped in a generally human sense [151] or to a man who merely borrows money to do business with it himself. The Greeks never distinguished between the two by nature totally different forms, the unproductive loan and the loan as an economical deed. And the incidental
nature of our records, drawn from the speeches of Athenian orators
and preserving a certain number of loans with the aim of making
them "work" [152], must not make us forget that in most cases the
money will have been lent to persons who stood in need of money
and in this way became dependent on the "usurer" [153]. In such a world
where borrowing in need was a rule and borrowing to do business
belonged to the exceptions, the demanding of interest could hardly
be distinguished from practising usury; *tokos* has in reality both
meanings: interest and usury, the later word in the sense of a prime of
money advanced to the man in need [154].

We possess a treatise, drawn up for this matter some centuries after
the period described here, from which we learn perfectly the nature of
the Greek way of lending; there has been but little change in these
centuries, though trade in the 4th century, was much more brisk. It is
a sermon of Plutarchus [155] about the perversity of borrowing, the text
of it runs as follows: "never borrow". The explanation of this advice,
incomprehensible in a time in which credit was to a certain extent
developed is to be found in the fact that the author thinks exclusively
of the borrowing of somebody in needy circumstances or of men who
run into debt in order to be able to spend much, so exclusively of the
unproductive loan. For by doing so one becomes the slave of the
trapezitès and his slaves; "pay back" is constantly threatening you.
"Luxury has produced the money-lender as well as the goldsmith, the
silversmith, the perfumer, and the fur-dyer." One does not only lose
one's liberty, but also one's honour to them. In short the money-lender
here is identical with the usurer, who makes victims.

As we have seen, however, this does not apply to all the money-
lenders of the 4th century. Part of them certainly played a rôle in

---

[151] [Aristot.], Oec. II, 1346 b 14 and 1349 a 5; Rhet. I, 5, 1361 a 12; Lys.,
XIX, 25; Xen., Oec. IV, 8; Inst. Cyr. III, 2, 19 sqq.; Isaeus, VIII, 35; Dem.,
XXVII, 7, 9 and 10.

[152] We remember that the Greek word for interest-bearing is "energos", operating
or producing (used also of land) as the contrast "argos" means non-operating, without interest. Cf. p. 112.

[153] Dem., IL, 22; LIII, 12 sqq.; Lys., XIX, 27.

[154] Harpocrat. s.v. obolostatoi; Aristot., Polit. I, 3, 19; Aristoph., Nub. 1155;
Athen., I, 108 e; Lucian., Necyom. 2.

[155] De vitando aere alieno VI (mè daneisèi. apodos).

trade and one of them could proudly declare before the tribunal, ingenuously overrating his economical significance, inherent to so many money-owners [156]: "the prosperity of traders does not originate from those who borrow money, but from those who lend it, for without his collaboration no ship, skipper or sailor can put to sea." But notwithstanding the useful part of relatively few in the process of production (trade inclusive) they were not held in very high esteem, a fate common to all money-lenders and tradesmen, as a rule foreigners; money-lending is brought on a level with trading upon the misfortune and distress of others. Elsewhere an orator declares briefly: [157] "the Athenians hate the money-lenders."

One form of credit grant often occurred, though, the credit with immovables, especially land and houses, as security, the only form considered safe. The placing of mortgages, very usual in Attica as well as elsewhere in Greece, is however, not at all to be considered as a token of a highly developed credit system. It did not take its rise from a strong need of capital, for agriculture with its little advanced technique needed but little capital. It was rather connected with the above mentioned predomination of the small farmer. It goes without saying that they were often compelled, unable as they were to bear a bad harvest, to raise money either to buy seed or foodstuffs, naturally with a plot of land as pledge. Hence that a considerable, part of Greece was covered with mortgage-stones [158]. The cancelling of mortgage-debts and the expropriation of the large landed estates were the principal revolutionary claims of the Greeks [159]. In order to safeguard themselves, the possessing class made eager use of the succour of the Macedonian usurpers who guaranteed the security of their property.

We readily understand Plato's and Aristotle's opinions about the taking of interest when considering that credit with a productive aim was very seldom given. In his "Republic" [160] Plato forbids summarily to take interest; whoever renders himself guilty of it, loses as well the right to claim the principal. Aristotle's [161] famous statement which

---

[156] Dem., XXXIV, 51.

[157] Dem., XXXVII, 52, cf. XLV; Athen., VI, 226 e. Bongenaar p. 44.

[158] Boeckh, Die Staatshaushaltung³ pp. 162-163.

[159] Cf. Bolkestein, Wohltätigkeit pp. 69 sqq. and 131 sqq. Id. Een geval van sociaal-ethisch syncretisme (A Case of Social-Ethic Syncretism). Mededelingen Kon. Ned. Akad. van Wetenschappen. Amsterdam 1931, pp. 21 sqq.; Id. Sociale politiek en sociale opstandigheid in de Oudheid (Social Politics and Social Rebelliousness in Antiquity). Amsterdam 1934.

[160] Plato, Rep. 551 sqq.

[161] Aristot., Pol. I, 3, 23.

has played such an important part in the later discussions about this subject deserves to be quoted in full: "the trade of the money-lender is justly hated because he makes profits out of the money itself and not out of that for which money has been made it is viz. made for the sake of exchange, but the interest increases by itself, thence its name (*tokos,* literally offspring of living beings); for the fruit is identical to the parents and the interest is money born from money. That is why this trade is the most unnatural of all." Instead of reproaching Aristotle not to have had an eye for the efficacious working of credit, we must conclude from the opinion of this sagacious observer that the productive credit was of slight importance, compared to the "unnatural" and immoral trade of the usurer; which is merely significant in trade which Plato as well as Aristotle want to keep at a distance from their State on account of the perils to the good old customs of the citizens.

In their judgment about the taking of interest the two philosophers hold with the moral of the people, especially of the farmers whose trade they esteem most. The farmer-poet Hesiod advised: [162] "if you borrow from your neighbour, give it back with the same or better measure, if possible; then you will find him inclined to help you anew, when you are in need of him." This is the loan which the farmer desires and appreciates, the mutual aid and assistance which by its reciprocity makes a reward almost superfluous. In a world like the Greek world, in which the agrarian element formed the majority, the farmer's moral which thought every other form of loan disastrous and condemned it as immoral, never gave way to a different conception which can only predominate in a society in which credit is not restricted to a part of trade, but has shown itself equally indispensable in industry.

[162] Hes., Erg. 347 sqq.

CHAPTER SIX

STATE AND TRADE

There is a wide-spread opinion [1] that the Greek State had so much power over her citizens, monopolized their bodies, their spirit, and their possessions to such a degree that the pride of their liberty, enounced so often by the Greeks towards subjects of the Oriental monarchies, cannot but have been a naive self-deception.

We cannot examine here what the Greeks meant by liberty which is in itself an exceedingly vague notion, and what it meant according to our standard. We may suffice here to remark that the conception of the Greek State making the lives of her individuals subservient to her own wants is chiefly the result of the circumstance that it only paid attention to the political development and hardly took the conditions of commercial life into account. If we do so, it is apparent that the power of the State asserted its influence very little upon this important point.

The concern of the State with trade may be of two kinds: it may participate directly by exercising a trade itself, either with the exclusion of private persons, as a monopolist, or it may step in as an entrepreneur beside them; indirectly it can interfere in trade life by leaving it, it is true, to private persons, but by intervening in different manners and with various purposes by administrative regulations.

The classical example of state exploitation in Antiquity with and without monopoly was Egypt under the rule of the Ptolemies [2]. Here the interference of the state in trade, in so far as it was still left to private persons, was so manifold and so excessive that we can hardly speak of liberty any more. In Egypt, indeed, the subjugation of the individual to the state was complete in almost every domain of trade; generally speaking, the individual is nothing; the state, that is to say the king, is everything. There is no better means to gauge the extent and the significance of Greek liberty in economic life than by comparing it to the situations in Hellenistic Egypt.

---

[1] Thus still K. R. Popper, The Open Society and its Ennemies. London 1925. I The Spell of Plato[3]. London 1949.

[2] Cf. Rostovtzeff, The Social and Economic History of the Hellenistic World I, pp. 255 sqq.

The Greek State did not know direct participation in economic life by exercising a trade itself. It never exploited, neither itself nor its *phylae* or *dèmoi* (sections of the population) its productive possessions cultivable land, orchards, forests, fishing water, mines and quarries, with its own servants. State agriculture and State workshops did not exist. No more did the State take industry in its own hands, leaving aside one single exception which we are going to discuss further on. It did not manage itself its principal source of income, the numerous indirect taxes; their collection was leased to private persons [3]. The erection of large and precious public monuments in the 5th and 4th centuries, as a rule temples, was let out in contract [4]. Below [5] we shall demonstrate that the waging of war may in a way be considered as a State-trade; it is the more remarkable that the necessary material for it was not manufactured by the State itself: the mightiest sea-power in the 5th century, Athens which used a good deal of men-of-war regularly, did not possess ship-building yards of its own for their construction; they were let out in contract [6]. It is still more characteristic that even the providing of the slaughter-cattle for the manifold public sacrifices was left to private persons and was allocated every time to the holder of the lowest tender [7].

The following important and necessary conditions for a government exploitation as existed in Egypt under the Ptolemies on a large scale were lacking: a well-ordered status of skilled officials and a properly administered and regularly filled treasury. To the little Greek state, (the largest of them, Athens, covered a territory of 1000 square miles, while in Egypt the cultivated valley-ground occupied about 12,000 square miles) it was sufficient to charge not the civil servants but the citizens with the performance of these little onerous functions. They took their turns annually. This profession was no means of subsistence, but a dignity, (*timè*) [8]. The lower officials, as a rule, slaves, were the only permanent elements in the management of State-affairs [9]. It was no more necessary to levy taxes regularly from all the citizens to deposit their proceeds into one State-treasury, because the few neces-

---

[3] Andocid., I, 133 sqq.; Lycurg., C. Leocr. 19, cf. 58; Plut., Alcib. V. Endenburg pp. 193 sqq.

[4] Cf. Francotte, L'industrie I, pp. 204 sqq. and II, pp. 54 sqq.

[5] Pp. 140 sqq.

[6] Cf. Francotte, L'industrie II, pp. 104 sqq.

[7] Isocr., VII, 1; Harpocrat. s.v. misthōma.

[8] Cf. Greenidge, A Handbook pp. 16 and 97.

[9] H. Wallon, Histoire de l'esclavage dans l'Antiquité. Paris 1879. I, pp. 195 sqq.

sary functions of the Greek State and the fixed expenditure required
for this were paid from a permanent post of certain revenues for every
recurring expenditure [10]. State-exploitation could hardly be possible
when such scanty means were available and skilled civil servants
capable of conducting a trade were not to be procured.

Indirectly too the State occupied itself little with trade. When saying
that it advocated the principle of free-trade, it is in so far inexact that
the question free-trade or protection was never raised. The idea of
protection never seems to have occurred: no trace has been found of an
effort to prevent or to hamper the import of certain goods by measures
of the government in order to support or stimulate home-industry or
agriculture; given the political power of the interested parties we may
conclude that the need of it has never been felt. The few import-
prohibitions known to us had an exclusively military and political
purport, as well as the taxes on im- and exported goods which a great
many of the Greek states raised bore a purely fiscal character; they
always concerned all wares without exception and notice was only
taken of their value [11]. The endeavours to concentrate the trade of
certain goods coming from abroad, or from the surrounding inland
by staple-compulsion, in some one town was likewise unknown.

The State was open not only to foreign goods, but it never excluded
foreigners either, as far as we know. On the contrary we know that the
number of "guests", *metics,* (this mediaeval denomination tallies
exactly with the Greek term) present in every town was considerable;
commercial policy always aimed at attracting foreigners as much as
possible, in so far as they carried on a trade or a craft [12]. They were,
it is true, not allowed to own land or houses [13] (hence we do not
meet with them among the husbandmen), they naturally missed the
political rights of the citizens, and they had to pay a pretty large
retribution in order to fix their domicile in a city [14]. However, by way

[10] Cf. Boeckh, Die Staatshaushaltung I[3], pp. 533 sqq: Von den Staatsleistungen
oder Liturgien im Allgemeinen, besonders den regelmässigen.

[11] Cf. J. Hasebroek, Staat und Handel im alten Griechenland, pp. 102 sqq.: Die
Handelspolitik im Dienste der Nahrung, and pp. 163 sqq.: Die Handelspolitik im
Dienste der Fiskus. [Xen.], Ath. Pol. I, 12; II, 1-7; III, 1-5; Dem., XXVII, 11;
Diod., XI, 43, 3; Plut., Sol. 24.

[12] Lys., XII, 4; Plato, Rep. I, 330; Plut. Vita X or. 835 c.

[13] [Aristot.], Oec. II, 2, 3; Xen., Vect. II, 6; Aristot., Pol. IV, 9, 5.

[14] Harpocrat. s.v. metoikion; Hesych. s.v. metoikoi; Poll., III, 55; Dem., XXV,
57; Lys., XXXI, 9, 14 (Oropos); Lyc., C. Leocr. 21, 145 (Megara); C.I.G. 1513
(Tegea); 2360, 10 (Keos); Dem., XXIII, 211 (Aegina); XXIX, 3 (Megara).

of distinction the right of owning land [15] or even civic right could be
conferred upon them [16]. For the rest, no impediment for the exercising
of their craft were ever thrown in their way: as well as for the export
of foreign goods as for retail sale in the State they shared the rights
of the citizens (this in contrast with the mediaeval guests). If we bear
in mind that besides these perfectly free outlanders there was still a
great number of slaves in many a town, also coming from abroad,
and who came in daily contact with the citizens, we may conclude
that many Greek towns were international and cosmopolitan to a
degree as was never realized again in later history.

Interference with labour-conditions, (the circumstances under which
the men worked or what wages were to be paid) cannot be expected
in a society where retail trade prevailed and where the work was done
by slaves in workshops. Real examples of it are unknown to us at any
rate. From the communication that in Athens a miller received capital
punishment because he had a free boy at work in his mill [17], we may
not deduct that a prohibition of child labour existed (there was but
little opportunity or temptation to do so); here the heavy punishment
is inflicted in the soul-seller. The legal regulations directed against
those who took away props in the mine-galleries or who let smoke
enter there [18], were not intended to protect labourers (mine-slaves!)
but to prevent other's property from being damaged.

In one domain, however, many Greek states encroached upon free
trade: when the supply of the most necessary foodstuffs was at stake.
As the size of the arable land was insufficient, the consumption in
many cities, particularly of corn, outgrew the production of the surrounding districts (cf. p. 4). This happened for instance in Athens,
Aegina, Megara, Corinth, Delos, and other regions [19]. Many measures
were taken to supply these wants.

As an export-prohibition, naturally, was not sufficient, all sorts of
decrees had in view to insure or to promote the importation. In Teos
impediments of it were placed on a par with the most heinous crimes,
murder and high treason [20]. In Athens most commercial laws, *empo-
rikoi nomoi*, referred to the supply of corn: to every inhabitant of
Attica it was forbidden to transport grain to any other than the

---

[15] Michel, Recueil 271 (Delphi). Cf. Guiraud, La main-d'oeuvre 152 sqq.
[16] Michel 653 and 306; Plut., Sol. 24.
[17] Dinarch., I, 23.
[18] Plat., Vitae X or. Lyc. 343 D. Cf. Michell, pp. 97 and 110.
[19] Bolkestein, Wohltätigkeit pp. 252 sqq.
[20] Ditt., Syll. [3] 344.

Athenian harbour under menace of the severest penalty [21]; two thirds of the cargo had tobe furnished to the town [22]; money-lenders probably were not allowed to lend money on a ship which did not take a return cargo to Athens [23]. Generally speaking, the principal aim of the Athenian commercial policy was the regular corn-supply of the citizens and therefore the safe-guarding of the lines of communication with the countries exporting grain: Sicily [24], Egypt [25], but especially the countries round the Black Sea [26]. In the 5th century when Athens' fleet ruled the sea, the import was insured. The "wardens of the Hellespont" were stationed at Sestos [27]; in the 4th century Athens was especially intent upon standing on friendly footing with the Greek princes of the Bosporan Empire whom they tried to oblige by conferring privileges and honours upon them: civil rights and freedom of custom dues on one hand and on the other gold crowns and statues [28]. They also tried to make Athens attractive to the, as a rule, foreign merchants, partly by practical measures as the guarantee of short justice (commercial lawsuits had to be decided at short date) [29], partly by the bestowing of all sorts of distinctions (the privilege of the front seats at feasts e.g.) [30] which were much more effective than the ones conferred nowadays since the whole public life enacted itself in the open and the privileged persons derived more pleasure from such honour.

Scarcity and dearth of corn were no unknown phenomena in the cities dependent on import, when traffic by sea was far from safe. So the need of the circumstances and the power of the people in the Greek democracies gradually led to an expansion of Government interference. When the supply of corn did not seem sufficiently warranted, the State took the purchase in its own hands: a special com-

[21] Dem., XXXIV, 37; XXXV, 20; Lyc., C. Leocr. 27.

[22] Dem., XXIV with scholia; Harpocrat. s.v. epimelètès.

[23] Dem., XXXV, 51. Cf. Büchsenschütz, p. 547; Boeckh, Die Staatshaushaltung I[3] p. 79.

[24] Theophr., Hist. Pl. VIII, 4, 4; Thuc., III, 86; Dem., LVI, 9; Athen., VI, 232 b; Polyb., XXVIII, 2.

[25] Thuc., VIII, 35; Dem., LVI, 3 and 9.

[26] Dem., XX, 31; Her., VII, 147; Thuc., III, 2.

[27] Ditt., Syll.[3] 75.

[28] Ditt., Syll.[3] 206 and 370; Dinarch., I, 43. Bongenaar p. 218 and Schäfer, Athenischer Volksbeschluss zu Ehren der Söhne Leukons von Bosporos. Rhein. Museum XXXIII pp. 418 sqq.

[29] Xen., Vect. III, 3; Dem., XXXIII, 23; VII, 12; XXI, 176; XXXII, 5-9 and 14; Harpocrat. s.v. emmènoi dikai; Poll., VIII, 63 and 101.

[30] Xen., Vect. III, 4.

mittee of grain-merchants, sitōnai, was appointed; it got a capital at
its disposal raised by more or less free contributions, in order to
provide the population with this indispensable food [31]. Formerly the
State had restricted itself to taking stringent measures against the
plotting of the corn-traders to force up the prices (the corn-wardens
could even be punished capitally in case of negligence or dishonesty[32]).
Gradually, however, the officials who in the beginning had merely
to supervise the validity and the exact weight of the market-wares,
concerned themselves also with the prices; either by persuading the
merchants or by supplying themselves, they succeeded in making the
merchants sell the grain beneath market-price [33]. Often the State did
not confine herself to attend to the importation, but she herself put
the corn at the disposal of the citizens at a lower price than the cost-
price, an advantage of which all the citizens, not only the paupers,
could profit. But the development of State-interference, as shortly
indicated above, and the model of the corresponding measures which
the Gracchi proposed and carried through in Rome [34], takes place in
the era after Alexander the Great and so lies beyond the scheme of
this sketch [35].

So the interferences of the State with economical life were neither
directly nor indirectly manifold or excessive. In the meantime there
is one trade, the most extensive, which Greek society ever knew, which
was naturally carried on by the State, viz. the waging of war. At first
sight we way wonder that war is ranged among the enterprises, de-
serving a place in a description of economic life, but we are entitled
so to do by the circumstance that their principal object often was the

[31] Dem., XVIII, 248; Poll., VIII, 114, cf. Plut., Praec. pol. XV, 9; Ditt., Syll.³
304; 951; 493; 671B; 976; 495; C.I.G.; II, 2334; II, 2140 = I G. IV, 2) : I.G. III
645; IX, 2, 1104; Ditt., Syll.³ 783, 15; Paton-Hicks, Inscriptions of Cos 108, 18
and 113; I.G. II, 252; 353; Ditt., Or. Gr. I. 458; C.I.G. II, 3080 and 3831 a;
I.G. VII, 1, 1719; Ath. Mitteil. VIII, 328; Bull. Corr. Hell. XI, 100; C.I.G. II,
3490; III, 3945; I, 1125; II, 1349; III, 4411 a; 4413 c; 1415 b; I, 378; II, 3422;
Bull. Corr. Hell. VII, 14, 100; XVII, 276; XII, 193; XI, 379; 73; 105; 473; 32;
XIV, 175; I.G. V, 1, 526; II, 2882; 2927; 2930; 2929; Ath. Mitteil. VIII, 321;
I.G. III, 708; II, 335; C.I.G. I, 1370. The sitōnai are first mentioned in Athens
in 359, viz. by Demosthenes, and last in Sparta ± 210 A.D. In 359 it was still a
commission ad hoc, in the days of Augustus it has become a permanent office.

[32] Lys., XXII, 16; Harpocrat. s.v. sitophylakes.

[33] Harpocrat. s.v. agoranomoi; Plato, Leg. 764b; VIII, 849a. Cf. Xen., An. V,
7, 2 and Aristoph., Vesp. 1406 sqq.; Acharn, 722, 824 and 968.

[34] Cf. Bolkestein, Wohltätigkeit pp. 364 sqq.

[35] The inscriptions from which this development can be traced are indicated in
note 31.

booty, to be distributed among the lucky participants. War was a means of securing a fortune or simply a livelihood instead or next to the other means of subsistence, consisting of labour. The Greeks themselves also considered war as belonging to the sphere of economic life.

It is a well-known and not surprising fact that in the oldest periods of Greek history, there was but a slight difference between war, robbery by land or by sea, and trade. With many especially sea-faring nations such was the situation at the beginning of their civilization [36]. The Greek word for booty, *leia,* is connected with the radical which means to profit, *apo-lauesthai,* and with the latin word for benefit, profit *lucrum.* Raids are repeatedly mentioned in the Odyssey [37]: it is difficult to decide whether the Taphians are to be called pirates or traders [38]. Hesiod [39] and the poets after him [40] still make use of the word *leïzesthai,* to rob, for to obtain; *acquérir* is still *conquérir.* In a law handed down to us under Solon's name [41], which indicates that it belongs to the complex of Athenian laws in the 6th century and later, (in Aristotle's time it was still known) the right is adjudged to to all companies to draw up their own regulations, provided not in contravention of common law. Besides sacrificial companies, societies of sailors or soldiers, of men going in search of booty or of traders are mentioned in it; a line has not yet been drawn between booty and trade in this law from historical times.

"After the Persian disaster at Marathon" [42], says Herodotus [43], "the fame of Miltiades which had before been great at Athens, was increased. He asked of the Athenians seventy ships and an army and money, not telling them against what country he would lead them, but saying that he would make them rich men if they followed him; for he would bring them to a country whence they should easily carry away abundance of gold." In this way the purpose of the expedition against Paros is explained; after this follows the description of the campaign itself. After the capture of Sestos and Byzantium, the ransom for the prisoners of war enabled Cimon to defray the upkeep of his fleet during four months and to deposit a considerable amount of gold in

[36] Thuc., I, 5 sqq. Cf. Ormerod, Piracy in the Ancient World pp. 69 sqq.

[37] Hom., Od. XIV, 230 sqq. and 245 sqq.; III, 301 and 312; IV, 90; IX, 40; XI, 401. Cf. Knorringa pp. 9 sqq.

[38] Hom., Od. I, 184; XV, 427; XVI, 426.

[39] Hes., Erg. 320. Cf. 700.

[40] Eur., Troad. 373.

[41] Aristot., Eth. Nic. VIII, 1160 a 14 sqq. Endenburg pp. 163-164.

[42] Transl. A. D. Godley.

[43] Her., VI, 132-135.

the Athenan treasury [44]. The victory near the Eurymedon procured
him 20,000 pieces of human ware to sell, besides an enormous
booty [45]. It is evident that the institution of slavery, to which the in-
cessant import of new material was indispensable, and which was
furnished to a large extent by slave-dealers, gave a peculiar spur to
waging war. For so they got hold of them in a cheaper way and the
prisoners of war yielded at least a precious booty of which the sale
was assured. Xenophon [46] describes a dance of two tribes from Central
Greece: a farmer is busy ploughing and sowing, the weapons beside
him. Every time he looks around him as if afraid of danger. A brigand
approaches and a quarrel arises about the yoke of oxen, which may
show us that in peace time too the plough and the sword were wielded
alternately. From the 5th century likewise an exceedingly important
treaty has been preserved between two little states on the Gulf of
Crissa [47]. They made a compact that their citizens were not to rob
each other, at least not in each other's domain and in the harbour.
In the offing, however, the right to plunder was emphatically acknowledged. The circumstance that on this coast everything meant for
Delphi had to be disembarked, will probably have contributed not
little to this decree, because Delphi was the sanctuary to which
presents were offered from all parts of the Greek world. According
to Thucydides [48], piracy was considered lawful not only with the
Ozolean Locreans in whose country these cities were situated, but also
with the Aetolians and the Acarnanians. So we are entitled to say that
some of the smaller and remote states were no better than organized
robber-bands: particularly piracy and privateering on behalf of the
State were always difficult to distinguish. In later decrees where the
states assured their mutual citizens *asylia* (that is to say free traffic
without the chance of being robbed), *agein,* to rob, and *polemein,*
to wage war, are put on the same level [49].

The manifold wars and their character as a means of enrichment is
closely connected with the fact that in Greece so many independent
states lived side by side which facilitated raids across the borders and
even justified them towards enemies: neighbours' quarrels were im-

---

[44] Plut. Cimon, IX.
[45] Diod., XI, 62. Cf., however, Westermann, p. 7.
[46] Xen., An. VI, 1, 7.
[47] Hicks and Hill 24.
[48] Thuc., I, 5, 3.
[49] Cf. L. Wenger, Asylrecht. Reallexikon für Antike und Christentum (Th. Klau-
ser) pp. 837 sqq.

mediately international contests. When in the beginning of the
4th century the Lacedaemonians, irritated as they were by various
unfriendly acts of the citizens of Elis, wanted to chastize this state,
they provoked them by demanding a restoration of self-government
to the cities subjugated to the Eleans. The latter, however, accounted
for their refusal by pointing out that the towns in question were theirs
as lawfully acquired booty. Then follows the punitive expedition of
the Lacedaemonians: the fruit-trees were cut down, the corn in the
fields was burnt, a great number of cattle and slaves were captured.
When hearing this, many inhabitants from the adjacent regions Arcadia and Achaea came rushing in in order to take part in the campaign and participate in the plunder. The historian from whom we
borrow this tale concludes as follows: "In this way this expedition
became so to say a source of forage to the Peleponnesus." [50]

Considering the great significance of the booty in these little states
we need not wonder that the sale of the plunder was properly managed and that special persons were charged with it, the so-called
laphyropōlai [51]; it is characteristic for Sparta that the laphyropolai,
as an instrument to oppress the people, formed here an official col-
lege [52]. In Tegea a special building was destined for this sale [53].

We are neither astonished that in the upper circles of the land-
owners belonging to nobility fight took the place of labour and the
lance that of the tool. Here the idea prevails, which Tacitus [54] ascribes
to the Germans, that it is unworthy to obtain by sweat of the brow
what may be got through blood. The opinions in democratic Greece
were but little different from the ideas of the upper class people in
Sparta. When Socrates asks a well-born citizen who wants to embark
in policy whether he is acquainted with the revenues and expenditures
of the State, the young man declares that he has not yet occupied
himself with it, nor was he convinced of the necessity of such study.
"For," he remarks, "it is also possible to procure wealth at the expense
of one's enemies." [55] Elsewhere Xenophon [56] describes how Socrates
put the king of the Persians as an example, who considered agricul-

---

[50] Xen., Hell. III, 2, 23-27.

[51] Xen., An. VII, 7, 56; Hell. IV, 1, 26; Athen., IX, 381 e.

[52] Xen., Ag. I, 18; Xen., Rep. Lac. XIII, 11.

[53] Pol., IV, 6, 3; Dion. Hal., IX, 56.

[54] Tac., Germ. 14.

[55] Xen., Comm. III, 6, 6 and 7.

[56] Isocr., XVII, 41 and 49. Bongenaar p. 167. Dem., L, 9; Thuc. III, 9; Lys.,
XXI, 1-3. Cf. Guiraud, La propriété pp. 522 sqq.

ture and warfare as the most dignified and necessary occupations. When the same author explains his proposition to let the Athenian State buy slaves on a large scale in order to let them out to the mine-tenants in Laurium and discusses the possibility to collect the necessary trading capital among the citizens, he bases his favourable expectations upon the fact that the Athenians had already often given money needed for some expedition by land or by sea without being sure whether the money would yield interest or not. The equalization of the assessment in a war tax and the share in an enterprise may also be deduced from the use of the same term: *eisphora* [57].

We can still see more plainly how much a war was considered as inevitable and normal when we watch the fact that in an Attic lease [58] a partial acquittance of the rent is promised not in case some natural phenomenon as hail or inundation should make the harvest miscarry, but when the enemy made working in the fields impossible or when they destroyed part of the crops. We have seen how difficult it is to draw the line between warfare and robbery. They both were such normal phenomena in the Greek world that Aristotle [59] in his con-siderations about the basis of economy enumerates piracy as a means of subsistence next to fishing and hunting. In an other passage [60] he mentions in the same breath sailors, associating in order to gain money by trade, and soldiers, going out together to obtain "money, a victory or a town". It follows that in the 4th century the Greeks still had the same ideas and knew the same practice as those known from Solon's society law in the 6th and 5th centuries.

In the meantime we must not forget that war was not only and not always waged by the State; it often happened that mercenary troops under private commanders who paid them, waged war too since the 5th century. For in the Greek world the use of mercenaries had also become general; in the Oriental states they had been known much earlier. Especially Egypt had often taken Greeks in her armies [61], while their use in Greece was restricted to the life-guards of the tyrants [62]. Many generals in Greece in the 4th century were entre-

---

[57] Cf. Guiraud, La propriété pp. 429 sqq.

[58] Cf. p. 32.

[59] Aristot., Polit. I, 2 and 3.

[60] Aristot., Eth., Nic. VIII, 1160 a 14 sqq.

[61] R. Cohen, La Grèce et l'Hellénisation du Monde Antique. Paris 1939, pp. 65, 68 (literature), 292 sqq. (Iphicrates), 309 (literature).

[62] B. Müller, Beiträge zur Geschichte des griechischen Söldnerwesens bis auf die Schlacht bei Chäroneia. Thesis Strassburg 1908; K. Grote, Das griechische Söldner-

preneurs, requiring a relatively large capital because they enlisted soldiers themselves and provided for them [63]; exactly like the slave-owner, he let out his soldiers and himself to the man who wanted his services; if there was no war in Greece, there was the Persian king or one of his satraps who were not averse from using them [64].

This waging of war was the most extensive trade known in Greece, the only trade where a large number of labourers were united under one man's guidance. The soldiers were called besides *xenoi*, foreigners, because many of them were recruited from abroad [65], also *misthophoroi*, wage earners; the mercenaries were the wage earners *par excellence*. It is worth while noticing that warfareinventions and corrections are manifold especially after the 5th century, the more so because tools and technique in general show but little development [66]. The word *mèchanè* which was to become our machine, often means without any addition *"battering-instrument"* [67]. While every one was sure of his livelihood in retail trade on account of the small fluctuations between production and consumption, (the few exceptions were not caused by crises in *economical* life) the phenomenon of unemployment often recurred in the uncertain wholesale trade of warfare. When a mercenary-army was dismissed, Greece was overrun by those out of work. Perhaps it is not incidental that the Governmentpensions, the support of the mutilated and orphans was limited to warvictims [68]; there was no need of the doles which are procured to victims of labouraccidents in an industrially highly developed society.

So warfare was the only governmenttrade and at the same time the only real wholesale trade. In this way the State played a highly important part in Greece's economic life: the State, the political organization of the citizens, procured a livelihood to its citizens by waging war;

wesen der hellenistischen Zeit. Thesis Jena 1913; H. W. Parke, Greek Mercenary Solddiers from the Earliest Times to the Battle of Ipsus. Oxford 1933; G. F. Griffith, The Mercenaries of the Hellenistic World. Cambridge 1935 (cf. Lammert, Phil. Wochenschrift 1936, p. 689 and Kahrstedt, Gött. gelehrte Anzeigen, 1936, p. 189).

[63] [Aristot.], Oec. 1348 b 22.

[64] Her., I, 61; VIII, 26; Thuc., III, 34; IV, 52 and 76; VII, 19 and 57; Xen., An. VI, 2, 10; Hell. VII, 1, 23; Isocr., IV, 168; VIII, 44 and 79; Paus., IV, 8, 3.

[65] Diod., XVIII, 21. Cf. Arr., An. I, 24, 2; II, 20, 5.

[66] Cf. R. Ménard-C. Sauvageaot, Le travail dans l'Antiquité I, Agriculture-Industrie, II, Architecture, Commerce-Beaux Arts.

[67] Thuc., III, 76; IV, 100.

[68] Thuc., II, 46; Plato, Menex. 248 e; Aeschin., III, 154; Aristot., Polit. 1268 a 8 sqq.; Dem., XXIV, 20 with schol. Cf. Bolkestein, Wohltätigkeit pp. 280 sqq.

still more than through the acquired booty it does so by the lasting
domination over other states. We shall leave undecided whether it
took its origin from the need of living at the cost of other communities; it is a fact, though, that it existed through. In the 5th century
the Athenian State did not prosper through revenues from economic
activity, nor through labour. The splendour of the Acropolis is paid
not from a surplus of commercial profits, but from the ransom of the
subjugated "allies" [69]. And when in 355 through the secession of the
principal allies the State loses the chance of enriching itself at their
cost, so by political means, the question was wittingly raised in Athens
how the citizens would be able to support themselves through economic
means in the future, a way of earning money which was at once
highly recommended as the most righteous way, now that the political
manner of earning a livelihood had become impossible. But even
under these circumstances the notion prevails that it is the State who
must provide for its citizens; only the means proposed are different.
Formerly the State conquered the enemy at whose cost the citizens were
going to subsist, with armies and fleets equipped by the wealthiest
citizens. Now the proprietors are invited to collect money in order
to buy slaves and the prospect is held out to them that the citizens will
almost be able to live on their labour [70].

The enormous development of the technique of the instruments of
production since the end of the 18th century came chiefly into being
by the strongly increased and large need of general commodities. The
fact that the highly gifted and ingenious Greeks hardly knew any
technical progress may be mainly explained by the circumstance that
the scanty and constant needs of life did not necessitate a large production. By the abundant supply of slaves the State had exceedingly
cheap labourers at its disposal who were by their indifference for the
labour imposed upon them hardly capable of handling finer instruments. So each stimulus was lacking to invent a manner of production
to eliminate human labour as much as possible. But this stagnation in
economic development will also undoubtedly have been due to the fact
that it was easier for many states to overpower and to ransom weaker
tribes or districts and so by their political power to procure material
advantages which also diminished the need of intense labour to many
citizens.

The important rôle which the State played in economic lify by

[69] Cf. Cohen, La Grèce p. 211 (literature).
[70] Xen., Vect. IV.

providing its citizens with revenues by the power of its political organization and not by labour but by subjugation or exploitation of other states has evidently also influenced the theoretical views. The slight development of economic life, the little circle in which the stable production and consumption concurred, because the State was self-sufficient, could hardly form a stimulus to trace its laws; as a matter of fact the Greeks have but touched upon economical science as such. This is the more remarkable because the science of the State, the investigation into its elements and its government, its nature and task had reached such a high degree of development. In this domain the conditions for study were exceedingly favourable in contrast with those of economic life: within a narrow compass some hundreds of little states were jostled together whose citizens spoke closely affined languages, but were very different as to composition and government, still more dissimilar in power which often increased or decayed rapidly, of transparent construction on account of the inner strife of the parties in public. All this could not but induce the looker-on with a contemplative disposition, to make comparisons and theoretical investigations. The circumstance that the State contributed so much to the material and intellectual welfare, the *eu zèn* of the citizen, will undoubtedly have enhanced this interest. Because political life predominated so much over the economical, political science was practised by the Greeks with zeal and excellent results; the history of political economy, on the contrary, may without injustice leave out the scanty and incidental remarks of Greek scholars.

SUMMARY AND CONCLUSION

Since Karl Bücher in his *"Entstehung der Volkswirtschaft"* of 1893 distinguished the following three degrees of economic development: *"geschlossene Hauswirtschaft* (self-sufficient family economy), *Stadtwirtschaft* (self sufficient town economy), and *Volkswirtschaft* (national economy) in which he put the *"Wirtschaft der Griechen, der Römer, der Karthager"* (the economy of the Greeks, the Romans and the Carthagenians) on the first degree [1], and Eduard Meyer in his lecture" *Die wirtschaftliche Entwicklung des Altertums"* (Economic development in Antiquity) of 1895 opposed him by saying that Antiquity knew *"eine ihrem Wesen nach durchaus moderne Kultur"* (an essentially modern culture) [2], many investigations in the realm of economic history in Antiquity have either directly or indirectly taken one of these statements as their starting-point, not always profitable to a good insight in this question. For even when acknowledging with gratitude that the fundamental consecutive degrees of economic development, like Bücher's other treatises contributed much to the theoretical training of the historian, still they are not very useful as a criterion for the judgment of the economical standard during Antiquity. As a matter of fact its determination did not originate from its study. A paraphrase of the *Hauswirtschaft,* which embraces as well the conditions in the demesnes of the crown in Egypt, as those in a poverty-stricken mountain-village in Boeotia in the 8th century B.C. and those in the latifundia in Italy in the time of the Emperors, does not clearly bring to the fore the characteristics and the differences. But especially with the second degree of the *"Stadtwirtschaft"* we can do very little in a country like Greece where the most important towns were situated on the sea, and the traffic with even distant districts was very easy also in ancient times, while all transport by land was exceedingly difficult, we may easily create the impression that the *"Volkswirtschaft"* had existed here since long, and, by doing so, form a mistaken notion of a degree of economic development, differing but little from the modern one.

Eduard Meyer [2], indeed, uttered the opinion since then endorsed by

---

[1] Bücher I, pp. 172 sqq.
[2] Kleine Schriften I, pp. 79 sqq.

many especially German scholars: *"Athen steht im 5ten und 4ten Jahrhundert ebenso sehr unter dem Zeichen des Capitalismus, wie England seit dem 18ten und Deutschland seit dem 19ten Jahrhundert."* (Athens in the 5th and 4th centuries stands as much in the sign of capitalism as England has stood since the 18th and Germany since the 19th century). This idea can only be sustained as long as we neglect to give a description of the term capitalism which by mentioning the principal characteristics of this conception enables us to judge about its appropriateness in a certain case.

A system of goods-production is called capitalistic when it requires the use of a considerable capital. It is characterized first of all by a wholesale production, outwardly possible by a regular and assured sale, inwardly based upon an advanced division of labour and combination of specialized labour in one trade. Furthermore it is characterized, on the one hand, by the existence of a class of men who own the capital and in this way dominate and guide the production; on the other hand, by a class of people deprived of capital and who, in order to earn a livelihood, are thrown on their working-power, which the owners of the capital engage: so by separation of capital and labour and by the lasting dependency of the labourer.

If we succeeded in formulizing this notion rightly in this sketch, it is apparent that economic life in Greece in the 5th and 4th centuries B.C. hardly showed any traits characteristic of capitalism.

Hardly a trace is to be found of a whole sale production engendering large trades requiring big capitals; retail trade predominated in all branches of production.

In many districts the cultivable soil was to a large extent the propriety of the small farmer himself, who tilled it either himself or with the aid of a few slaves or together with his sons, often also with his brothers. Next to these freeholders we also meet with tenants of wealthy lords whose properties were cultivated in some parts by serfs; but their trade was so little intensive that the need of big capital was out of the question.

Similar conditions are to be observed in industry. For the greater part it was practised in small crafts which procured a modest, but secure livelihood to the master and one or more slaves. A combination of a large number of labourers, always slaves, in one workshop under common management and in the possession of one man is found, though distribution of labour as well as the expensive outfit requiring much capital and characterizing modern industry was absolutely

BOLKESTEIN, Economic Life.   11 lacking. But the principal conditions for the frequent occurrence and the durability of such large trades were missing, e.g.: an urgent need which would have provoked a large production, the certainty of selling, guaranteed by undisturbed traffic and in general the productiveness of the invested capital. Only a few will have risked the whole or a part of their fortune in such a craft; a status of workshop-entre-preneurs, the "manufacturers", did not exist. How much so, we can deduce from the following particulars: our records teach us that it often happened that a craft changed proprietors [3]; this was possible because it was exercised by slaves, among whom one was not only looking after the technical management but was also charged with the whole exploitation [4]. So the carrying on of such a trade was meant more as an investment than as an enterprise. It follows as well that the status of wage labourers was lacking too. Even when taking this term in its widest sense and including the workshop slaves, and referring to Aristotle's [5] description that the slave receives his wages in the form of his maintenance, the number of workmen who worked in permanent large industries regularly and exclusively, was not great, the miners excepted. For this matter the significance of slavework for the economic and social development has been amply dealt with before.

It was trade which yielded most profits and of all professions it was trade which was most developed at least in the states which parti-cipated in traffic by sea. But because the much used daily necessities of life were produced by each region itself on behalf of its inhabitants and staple goods could hardly be transported, sea-trade though ex-tending over far distances, never became very brisk. It was especially the "*Wanderhandel*" (travelling-trade) which was carried on in the era discussed above: the merchants themselves sailed with their cargoes in small vessels from coast to coast; making a port, they often had to sell their merchandise themselves by retail. On one hand the extent of their trade was not so large that it justified the term of wholesale trade, on the other a status of men exclusively occupying themselves with wholesale purchase and sale did not exist. The circumstance that during a large part of of the year all traffic by sea was laid up, formed a serious impediment to its development.

The phenomenon that in industry as well as in trade (goods trade and money-trade) a large number of professions was exercised by non-

---

[3] Dem., XXXVII, 4-5.
[4] Aristot., Polit. I, 2, 23; Hyperid. c. Athenag. XII, 1. Cf. Dem., XLVIII, 14-15.
[5] Aristot., Polit. I, 5, 3.

citizens, "guests" (*metics*) partly accounts for the subservient position which these means of existence occupied in economic life and in the estimation of public opinion.

In trade especially, it often happened that more than one person collected money, not for the establishment of a permanent business but to undertake a trade by itself. This, however, was not necessary on account of the extent of the enterprise which might have required big capital but exclusively as a result of the endeavours to participate the high risks of sea-trade, threatened as it was by all sorts of dangers from nature and from men. Besides participation, there was another means of making money bear interest outside the circle of the merchants: the institution of bottomry or ship-credit in its ancient form. Pooling of transactions as well as the *nautikon daneion* strongly bore the character of an insurance.

The need of raising money in trade, partly a result of the fact that the greater part of the merchants were craftsmen with few or no possessions was furthermore connected with the circumstance that in trade payment in cash, in silver or gold, was a rule with hardly any exception; delivery of goods on credit was unknown. But credit in its other meaning, the procuring of money against interest for a productive purpose, was of no significance either, as may be concluded from the fact that every form of credit-money remained unknown. The most usual form of investment and the only one which was considered safe, was the lending against the security of immovables, as a mortgage [6]. On an earlier page [7] we saw how much the need of it was increased by small farming. It was an exception for wealthy men in so far as they were not contented with the revenues of their landed property to become exclusively entrepreneurs in a branch of trade. They made their money bear interest alternately in trade by lending money or by exploitation of slaves in a craft of their own or by letting them out to third parties. The circumstance that the Greek state was wont to let out in contract the performance of all sorts of work, not only the collecting of taxes, even the most paltry ones, but also for instance the supply of sacrificial necessities, formed also a means of earning a livelihood without having a permanent trade. It was the Roman empire only with its rich, subjugated provinces where the governmentrent was to become the most profitable profession [8].

[6] Poll., III, 84; VIII, 141.

[7] P. 133.

[8] J. Marquardt, Römische Staatsverwaltung II. Leipzig 1884: Dritter Abschnitt: Die Einnahmen des Staates.

Private life also offered such possibilities: the administration of the fortunes of minor orphans was let out (*oikou misthōsis*) when the tutor was not willing to manage them himself [9]. This also meant a means of subsistence for the unemployed.

When considering that no large trades existed unless as scarce and short exceptions, that there was no or little need of working-capital of any importance, we cannot but conclude that capitalism was out of the question. The few traits to be found are also met with in the Middle-Ages, but then more sharply outlined. Greek society of the 5th and 4th centuries exhibits not one of the characteristics familiar to the capitalism of the 19th century.

This conclusion to be drawn from the facts is confirmed strikingly by the way of viewing the question by the Greek social theorists.

Plato [10] when describing in his work on the Republic his famous cyclus of Governmentforms indicates a.o. through what means the big fortunes are gained in oligarchy (what we are accustomed to call plutocracy). He mentions these causes: the accumulation of landed property which becomes possible because everybody has the absolute right to alienate it; the lending of money on usury to young men leading an extravagant life, and theft or embezzlement of goods particularly occasioned by the administration of orphans' fortunes. The pre-capitalistic character of Greek society in the 4th century is proved nowhere more clearly than by the criticism of its ingenious reformer. Moreover it confirms once more that the striving after riches and the greed of gold were certainly not lacking, but how different the means of indulging in them from those usual in a society which produced the system of entrepreneurs. We must surely take into account that Plato was a reactionary in his social ideas and that his longing for a self-sufficient state made him underestimate the significance of trade which he condemned for its risks of moral pollution whereas it is chiefly in trade that the love of gains expresses itself, a statement absolutely failing in his critical views. But it is evident all the same that he would not have neglected to notice and to scourge this if a considerable part of the population had taken part in it and if it had put its stamp on economical life. Contrary to the capitalistic society which created the conviction that man is a money-grubber by nature,

---

[9] Dem., XXVII, 58, 64; XXIX, 60. On the concept oikos: Xen., Oec. I, 4, 5; Lys., XXXII, 23; Isaeus, VI, 36; Poll., VIII, 142 and 89; Hesych. s. v. apotimèmata.
[10] Plato, Rep. 551 sqq.

the making ot profits, not yet obtained regularly without cheating, was generally considered as morally inferior.

The greater majority of the Greeks, more in particular the independent and small proprietors had no other view when working than earning their livelihood. Labour is not yet the cheerless occupation which made it necessary later on to proclaim it a boon: the craftsman not separated from his utensils nor bereft of the free disposal of his labour-product did not only enjoy material but also moral satisfaction which the love of one's own labour procures; art and industry were mainly identical. Economic life was not ruled by the hurry to increase production and to furnish the goods more cheaply; one spent so much time on a piece of work as necessary to part with it with satisfaction. The struggle for life had not yet exalted competition to a social principle, in nature absolutely different from the emulation natural among colleagues; but the desire to be known as a skilled craftsman, specific as well to the potter as to the physician, and the rivalry created by it often made life to an *agōn,* match, often festively celebrated. There was less need of a steady exertion of will-power, but the faculties of the mind and of the senses were more developed. Labour was not yet the predominant factor in human life: the Greek language formed the word for activity, *ascholia,* as a contrast to idleness, *scholè,* which was considered normal. They could still afford to take long and many hours of repose without becoming victims of unemployment; time was available for immaterial values: *time was not yet money* [11].

As well as to the individual this was applicable to the community of the State. We may calculate that in the era from 447 to 438 B.C. the Athenian state spent more than half its yearly income (chiefly formed by the contributions of the allies) on the erection of temples, images and other adornments of the Acropolis, furthermore it payed the expenses of its numerous public festivities [12]. This way of living has been strongly disapproved of by a modern economist: "with such revenues at their disposal", he writes, "the Athenian might have built a town enjoying lasting prosperity." Quite injustly, though: when considering the status of the economic development where not a single trade required a large capital the opportunity was lacking to make important sums productive. It goes without saying that this does not

[11] Cf. also Aristot., Pol. 1338 a 1 sqq.; 1137 b 31 sqq.
[12] R. Cohen, La Grèce p. 211 (literature).

explain why the Athenians spent them on the creation of art (they might have squandered them) nor does it explain that this art belongs to the very highest ever produced; we have merely indicated, the circumstances which made possible the intellectual wealth: the building of the temple of the Athenian Acropolis as well as later on the cathedral of Amiens.

Will a society in which the supply of the material needs requires and must require the labour and energy of millions, ever again be able to spend such fortunes for the adornment of life?

LITERATURE

(Only the principal works are mentioned)

GENERAL WORKS

A. BOECKH, Die Staatshaushaltung der Athener. 3th ed. revised by M. Fraenkel, 1886.

B. BÜCHSENSCHÜTZ, Besitz und Erwerb im Griechischen Altertume, 1869.

R. PÖHLMANN, Geschichte des antiken Kommunismus und Sozialismus, 1893. 3th ed. entitled: R. VON PÖHLMANN - F. OERTEL, Geschichte der sozialen Frage und des Sozialismus in der antiken Welt, 1925.

K. BÜCHER, Die Entstehung der Volkswirtschaft, 1st ed. 1893, 17th ed. 1926.

ED. MEYER, Die wirtschaftliche Entwicklung des Altertums, Jahrb. für Nationalökonomie und Statistik, 3e Folge, Bd. IX, 1895. Reprinted in Kleine Schriften, 1910.

O. NEURATH, Antike Wirtschaftsgeschichte, 1st ed. 1909, 2nd ed. 1918.

M. WEBER, Agrarverhältnisse im Altertum, Handwörterbuch der Staatswissenschaften, 3:d ed. I, 1909. Reprinted in Gesammelte Aufsätze zur Sozial- und Wirtschaftsgeschichte, 1924.

A. E. ZIMMERN, The Greek Commonwealth, Politics and Economics in fifth-century Athens, 1st ed. 1911, 5th ed. 1952.

G. GLOTZ, Le travail dans la Grèce ancienne, Histoire économique de la Grèce, 1920.

J. TOUTAIN, L'économie antique, 1927.

J. HASEBROEK, Griechische Wirtschafts- und Gesellschaftsgeschichte bis zur Perserzeit, 1931.

H. MICHELL, The Economics of Ancient Greece, 1940.

F. M. HEICHELHEIM, Wirtschaftsgeschichte des Altertums, 1938.

E. CAVAIGNAC, L'économie grecque, 1951.

SPECIAL LISTS

CHAPTER ONE

J. NEUMANN-PARTSCH, Physikalische Geographie von Griechenland mit besonderer Rücksicht auf das Alterthum, 1885.

A. PHILIPPSON, Das Mittelmeergebiet. Seine geographische und kulturelle Eigenart, 1904.

A. STRUCK, Zur Landeskunde von Griechenland, 1912.

M. CARY, The Geographic Background of Greek and Roman History, 1949.

J. L. MYRES, Geographical History in Greek Lands, 1953.

CHAPTER TWO

P. GUIRAUD, La propriété foncière en Grèce jusqu'à la conquête romaine, 1893.

W. E. HEITLAND, Agricola. A Study of Agriculture and Rustic Life in the Greco-Roman World from the point of view of Labour, 1921.

R. GRAND, L'histoire de l'agriculture dans l'Antiquité, 1935.

A. JARDÉ, Les céréales dans l'Antiquité grecque, 1925.

CHAPTER THREE

P. GUIRAUD, La main-d'œuvre industrielle dans l'ancienne Grèce, 1900.

H. FRANCOTTE, L'industrie dans la Grèce ancienne, 1900/1901.

P. CLOCHÉ, Les classes, les métiers, le trafic, la vie publique et privée des anciens grecs, 1930.

CHAPTER FOUR

ED. MEYER, Die Sklaverei im Altertum, 1898. Reprinted in Kleine Schriften, 1910.

E. CICCOTTI, Il tramonto della schiavitù nel mondo antico, 1898. French translation: Le déclin de l'esclavage antique, 1910. German translation: Der Untergang der antiken Sklaverei, 1910.

W. L. WESTERMANN, The Slave-Systems of Greek and Roman Antiquity, 1955.

CHAPTER FIVE

J. HASEBROEK, Staat und Handel im alten Griechenland, 1928. English translation: Trade and Politics in Ancient Greece, 1934.

H. SCHAAL, Vom Tauschhandel zum Welthandel, 1931.

E. ZIEBARTH, Beiträge zur Geschichte des Seeraubs und Seehandels im alten Griechenland, 1929.

G. M. CALHOUN, The Business Life of Ancient Athens, 1926.

INDEXES
SUBJECTS

NAMES [1]

[1] Left out: Attica, Athens, Athenians, Greece, Greeks.

GREEK WORDS